Providing materials for library users

David Spiller

Library Association Publishing
London

© David Spiller 2000

Published by
Library Association Publishing
7 Ridgmount Street
London WC1E 7AE

Library Association Publishing is wholly owned by The Library Association.

First published 1971 as *Book selection: principles and practice*
Second edition 1974
Third edition 1980
Fourth edition 1986
Fifth edition 1991
This edition as *Providing materials for library users* 2000

British Library Cataloguing in Publication Data

A catalogue record for this book is available from the British Library.
ISBN 1-85604-385-1

Typeset from author's disk in 11/14 Elegant Garamond and Humanist by Library Association Publishing.
Printed and made in Great Britain by MPG Books Ltd, Bodmin, Cornwall.

Providing materials
for library users

Contents

'You may say that one doesn't really need to read every single book. My retort to that is − in warfare, too, one doesn't need to kill every single soldier, and yet every single one is necessary. Now you will say every single book is necessary too. But there you are, you see, even *there* there's something wrong. For it isn't true. I asked the librarian!'

Robert Musil *The man without qualities*

'He was interested in what was taken from the shelves.' Ruth Bowman about Philip Larkin, Wellington public library, 1944. In Andrew Motion *Philip Larkin: a writer's life.*

Preface

This book has grown out of a previous work – *Book selection* – which was published in its fifth edition in 1991. *Book selection* outgrew its title round about the third edition, and I have at last adopted a new handle more suited to the complexities of the subject matter – in particular, the galloping growth of electronic materials (the word 'Internet' was not even mentioned in the 1991 edition of *Book selection*), and the related 'holdings v access' discussion. Some elements of the old book remain, but in essence *Providing materials for library users* is a completely new book.

The word 'users' features in the title as a statement of intent. The aim – I hope at least partly achieved – is to consider user needs, and what we know about them, at every stage of the provision process. Users are not of course the only consideration in provision, but they are a good deal more significant than our library systems and procedures, with which we are so mightily impressed. Everything librarians do should improve the interface between what users need and what is 'out there' in the complex world of information. Providing the right materials is *the* essential component of that interface.

The book is primarily aimed at staff in libraries who have to make decisions about provision, and so is fundamentally concerned with practicalities. But practice has to take on board recent literature and research, so the extensive references in the book should also be of use to students. The range of examples from LIS practice is broader than in *Book selection*, and includes academic, school, workplace and public libraries – mostly from the UK.

My strong impression is that not enough attention is now paid in libraries to key techniques connected with library stock: selection, weeding, logistics and particularly stock revision (which seems to belong in a museum). An extraordinary tendency for librarians to lean upon suppliers for selection is a symptom of a general malaise. The much-increased staff time given to identifying what users want seems only rarely to be translated into stock provision measures. The increasing importance of electronic sources does not diminish the need for such measures, since electronic sources still have to be evaluated and promoted, and often 'selected' too.

I have been fortunate in working relationships over the past 40 years which have influenced thoughts on this complex subject. Two individuals made a particular impact – both, coincidentally, former stock editors at the London Borough of Lambeth, where my own interest in this subject was sparked off: in the 1960s, Marion Wilden-Hart gave me a thorough basic grounding in the practice of stock management; and in subsequent years, Brian Baumfield has been generous in making available to me his considerable time and expertise.

Further reading and references

Recommendations for further reading are marked by number in the text and are listed chapter by chapter at the end of the book (page 175).

References are marked in the text by author and date, and are listed alphabetically under author at the end of the book (page 194).

David Spiller

Acknowledgments

I would like to thank the following for help and advice:

Tom Jackson of Chadwyck-Healey for responding to enquiries about the *KnowUK* product.

David Brown of Askews Library Services for sending details of Askews selection support tools for librarians.

Moira Arthur of Peters Library Service for sending details of the *Children's ROMREAD* CD-ROM.

Mike Hosking, Chris Heaton and Steve Bending of Cambridgeshire library service.

Michael Humphrey for advice on sound recordings.

Ann Chapman of UKOLN for recent information on BNB hit rates.

1
Library policy and provision

Background

Throughout this book there is an emphasis on users: on discovering what users want, and what they think of library services; and on developing services accordingly. But pre-eminent as they are, users' expressed wants cannot on their own dictate policies for the provision of materials.

Sometimes users want services which are not on the agenda of the library's funders, and have to be referred elsewhere. For instance, if students request extensive recreational reading from their university library, most university librarians would explain that they want to concentrate their limited funding on supporting teaching and research, and that students should go elsewhere for recreational reading. Another example might be if student users of public libraries wanted multiple copies of course textbooks; most public librarians would in turn give this request short shrift, saying that course texts were the responsibility of the university.

More often, the depth and variety of demands from valid groups of users add up to more than the library can afford, or find space for – and someone in the organization has to make decisions about priorities. This can be really difficult when institutions have two or more key functions which are different in kind, as with the teaching/research function of universities, or as in the case of UK public libraries, where an over-ambitious brief requires them to service the demands of *all* sections of the community.

In these circumstances, the objectives of the library's parent institution (ie funders) are likely to be paramount in identifying the priorities. Library managers have to discuss and clear library policy with institutional managers, clarifying the issues involved, and setting out ways that policy and funding decisions may translate into different levels of access to materials.

Perhaps the fewest policy dilemmas occur in workplace (or 'special') libraries, where corporate policy is generally clear-cut. In most commercial organizations, for instance, the main objective is related to profits, and the library/information centre's purpose is to contribute to maximizing profits. That said, there are types of workplace library where conflicts might arise between different user groups – for instance, in professional association libraries, between the interests of the association's staff and researchers, and those of external members of the association.

We describe below three situations where there are conflicting demands for the provision of materials, and where priorities have to be established. These show some of the complexities that can arise, and a number of others are touched upon throughout the later chapters of this book. They include the whole question of the desirable *size* of collections, linked to the 'holdings v access' discussion (see Chapter 9).

University libraries: teaching and research

Prioritization is particularly important in universities with heavy research programmes – more commonly the older (pre-1992) universities. These institutions combine two very different functions: the teaching/learning operation, and the research programmes. The functions are characterized by the relatively simple information requirements of students (particularly undergraduate students) on the one hand, and the wide and unpredictable needs of researchers on the other. In crude terms, undergraduate needs are largely served by textbooks, housed in short-loan collections and drawn from lecturers' reading lists. Researchers' needs are served by the bulk of the remaining resources: electronic services, very substantial monograph collections, and above all the current and retrospective runs of serials. In even cruder terms, a very small proportion of the 'materials' serve large numbers of students, whilst most of the materials serve relatively small numbers of researchers. How far is this allocation of resources justified?

The 1997 Dearing report[1] observed a significant tension between the two functions in terms of academics' career development. On the one hand, research was 'currently the main basis for professional reward and advancement'; on the other, universities needed to 'establish higher education teaching as a profession in its own right'. The case for the latter was strengthened by a rapid rise in student numbers, especially during the period 1988–93. Another Dearing report[2] also noted an increase in independent learning amongst students: the average full-time student spent eight hours a week attending lectures compared to 15 hours in independent study (and four hours at tutorials, six on projects and four on other teaching situations).

In university library terms, both these student-related developments – the higher numbers and the move towards independent study – greatly increased the use of library services. So what are undergraduates' views on access to library materials? There is little doubt about their strength of feeling, and it is largely directed at a shortage of textbooks. A survey carried out for Dearing[2] asked a wide range of students the open-ended question: 'What changes or improvements would you like to see made to your institutions or your course?'. Amongst diverse responses related to all types of university services, the issue attracting the highest proportion (12%) was 'A more relevant/wider range of books in the library'. (The second and third issues, each at 9%, were concerned with more time spent on tutorials and remedial teaching, and better communications between staff and students.)

A related question explored student satisfaction with various 'academic-related facilities'. Amongst these, 'Availability of books in the library' attracted:

- 38% 'satisfied or very satisfied' responses
- 15% 'neither satisfied nor dissatisfied'
- 47% 'dissatisfied or very dissatisfied'.

The high (47%) 'dissatisfied' figure was more than double the proportion who felt dissatisfied with the 'range of facilities' in the library, and over three times those unhappy with library opening hours; and in other areas, double those dissatisfied with computing facilities, and with specialist equipment in laboratories.

Should the point need further emphasis, a 1996 survey of university 'stake-holders'[3] on the importance of different aspects of library services found that four groups of stake-holders – part-time and full-time undergraduate and post-graduate students – all gave 'multiple copies of items in high use' the highest priority, amongst 99 different indicators. And Horrocks (1998) reported that 'more books' came top of the list in Priority Search student surveys conducted at Kingston, Leicester, Brighton and Brunel.

On the other side of the user coin, Erens' 1995 survey of academics in UK universities (see Appendix) found a milder picture of dissatisfaction. In all, 12% said the university library met their research needs 'very well', and 55% 'fairly well', whilst 26% said 'not very well' and 7% 'not at all well'. However the 66% figure in the two top categories had fallen from 77% in a similar survey question put six years earlier. Asked about the detrimental effects of recent library changes on their research:

- 27% agreed that they were 'less aware in their subject', but 40% disagreed
- 16% agreed that their 'research was less rigorous', but 50% disagreed.

Finally, asked which two improvements to their university libraries would most benefit their areas of research:

- 53% specified the journal collection as first choice, and 22% as second
- 18% gave the book collection as first choice and 26% as second
- 11% gave 'improved access to external databases' as both first and second choice.

Summarized crudely, the impression we get from these surveys is that students want more books and academics want more serials, but that students are a lot more dissatisfied with existing provision of these materials. How does actual expenditure on materials for these groups look in relation to the pre-1992 UK universities, where much of the higher education research is done? Expenditure is analysed (Library and Information Statistics Unit, 1999b, 111) under serials, books, 'other' (increasingly, electronic services) and staff – but not running costs. In 1997–98, 17% of this expenditure went on serials, 11% on books, 21% on 'other services' and 49% on staff. Compared to the situation ten years earlier, in 1987–88, the proportions of expenditure on these items had fallen: by 15% for serials, 26% for books and 10% for staff. The 'other services' figure had risen by 159%, largely because of the increase in electronic resources.

In other words, despite the intense pressure from students for more books, and the very big increases in student numbers, expenditure on books has fallen more sharply than expenditure on periodicals; and for that matter, both have fallen more sharply than expenditure on staff. Here is a pretty clear example of university and university library managers pursuing a policy which runs in the face of expressed demand from a majority of their users, and against the recommendation of the 1993 Joint Funding Councils' Libraries Review Group[4] – that multiple copies of texts should *not* be reduced to meet journal requirements. There are arguments that can be mustered in support of the strategy, and the policy of investing primarily in research materials (and especially journals) is clearly affected by the high status accorded to research and the strong influence of academics in universities. It becomes harder to defend, though, when we consider the extraordinary price increases in academic serial subscriptions – 162% during the period 1989–99 (Library and Information Statistics Unit, 1999b, 8) – and the scant investigation into serial use in universities; not to mention the findings of a 1998 study[5] that the size of serial collections is not necessarily correlated with gradings in the Research Assessment Exercise. These are matters explored further in the chapter on serials.

Public libraries: user groups and user needs

Priorities in academic libraries appear positively clear-cut when compared with those of their public library counterparts. In part, the public libraries' problems arise from the very broad claims made for them in various official statements in relation to different groups of users and different types of user needs. These look good on paper; but librarians, with limited budgets, have to pick and choose from the official claims as they translate them into services and collections.

For instance, the UK Public Libraries Act (1964) requires public library authorities 'to make facilities available for the borrowing of, or reference to, books . . . and other materials sufficient in number, range and quality to meet the general requirements and any special requirements both of adults and children'. Subsequent government statements have fleshed out this already considerable brief. In 1995 the then Department of National Heritage's *Guidance for local authorities*[6] referred to encouraging individual participation in cultural, democratic and economic activity, and to educational development, as well as making good use of leisure, and promoting literacy. Three years later, the same department, renamed as the Department of Culture, Media and Sport, set out a similar agenda[7] for all publicly funded libraries: formal education and 'economic endeavour' were again singled out, together with the more political agendas of life-long learning, access to information, social inclusion, and 'modernisation of the delivery of central and local government services'.

Given these official statements of library purpose, it is certainly helpful that we now know a good deal about the expressed needs of public library users – though in a sense the breadth and depth of their demands merely underline the practical difficulties. Aslib's 1995 *Review of the public library service in England and Wales* (see Appendix), for instance, reported a heavy emphasis amongst borrowers of fiction and non-fiction books on reading for pleasure, on supporting recreations and pastimes, acquiring information, and supporting educational development – but little work-related use. Patrick Timperley's survey[8] took this process a stage further, refining the 'reasons for borrowing' categories, and assigning to each a percentage of the borrowers of 400 non-fiction titles, viz: borrowing for practical purposes (29%), hobbies (27%), reading for pleasure (14%), study (13%), 'personal development' (13%), and – again a small proportion – work (5%).

Surveys of user needs are a form of marketing activity, but librarians have some difficulties in following through a classical marketing approach. The needs of individual users have to be combined with government agendas for libraries, which relate to society as a whole. In the UK this concerns both central and local government, the two principal funding sources for public libraries, and their corporate objectives are fundamental to library policy. It would be counter-productive, in pragmatic political terms, for any library authority to ignore its funders' broad objectives. In any case, librarians could hardly go out on a limb in this way, because local authorities now develop corporate strategies which cover all their departments. As it happens, at the start of the 21st century the UK government's political agendas are likely to be in tune with public librarians' preferred approaches – as references above to 'access' and 'life-long learning' make clear.

There was some discussion of these matters in the influential 1976 Hillingdon report,[9] which examined the effectiveness of public library attempts to satisfy user needs. The authors concluded that most public library services were 'supplier oriented' – ie that 'needs have a predetermined boundary deriving from the people who are supplying the library service and reflecting their own cultural and educational goals. In this situation the distinction is almost always made between significant needs and by implication unimportant wants or desires'.

There is a reasonable warning note here against ignoring users' views, but we may also argue that 'needs' are simply 'wants' which are as yet unrecognized by users, and that public libraries should make available materials which permit users to satisfy both wants and needs. Getting a balance between the two (there probably is no 'right' balance) is extremely difficult.

In fact, as librarians get to know more about user needs, we find that the gap between official goals and users' expressed needs is not very wide – as the detail of Timperley's survey above reveals. But in all library services there are crucial decisions to be made between conflicting sets of requirements, not least in providing access to materials: between fiction and non-fiction; between recreational reading and reading for information; between the relatively small proportion of heavy borrowers and the much larger numbers who borrow infrequently; between new material and older 'classic' texts. These issues, and others, are explored further in subsequent chapters.

Two further quotations reflect the complexities of policy in this area. Ronald Benge, in a valuable section from his *Bibliography and the provision of books* (Benge, 1963a), wrote:

> . . . those who state simply that a library exists to provide people with what they want forget that the library service itself is one of the agencies which determine what they want. All agencies of mass culture, ie the press, the radio, the television and the cinema, stand in this dialectical relation to the individual and must in the last resort concern themselves with value judgements.

Secondly, Richard Hoggart (1993) quotes T S Eliot responding to the statement

'We aim to give the people what they want, not what we think is good for them.' Eliot replied: 'Those who claim to give the public what the public want begin by underestimating public taste; they end by debauching it'.

This is a policy minefield, and when they cross it – as they have to – librarians are vulnerable to a critical blast from users who are adversely affected by their decisions. We cannot conclude the debate, but it can be summarized: these are highly complex matters, which do not lend themselves to an ideal solution; library managers must be well informed about user wants *and* their funders' agendas; they must set out a scheme of priorities which take both into account, and which are based upon judgement; they must also find ways of translating priorities into collections, through stock management guidelines, budgeting to priorities, and monitoring expenditure accordingly.

School libraries: curriculum support and reading for pleasure

School libraries are always short of funds, and there is a good case for them to prioritize between materials for curriculum support and those for recreational purposes. The 1988 UK Education Reform Act created a compulsory National Curriculum for state schools in England and Wales, which set down curriculum structure, content and timetables. The National Curriculum required an increased emphasis upon the skills and processes of learning, in contrast to the former stress upon content. These changes had clear implications for the role of the school library. The Department of National Heritage's seminal report *Investing in children: the future of library services for children and young people*[10] observed that 'there should be a requirement upon schools to demonstrate how they will provide adequate learning resources' to support National Curriculum teaching.

Helen Spreadbury's *Survey of secondary school library users*[11] contained information about curriculum-related library use compared to recreational use in both state and independent schools. Just over half of 400 pupils used their school libraries solely 'for schoolwork', whilst 18% went solely 'for pleasure' and 31% for both schoolwork and pleasure. The proportions using the library solely for schoolwork increased to over two-thirds amongst the older pupils in years 10–13.

Of course, the 'schoolwork' and 'pleasure' motivations are often linked (particularly in English language/literature studies), and one cannot envisage a school library which did not stock some recreational materials. That said, the primacy of the teaching/learning objective in schools suggests that curriculum support should attract the bulk of a school library's resources; the survey suggested that pupils see it that way too.

Spreadbury also found that nearly 80% of pupils who used the school library also used their public library, regularly or occasionally, prompting the thought that public and school libraries might more often plan provision jointly. Genuine cooperation on acquisitions between different libraries is a rare beast, but given the chronic underfunding of most school libraries, here is an area where rationalization of resources might pay off.

Spreadbury further reported that many teachers failed to refer children to the school library for study-related materials, with a quarter of pupils being directed 'always or most of the time', 43% 'sometimes' and 32% 'not very often or never'. A survey by Gillian Shakeshaft[12] – this time of independent school libraries – showed how many school libraries are distanced from the main teaching/learning function of the school: most said that communication with their line managers was rare, and nearly a quarter of them said that they *had* no line manager; only 11% attended curriculum development meetings. Clearly, if collection development policies are to be concentrated on curriculum support, libraries must first be integrated into school management structures.

Censorship

One unwelcome visitor to the forum on policy is the heavily masked delegate for censorship. There is a very clear distinction between, on the one hand, attaching priorities to different types of service or services to particular user groups, and on the other hand (the censor's agenda), ensuring that certain types of material, reflecting certain user views, are excluded from libraries altogether. An article on this theme[13] brought both censors and defenders of free expression out of the woodwork and into the correspondence columns of the *Library Association Record*. There appear to be quite a number of librarians who believe that they may legitimately proselytize for political and other beliefs through their work, unaware that these are highly damaging views for librarians to hold. The euphemism 'positive selection policies' is sometimes used to soften the censor's image. Bob Usherwood's comment (Usherwood, 1989) that there is 'a degree of tension' between 'positive selection policy' and 'commitment to intellectual freedom' adopts a distinctly uncomfortable posture on the fence. McClellan (1973, 45) provided some definitive guidance:

> The public library is the only channel of communication of ideas and feeling which is not controlled either by powerful minority interests or by monopolies. The public library uniquely affords the expression of all minority views, gives all of them the opportunity of acceptance, or of withering away. Its existence in the form we know is a guarantee of intellectual and political freedom.

Policy statements

It has become fashionable for libraries to produce policy statements on collection management, often as part of a more general process of turning out (in the case of university libraries) strategy documents or (in the case of public libraries) library plans submitted to the Department of Culture, Media and Sport. In Sumsion's 1993 *Survey of resources and users in higher education libraries* (see Appendix), 49% of university libraries had formal collection management policies or guidelines – though, disconcertingly, only 24% had policies agreed by their institution; 52% had a formal stock review or stock disposal policy.

In the case of public library authorities, the 1998 survey of *Information used in public library book selection*[14] found that 39% of 109 responding authorities had a stock management policy, 14% did not, and 48% had one in preparation. A larger proportion of authorities had a book selection policy (51%), whilst 15% did not, and 35% had one in preparation.

The *Guidelines on public library stock management*[15] were jointly instigated in 1998 by The Library Association and the National Acquisitions Group. They recommended that stock management guidelines should be prepared by all authorities, and annually reviewed. They should cover: the range of stock; the requirements of different user groups; the stock management process; criteria for the inclusion and exclusion of materials; qualitative and quantitative targets; stock rotation targets; refurbishment, relegation and withdrawal policies; and stock security policies.

A publication edited by Futas[16] has some actual examples of policy statements, though these are all from American public and academic libraries in the 1970s. Wood and Hoffman's *Library collection development policies*[17] included examples of policies from academic, public, special and school libraries. Cole and Usherwood[18] in 1996 examined different approaches to stock management taken by UK public library authorities. A survey by Capital Planning Information Ltd in 1987[19] listed the kinds of information that were found in UK authorities at that time.

It is hard to know how much use policy statements really are. Good ones can ensure a consistency of approach amongst staff, and serve as a planning tool for managers, as a statement of purpose for funders and/or committees, and even as a source of information for library users – though not all libraries will find it politic to make their priorities known so openly.

But there are difficulties about producing genuinely useful policy documents. Broad statements of intent ('the library takes account of varying needs . . . anticipates future requirements and current demands . . .' etc) are of little practical use – although some policy statements consist almost entirely of generalizations along these lines. The documents need to define priorities and services in a way that is meaningful to both policy makers and policy executors. Whilst it is possible to state the priority given to different user groups, and even to different user wants, there are problems about translating these into actual services or materials. For instance, one may easily state that no more than 25% of fiction funds will be spent on light fiction, but the statement is unhelpful unless all parties involved agree on the definition of 'light fiction'. Definitions become even more complex when we consider different categories of non-fiction.

The title of Snow's article – 'Wasted words? The written collection development policy . . .'[20] betrayed where the author was coming from. Snow argued that, to write a policy, managers must indicate what they have already as well as where they want to go. All the same, he did not rate the American 'Conspectus' system, which offers a numeric grading system for evaluating academic library collections, and which has only been taken up by a handful of UK librarians. Summarizing, Snow believed that a written collection policy was too inflexible to justify the significant investment necessary for its creation and maintenance, and that it was better to evaluate how the library was used, and why.

In conclusion, we may say that where policy guidelines are used, they cannot be effective on their own. They depend upon good communications between policy makers and other staff – through, for instance, staff seminars and workshops – as well as unambiguous statements in the documents themselves. Even then they are likely to remain pious statements of intent unless backed by financial allocations to stated priorities, with subsequent monitoring to ensure that funds are actually spent as directed.

2
Budgeting

Under the headings of academic and public libraries, this chapter examines two aspects of budgeting:

- how is a library's budget figure for materials reached?
- how is that figure divided up, or allocated, within the library system?

Academic libraries

Baker's work *Resource management in academic libraries*[1] is essential reading, and much quoted below; see also Ford's contribution on finance and budgeting,[2] and Breaks's chapter on the management of electronic information.[3] Graham's earlier contribution on university library finance in the 1980s[4] and Fletcher's chapter on financial management systems[5] are very clear statements, but both now over a decade old.

Despite the diversification of income generation, most university funding still comes from the state; Baker observed that typically 90% was from taxation and 10% from income generation. Since 1992, UK higher education institutions have received core state funding from the higher education funding councils: the Higher Education Funding Council for England (HEFCE), the Scottish Higher Education Funding Council (SHEFC), the Higher Education Funding Council for Wales (HEFCW) and the Department of Education for Northern Ireland (DENI). Baker commented that a university's financial position was increasingly uncertain, since the size of these central grants was rarely known well in advance of the academic year – and library budgets were correspondingly often guessed at until after the year had begun.

Funding mechanisms for UK higher education institutions are generally more transparent than they were. The funding council allocations distinguish explicitly between the universities' two main functions: teaching, based upon student numbers in different disciplines; and research, based upon grades received in the previous research assessment exercise. University librarians – and others responsible for central support services – need to be aware of the detail of these allocation procedures, and to press for clear mechanisms for channelling funds from the various income streams into their service areas. Some libraries receive their grant as a percentage of the university's central grant – though, as Baker observed, this creates problems if only 50% of an institution's income comes from the government.

In universities the major resource areas of staffing, plant and running costs are normally handled centrally, so the library's contribution to resource management has concentrated on the acquisitions process. Baker commented that, historically, resource management for academic librarians meant – and for some, still means – three types of activity:

- making an annual bid for funds to cover materials, based upon estimates of need and previous budgets
- allocating resources between different spending headings (books, serials etc)
- monitoring the rate of expenditure.

But the current trend is towards full devolution of resources to spending departments. Everest's report of a 'devolved budgeting workshop' (Everest, 1999) summarized the advantages and disadvantages of devolution.

Where libraries use the 'historical' procedure of bidding for funds based upon an increase on the previous year, an indication of the increased costs of materials is needed. LISU's *Average prices of British academic books* (Library and Information Statistics Unit, twice yearly) provides this for monographs, and Blackwell's information on serial prices is published annually in the *Library Association Record*.

We examine below the use of formulae for allocating funds to individual university departments. Whether funding is decentralized in this way or coordinated centrally by the library, a number of other (increasingly complex) decisions must be made about the way funds are divided up between functions and/or types of material.

Books versus serials

In practice, serials are absorbing increasing proportions of materials budgets – a problem discussed in Chapters 1 and 10. In crude terms, the choice between serials and books could be represented as one between research and teaching functions – although there is of course a considerable overlap between these functions and the two types of material.

Print versus electronic

The expenditure of pre-1992 universities on 'other costs' (primarily consisting of electronic materials) has increased from 8% of all library costs in 1987–88 to 21% in 1997–98, and we may expect this percentage to go on rising for some years. In addition to purchased materials (notably CD-ROMs), this heading includes commercial service charges, and hardware/software costs to support access. For a variety of reasons, many of the electronic materials costs are best handled centrally: items such as CD-ROMs are often costly and multidisciplinary in coverage; JISC-funded datasets such as BIDS-ISI (see Chapter 4) are subscribed to in bulk (formerly on a flat charge, now charged according to use); and electronic journals are usually handled through a single supplier, or through bulk agreements with commercial publishers. Electronic information resources are generally more expensive than print resources, and networked resources are more expensive than standalone facilities. At present, many electronic publications can only be subscribed to *along with* their print equivalents. The use of secondary sources – which currently dominate the electronic market – tends to *increase* the demand for print resources (so there is no print 'saving' to be offset against increased electronic expenditure).

Ownership versus access

The choice between buying and borrowing is discussed in Chapter 9, including Cranfield's BIODOC experiment, where print serials were cancelled in favour of electronic contents listings and rapid document supply. Developments in this area are most likely to affect serials collections in the near future. Budgeting for interlibrary loans (ILLs) is becoming increasingly important, and most universities already operate quota and rationing systems to restrict demand. Baker suggested that suballocating an ILLs budget to departments might also contribute to controlling costs overall.

Special collections

Funding for special collections often comes from a separate source.

Many universities now use formulae as an aid to dividing up materials funds between different departments or different subjects – most often for book funds – but these could and perhaps should be extended to other types of materials, particularly serials and interlibrary loans. Hutchins's chapter on this theme[6] in Baker's book is essential reading. Ford[2] also discusses formulae in detail, and cites articles on the subject by McGrath (1975) and Kohut (1974). Budd[7] wrote on the subject in 1989.

Ford noted that, in 1998, 19 out of 25 academic libraries surveyed used formulae of some sort, mostly to 'slice a given cake' rather than to decide the optimum size of the cake. He noted the difficulty of constructing a formula from the large number of possible variables:

- staff and student numbers (the most common feature, often weighted to take account of postgraduate numbers)
- size and/or use of existing stock
- amount of research activity
- previous expenditure
- average prices of published materials
- amount of publishing output by subject field
- obsolescence rate of subjects
- relative importance of books and serials by subject
- relative importance of split sites
- importance of departments
- differences between hard and soft disciplines.

Hutchins[6] summarized the reasons for using formulae:

- they were more equitable, and seen to be more equitable (and for this reason should be based upon wide consultation)
- they increased the library's efficiency
- they maximized benefits in relation to costs.

On this last point, it was important to define *who* would benefit:

- the university, in terms of research output
- students, in terms of examination results
- the library, in terms of satisfying needs.

Hutchins included some pragmatic advice on developing formulae. On the key measure of 'numbers of users' (teachers, students and researchers), he suggested a weighting system making one member of lecturing staff worth four undergraduates, and a postgraduate worth two undergraduates. An alternative to absolute numbers of students was to count the number of student course hours. Some universities might want to weight *subjects*, where they intended to increase research performance over a given period. Use data could include stock turnover (average issues per item per year), the length of time that items were borrowed, or the number of items on loan at any one time.

Hutchins advised that libraries needed to come to an agreement with departments about the time span over which the formula would apply, and recommended a minimum of three years. He also noted the strong influence exerted by historical precedent; this was a poor guide to the division of funds, and had to be supplanted, but it was politic to do so gradually – fixing initial allocations close to the traditional ones, then moving to a more logical system by stages.

Whatever the allocations decided upon, universities normally put aside a substantial reserve for the library to cover general material which does not fall under subject or departmental headings: reference material, government publications, subject areas which are of interest but are not taught, abstracts and indexes. The reserve can also help to correct any of the imbalances which arise from departmental ordering.

Yeadon and Cooper's 1995 article on book selection and bookfund management at the Imperial College libraries[8] summarized the complexities that can occur in an institution with 15 departmental libraries plus a central library. Departmental funds covered the research requirements of the departmental libraries, independently from the central library. Special collections received funding both from departments and from the centre. The central library handled background curricular reading, interdisciplinary and reference materials, and student texts – the last of these on the basis of an agreed formula.

Public libraries

Public library budgets derive from local authority budgeting procedures. For various reasons, the size of a library authority's book fund is more often the result of circumstances and local politics than reasoned calculation. In the 1970s the librarian's aim was usually to achieve as large an increase on the previous year's fund as the finance committee would tolerate. In the economic climate of the past two decades, most librarians would be happy to achieve a figure equal to the previous year, with an increase to cover risen costs if they are lucky.

Records of public library budgets – estimated and actual – are issued annually by the Chartered Institute of Public Finance and Accountancy (CIPFA, annual). The figures for 1997–98 show that, over the UK as a whole, 55.4% of expenditure went on staff, 12.0% on premises, and 11.4% on books (compared to percentages a decade earlier of 51.4%, 10.5%, and 16.1% respectively). There is more detail on the decline in book funds – compared to increased staffing and administrative costs – in LISU's *Public library materials fund and budget survey*

(Library and Information Statistics Unit, annual).

In 1973 McClellan[9] tried to systematize calculations to determine the size of bookfund required by defining all the factors involved:

- the total population of the authority, and the number of users
- the numbers of new books published per year, and their risen costs
- the longevity of stock on open shelves (or depreciation rate)
- the range and condition of existing stock.

Information about 'depreciation rate' – or the rate of physical decline of existing stock – is available from various sources. McClellan gave a crude yardstick of 60 issues for fiction and children's books and 75 issues for non-fiction. Houghton[10] suggested 80–100 issues over 5–7 years for hardbacks, and 30–40 issues for paperbacks. A Hertfordshire survey (Herts Library Service, 1984) gave an average of nine years for a hardback, and an Australian survey gave eight years (*Public Libraries in Australia*, 1976). For greater accuracy, taking local circumstances into account, authorities are advised to conduct their own investigations. Once a reliable figure has been reached, they can derive from it an annual replacement figure for the total existing stock (as long as outdated material has first been weeded out).

Authorities sometimes content themselves with quantifying increases in the numbers of books published, and an average price increase. Six-monthly lists of average book prices, broken down by subject field, are published in the *Bookseller* (weekly). Some authorities take from the automation system their own average book prices, based upon the previous year's accessions to stock.

In theory the quality of existing stock is an important contributory factor to the size of book fund required, but in practice it is extremely difficult to quantify – unless stock has fallen to gruesome levels.

As remarked earlier, national trends and local politics are often more influential in fixing book funds than any figures put forward. That said, the most useful lever for librarians wanting to increase their book funds can be their authority's 'expenditure per capita' figure in a league table of similar authorities – or better still, a benchmarking exercise showing expenditure, additions and use against other authorities over a period of time.

Once a book fund figure has been decided upon, the key management role is to allocate funds and monitor expenditure to see that allocations are adhered to. This is *the* main mechanism for ensuring that priorities set out in policy statements are translated into reality.

The CIPFA statistical return requires authorities to report expenditure allocations under a number of materials headings, in addition to books. In 1997–98 the proportions of total library expenditure reported for the whole of the UK were:

- newspapers and periodicals 0.9%
- sound recordings 1.2%
- videos 0.5%
- other acquisitions 0.8%
- computing costs 6.7%.

One may assume that these rates of expenditure are consistent with *allocations* for these materials – though this is not necessarily so. A 1987 survey[11] showed that about 20% of authorities at that time did not even allocate amounts for adult fiction or children's books; we do not have any more recent information on allocations practice.

There are a number of different ways that bookfunds can be carved up – some widely used, some rarely. Possibilities include:

Regions/service points

We comment in Chapter 7 that making allocations to regions or service points, rather than coordinating provision centrally, criminally misses out on the opportunity to stock the widest possible variety of relevant titles. Nevertheless, geographical allocations still occur.

User groups

Children's provision is invariably separated. The *Investing in children* report[12] recommended that children's services should receive allocations at least in proportion to the percentage of children in the authority's population. Other user groups commonly separated are housebound users, hospitals and prisons.

Function

Possible headings here are recreational reading (or light fiction), adult literacy materials, open learning, textbook collections, reference material, local studies and foreign language books.

Subject

Allocation by subject is relatively rare – unless 'fiction' is counted as a subject. Some authorities separate 'music' (comprising print and recorded sound materials).

Format

Many public libraries now spend large sums on paperbacks, and some budget for them separately (see Chapter 16).

Level

Most authorities put a high priority upon introductory and standard works, rather than advanced material, but this is rarely quantified in the budget.

Stock revision

Expenditure on stock revision – as opposed to newly published books – is included in this list more in hope than expectation. The subject is discussed in Chapter 5, where we suggest that the quality and coverage of stock *on the shelves* can only be maintained through extensive stock revision, backed by allocation of up to 50% of total funding. That this rarely occurs does not diminish its desirability. Valentine[13] described how new book selection in Hertfordshire was centrally controlled, but allocations were made to service points for stock revision purposes (see Chapter 7).

3
Evaluating print materials

In this chapter we discuss the different sources and factors which librarians use to evaluate material – price and date of publication, physical characteristics, publishers' information, reviews, reservations, and a whole range of bibliographies – and the ways that these are combined to reach a selection decision. Two recent surveys[1,2] – of public and special libraries respectively – reported on how intensively these various sources were used for selection purposes. Electronic materials and special materials such as serials and fiction are covered elsewhere, in the relevant chapters.

In practice it is rare for all the sources mentioned to be taken into account before items are selected. Some books (or other items) almost select themselves if they fit a library's aims – though someone must still decide upon the number of copies to be ordered. Others are virtually ruled out by one unsuitable feature – inappropriate subject matter, an astronomical price, a spiral binding and so on.

Information about a new book does not all become available at the same time. Publishers' catalogues can arrive several months in advance of the books they announce. Publication of the book itself is followed shortly afterwards by its listing in a book trade bibliography, then in a national bibliography, and by some of the reviews. During this whole period, reservations may be received from users. Specialist reviews appear later still (up to several years, in extreme cases), and listings in subject bibliographies even later.

With all this information available, when is the right moment to select? We believe that far too little attention has been given to this crucial subject. In one way, selection made several weeks after publication is better than an order on or around publication date, because it allows more information to be collated, and is more likely to lead to a considered use of funds. But there are other pressures for an early decision: the most intensive use of material in research libraries (and some others) is in the year after publication, an argument for getting new books onto the shelves quickly; a title may go out of print if orders are delayed for too long (though this is unlikely in the first months after publication); and there is often reservation pressure for certain types of material.

The cost-effective approach is to centre selection on a single base source (probably a trade listing or national bibliography), and then back it up with other types of information. A base source is especially important in a library system which has centrally coordinated selection for a number of service points (see Chapter 7). A system which can coordinate orders in this way is likely to negotiate better terms from its suppliers. (This also applies when several systems combine in a consortium.) On the other hand, not using a base source leads to staff investigating titles via different sources at different times, wasting a lot of time, and – in all probability – placing unintentional duplicate orders. Despite these fairly obvious advantages and disadvantages, many library systems do not opt to coordinate selection around a single tool.

Many library managers insist on seeing books before ordering, through the use of 'approvals' copies obtained from library suppliers. (About half of public library authorities used approvals in 1998.) This approach is taken to some lengths by children's librarians, who often 'review' books before buying them (see Chapter 13). Though the practice is widespread, it is hard to see the logic of using approvals copies, since there are relatively few instances when seeing the book helps a selection decision, and even fewer where it is significant – especially since the biggest consumers of approval copies are public libraries, which number few subject experts amongst their staff. Can there be any meaningful communion – in a five-minute inspection – between a librarian and a novel, a biography, a book on plumbing or thermodynamics – or even a work on library classification?

There is no evidence that books ordered from approval collections are any more 'successful' (success being measured in terms of use) than books ordered by other methods. In fact, Peasgood (1988) demonstrated in an academic library that they were not. As it happens, approvals services appear to be waning; following the discontinuation of the Net Book Agreement, libraries prefer to take cash discounts rather than approval copies and other 'hidden' services formerly extracted from suppliers.

A good deal of pre-publication (or advance) ordering takes place in all kinds of library. The ultimate form of this is the 'standing order', usually used for annual publications. In their case it makes sense because much is known in advance about the content of annuals, and they tend to go out of print soon after publication. Standing orders are also sometimes used for all the titles in a series; this is more questionable, because the quality of individual titles in a series can vary so much.

Another type of advance ordering occurs when public libraries order multiple copies of fiction or non-fiction by well-known authors, on the basis of information received from library suppliers. Though this is common practice, its value must be open to question. The individual titles of (for instance) a well-known novelist are rarely uniform in quality; moreover, this is the one type of material where reviews are almost guaranteed soon after publication, and can be used to estimate how much duplication is sensible. Reservation pressure – from a minority of the library's customers – should not be allowed to distort provision in these cases.

Price

Judgement of price requires an awareness of the pricing structure of publishing, which has produced a given price at any given time. The selling price of a book stems principally from the number of copies which are printed, which in turn depends upon the publisher's estimate of likely demand. A work of scholarship on an esoteric subject will sell for a significantly higher price than a novel of approximately the same length and format by a popular writer. Also, books deliberately produced to a high standard of physical appearance cost more than the average.

Judgement of 'a good buy' is only one element of selection, very much subordinated in importance to the subject and quality of the book. In theory, there should be few cases where a 'good' title is not ordered at all because the price is considered too high. In practice, price does often seem to weigh quite heavily in selection decisions. Chambers and Stoll[3] provided some impressionistic evidence to this effect for public libraries. The average price paid for a book in UK public libraries in 1997–98 was £8.65 – extraordinarily low, even given post-Net Book Agreement discounts and a high proportion of paperback purchasing. This price showed an increase of only 38% over the past 10 years, compared to an increase of 50% in the *Bookseller* price index. The average price for 1997–98 was actually lower than average prices for the years 1992–97 (Library and Information Statistics Unit, 1999b, 36).

In UK higher education libraries, the average price per book purchased in 1997–98 was £16.77 – an increase of only 3.4% on the average price for 1993–94 – compared with an increase of 13% over the same period in the LISU *Average prices of British academic books* (Library and Information Statistics Unit, twice yearly).

Some further evidence on prices came from a trend analysis of acquisitions,[4] which looked at the ratio of the median acquisition price to the median published price. In public libraries, this fell during the period 1986–97 – from 0.50 in 1986 to 0.43 in 1996, before rising in 1997 to 0.47. In academic libraries the ratio fell from 0.73 in 1984 to 0.55 in 1994 – rising to 0.63 in 1998.

The picture described here is one of low – and diminishing – average prices in both public and academic sectors. Other information suggests that high price is a key element of many titles requested through interlending systems. The situation gives rise to some concern, since there is a strong argument for libraries giving *priority* to the high price titles which individuals cannot afford to purchase. 'Getting a bargain' is not the main purpose of library purchasing.

It would be worthwhile to research more information on the 'thresholds' above which librarians in different sectors are reluctant to purchase. There were several mentions in the Chambers and Stoll survey[3] of £20 as the threshold for some public librarians. In special libraries it is very much higher: a 1995 survey of 326 special libraries (see Appendix) found that £172 was the average price below which libraries would usually buy a book, whilst £346 was the average above which they would never buy.

Identifying new book prices is increasingly a problem, as price information tends to be omitted from publishers' catalogues, and from national bibliographies – and any advance prices given may have risen considerably by the time of publication. Despite these difficulties, it goes without saying that no book should be ordered unless the price is known.

Date

Clearly, the date of a book's publication is a much more significant selection factor in some subject areas than in others. All the same, it is difficult for librarians to apply any general principle of obsolescence for selection purposes (see Chapter 8 for a discussion of this). For instance, Peasgood's study of researchers' borrowing in a university[5] noted an often unexpected dominance of recent publications. On the other hand, Smith's analysis of popular non-fiction in a public library authority[6] reported that very few of the most popular titles had been published recently.

We discuss in Chapter 5 the apparent lack of stock revision in UK public libraries, and the relatively small numbers of 'old' books being ordered. A trend analysis of acquisitions in the UK[4] provided some further information about the dates when books were acquired in relation to their publication dates, breaking this down into four large subject groups. The subject breakdowns do not always pan out as expected. In public library authorities, the largest proportions of the samples ordered 'new' (ie in the year of publication or the following year) came from the 'language, literature and biography' group, where getting books onto the shelves quickly does not seem to be a priority, at least in terms of their rate of obsolescence. This probably happens because many of the titles in this group are heavily publicized on publication, especially through reviews. On the other hand, the smallest proportions ordered new came from the 'law, medicine, computing and technology' group, where making material rapidly available *is* a priority.

In the academic library samples there were – very surprisingly – larger proportions of 'old' acquisitions than in the public libraries, with only about two-thirds of all acquisitions made in the year of publication or following year. Given that stock revision is relatively rare in higher education libraries, we may only speculate as to the reasons for so much older material: a holding back of orders because of budget cuts; slower appearance of reviews; upgrading of stocks in the new universities; larger proportions of short-loan collection orders; or more second-hand material?

In the subject breakdown for academic libraries, the largest proportions of 'new' acquisitions (ie in the year of publication or following year) were in the social sciences (74%) and science and technology (70%). Even so, this meant that 30% of orders in science and technology were delayed by at least a year – a high proportion in collections largely devoted to research, where users want to get hold of new titles quickly.

Level

Audience level is an important feature of material purchased for libraries, but until now it has largely resisted accurate definition. Sweeney (1977) and Jones and Pratt (1974) made some early attempts to produce definitions – the latter carrying out experiments based on six 'level' categories:

- compendia
- light, popular
- serious popularized
- elementary
- standard (authoritative works and standard factual presentations)
- advanced.

McClellan (1973, 68–73) proposed a different series of categories based upon what he called the function of material rather than level alone:

- prospective (popular and general reader guides to the subject)
- instructional and structural (for mastery of the main elements of the subject)
- bibliography and reference
- interdisciplinary and specialist (related fields of knowledge as they bear on

the main subject, as in history and sociology)
* critical and projective (research and innovatory thought).

To date, none of the various definitions of level have been widely accepted, and interest in this subject seems to have died down. Published bibliographies rarely give level indicators, and information deriving from publishers – which is potentially the most useful source – is often highly unreliable. Probably the most helpful indications are provided by the contents lists given in the fuller bibliographical records from Book Data. The need to define level remains important, and deserves further attention.

Readability

In theory, a book (or any other information vehicle) which scores high on readability is a better buy than one which does not. That said, it is doubtful whether librarians can take much account of the concept of readability in selecting material. In novels and other creative writing, literary style is no big deal to many users. One survey[7] observed that two out of three fiction readers in libraries did not look at the text of a book before choosing it. In literary fiction – where style is often considered important – there is unlikely to be much agreement between library users, literary critics or librarians as to which authors 'write well'.

In academic and practical books, a clear and readable style which allows the reader to absorb information easily is certainly a desirable feature. Given time, a group of librarians would probably reach some consensus as to which books fell into this category; but time is rarely available. This sort of analysis will become possible as and when more works are digitized, and computer analysis is made of features such as sentence length. But in any case, in most works of an advanced nature (research material, monographs etc), the content is unavailable in any other form, and the user's interest and motivation overcomes any stylistic deficiencies.

There is perhaps a role for analysis of style where libraries are carrying out major stock revisions, and making comparisons between a number of different books on the same subject; this chiefly applies to popularizations, introductions to a subject field, and textbooks, where badly written works may be rejected because there are alternatives available.

Physical features of books

To what extent is selection influenced by a book's physical features? A well-known publisher, Anthony Blond, wrote (Blond, 1971, 43):

The design and appearance of a general book matters but not too much: after all, printing is only a form of communication and rarely an end in itself. A book should be readable and clean, and the design should not obtrude to the extent that it distracts the readers from the author's thoughts.

This statement holds good for anyone selecting books for libraries. Content is the main consideration, and it is rare for physical characteristics to make a decisive contribution. This is particularly the case in academic or special libraries. (Before the onset of desktop publishing, perusal of duplicated or varityped documents was an occupational hazard of the research worker.)

There are a few exceptions to this general rule. Oversized books suffer from quite a serious disadvantage in that they are housed in a separate sequence from the main stock and invariably less well used, and this often influences librarians to buy them in more modest quantities. Some libraries avoid spiral bindings. All libraries should, if possible, avoid books which are so tightly bound that they have to be held forcibly open.

Similarly, standards of typography are rarely a decisive factor in selection, but there is no doubt that small print is disliked by many readers – including those with good eyesight – and should be avoided on the relatively rare occasions when alternatives are available (as, for instance, with different editions of popular classics).

Publishers' information

The use of publishers' information for selection purposes varies according to the type of library. A 1998 survey[1] found that 20% or less of UK public library authorities used publishers' catalogues for selection. Academic libraries are likely to make more use of publishers' information. (We have no recent data available, but a 1979 survey (Smith, 1979) found that 35% of academic libraries used publishers' catalogues. Special libraries perhaps use them most: a 1995 survey by the Council of Academic and Professional Publishers[2] found that 67% used publishers' mailed circulars, and 62% publishers' catalogues. Along with 'user requests' and 'reviews' these were the main selection sources used.

From a selection point of view, the self-evident limitation of publishers' information is that it is a form of advertising. It promotes – but does not evaluate – the product. Selectors using such information soon become wise to typical selling wheezes, such as over-claiming for audience ranges ('the book is aimed at undergraduate, postgraduate, research and professional audiences' etc). That said, publishers' catalogues and circulars cannot help but give out some useful information about the *content* of books. In some cases, and especially if a pre-publication order is being contemplated, this is often the only kind of information available of any kind.

The more specialized the catalogue, the more likely it is to be used for selection – as, for instance, with the catalogues of local publishers, of specialized formats (such as large print), or of subject areas which are dominated by the works of one or two publishers. To these we may add the catalogues of grey literature, which is largely neglected by the library suppliers. Atton (1994) discussed the thousands of small UK publishers in areas such as politics and poetry; in his view, their non-standard work provided an alternative to what he called 'the dominant paradigm' of democratic capitalism sustained by the mass media channels.

Selecting from publishers' catalogues throws up two practical problems. Their information about price and publication date often proves to be inaccurate when the books appear, because of their inclusion before the final details were known to the publishers themselves. And there are logistic problems involved in selecting from a very large number of catalogues; it is easier to use a single bibliographical source, cross-checking to publishers' catalogues if more details are needed about particular titles.

Reviews

In a 1995 survey,[2] two-thirds of UK special librarians said they used 'reviews in the specialist press' as a selection tool; and in a 1998 survey,[1] about a third of UK public librarians reported using reviews – 32% for adult non-fiction, 37% for adult fiction and 27% for children's books.

There are several different kinds of reviewing source. The broadsheet newspapers (daily and Sunday), and weeklies such as the *Spectator* and the *New Statesman*, devote generous space to book reviews. These refer mainly to fiction and biography, and to a sprinkling of popular books on art, history, humour, poetry and natural science. Some also review children's books. Most of these reviews appear just before or soon after the publication of the books they cover – a promptness which is their most valuable feature, and which contrasts with reviews in the specialist press. Between them they produce at least one review of most 'serious' fiction, and most biographies of well-known people; and they also generate a good number of reservations for these categories in public libraries.

There are a few general reviewing journals. The *Times Literary Supplement* is almost an institution, publishing about 50 full scholarly reviews a week, from most fields except science and technology. The *London Review of Books* publishes very lengthy reviews of a political and literary nature. In both these journals, reviews customarily appear well after publication date. The *Good Book*

Guide is a useful reviewing tool for public libraries, though is produced by a bookseller, and therefore designed to sell books; but its coverage – fiction, biography, travel, hobbies, popular science, reference works – includes many subjects not given critical attention by other sources.

In addition to these sources mentioned above, numerous book reviews appear in specialized journals. Little investigation has been done on coverage, though it is probable that the majority of books do eventually get covered. 'Eventually' is the keyword; their appearance is usually six months to a year after publication, and often much longer.

Librarians need to know about the main reviewing agencies of interest to their type of library: their frequency and coverage; the authority and quality of their reviews; and the time lags in their appearance. But however good the reviewing agencies are, there are likely to be three main problems about using them. The review coverage, when measured against the total number of books of interest to the library, is inadequate. Delays in the appearance of the reviews mean that librarians must make selection decisions before they appear – or risk material going out of print. And the reviews which are published will often be difficult to trace when the library needs them.

For a few subject areas, libraries should probably make more use than they do of reviews. For instance, in public libraries some form of home-made index to fiction and biography reviews in broadsheet newspapers can guide decisions on the numbers of copies to be bought in these subject areas. Beyond this, most librarians read reviews as a form of long-stop, to make sure they have not missed important titles on their initial selection, or to buy extra copies of titles which have been particularly well received. Potentially the most important use is retrospective, in stock revision lists, to identify the key titles in a subject field; however there is no evidence that reviews are widely used in this way.

Reservations

Reservations (or requests) influence selection in two ways. First, they are often received just before or just after a book has been published, indicating demand for the title; this is a particularly significant feature in public libraries, where quite large numbers of requests may be received for the same title. Secondly, they are received for older books, not in stock but still in print, requiring the library either to purchase the title or to borrow it through interlending systems (or just occasionally, to return the request unsatisfied).

In higher education libraries, many of the data collected concentrate on interlibrary loans rather than requests. However, some of the literature relating to shelf availability is also relevant to studies of requests (see Chapter 5). Sumsion's survey of the period 1986–92 (see Appendix) reported that the proportion of requests to total loans was about 5% – much more than the 1.7% in public libraries (1997–98 data). The figure reflects the importance of purposive use in academic libraries, and particularly the high proportion of student users following up reading list recommendations for specific titles.

Sumsion also found that requests had increased in academic libraries by 96% during the five-year period. He concluded:

> The fact that reservations and recalls increased by so much more than total loans is a significant indicator pointing to an increase in unsatisfied demand and to inadequate copies provided.

His conclusion may hold good for all kinds of library, despite the trend in public libraries for large numbers of requests to be considered 'a good thing'. (Essex County, for instance, trumpeted the news (England and Sumsion, 1995, 200–201) that requests received had trebled 'in recent years'.) A neutral stance to high request rates is perhaps more appropriate, since the implications are not particularly favourable: requests for older material not in stock suggest that important titles were not selected, or have been mistakenly withdrawn; requests for older material already in stock suggests a high rate of failure at the shelf; and large numbers of requests for new titles is merely an indication of demand for fashionable material – a demand which, if satisfied quickly, may signify overstocking of titles which then go quickly out of fashion.

There is some information available on public library requests – though not a great deal – in the shape of two sizeable surveys: Roberts's analysis of the request and reservation service of Nottinghamshire County Library[8] in 1973; and Ian Smith's survey in 1999 of requests in a London authority.[9] The subject content of reservations in these two surveys was rather different – perhaps because of changes over time, and/or because the surveys were conducted in different types of authority. In the Nottinghamshire survey, the majority of requests were for fiction (47%) or popular non-fiction (22%); only 10% were for advanced material and another 12% for a category defined as 'standard works'.

In Smith's survey of nearly 2,000 requests received over a two-week period, fiction took 26% and non-fiction 52% (with children's books, audiovisual and other material also included). Of the 52% of non-fiction, 30% were for new or best-seller material, 37% for practical works or text books, and 32% for books of general or academic interest. In a subject breakdown, the most popular categories were biography (17%), history (11%), 'the body' (10%), travel (8%), society (8%), business (7%) and computers (6%). There was also a breakdown of fiction requests by date of publication: 39% had been published three or more years earlier, 20% one to two years earlier, and 41% in the same year.

Of all the requests made, 1% were for older titles 'not in stock' and out-of-print, and 9% for titles 'not in stock' and not current. Another 10% were not in stock but current.

There is also information about the frequency with which public library customers use the reservation service. Overall, most customers do not use the service at all, and most of those who do use it infrequently. For the whole of the UK, the number of requests per head of the population in 1997–98 was only 0.14 (Library and Information Statistics Unit, 1999b, 85). Of those users seeking a specific book (by author, title or subject) on a given day, only 6% placed a reservation for it.[10] Three surveys of fiction use (Spiller, 1980; Steptowe, 1987; Goodall, 1989) also reported the frequency with which reservations were placed for novels: in one survey 6% frequently, 31% occasionally, and 63% never; in a second, 4% frequently, 42% occasionally and 54% never; and in a third 8% frequently, 15% sometimes, 35% rarely and 43% never. Another survey[11] reported that 78% of fiction readers had not reserved any fiction in the past six months.

As happens with most types of library service use, a small number of people account for a fairly substantial proportion of the reservations placed. Smith found that one-third of those reserving accounted for two-thirds of the requests, and the 23 most prolific 'requesters' averaged 11 requests each. But two-thirds of the users submitted just one request during the two weeks, 18% submitted two requests and 7% three.

What kind of sense can be made from this information about requests for selection purposes? We would argue that reservations are a helpful and necessary service for users, but that large numbers of reservations received in a library do not signify 'success' in any sense. Most users do not submit reservations, and 'reservations pressure' is therefore not a representative or significant indicator of demand, and should not be allowed to distort overall provision of materials. Large numbers of requests for older material – especially if they fall in particular subject areas, or on particular titles – may indicate failures of selection or weeding policy, and prompt corrective action accordingly.

Large numbers of requests for new titles are a different matter. These tend to create a short-term demand which can, if allowed to, dictate acquisitions policy. Comments reported by public librarians in the Chambers and Stoll survey[3] – 'If I had two requests, I would probably buy it'; 'We always have the criterion that we don't allow the request-to-copy ratio to go above five to one' – suggest that some authorities get landed with a lot of duplicates on the shelf after initial demand has died down. Smith's survey of fiction use[12] reported an authority where the most popular 15 hardback fiction titles on a particular day had generated an average of 47 requests each, with the top five responsible for over 100 each. He noted that of the 213 copies of these books in stock in the authority, not one was available on the library shelf; and the titles had generated a measly average of one loan per month, because of the time books spent on the reservation shelf awaiting collection. Figures such as these suggest that the authorities which refuse to accept reservations for fiction in the first year after publication are getting it right.

Bibliographies of current publications

There are now a number of comprehensive tools available in print and electronic formats to assist librarians in selecting and ordering books. CD-ROM is the most common format for these, but they are also increasingly to be found on the Internet. These are essentially tools which aim to list either all the books 'in print' or all those which have been published over a specific period; that it is to say, they cannot be used to evaluate one title against another. But the different degrees of detail provided in the individual entries – detail which assists the evaluation process – is a factor for libraries trying to choose between them. Their coverage also varies between UK publications only and world coverage of books in English.

Where a single source of information on new publications is used as a 'base source' – as suggested above – it is likely to be a trade listing or the national bibliography. In the 1998 CPI survey, *Information used in public library book selection*,[1] 42% of public library respondents said they used the *Bookseller* – the UK's main trade listing of new books, published weekly – as an 'on-publication' source of information; and 24% used *Bookbank* – Whitaker's list of in-print books available on CD-ROM. (The survey also reported that much of the *Bookseller* use was of the seasonal *Buyers Guides* – so use of the weekly main lists may be much smaller.) Whitaker also produces the *Bookbank OP* CD-ROM – a list of titles which have gone out of print since 1970, updated quarterly.

The *Bookseller* aims at complete coverage of large and small UK publishers, and it normally lists new titles in the same month as their publication. David Whitaker (1988) claimed an 86% hit rate for *Bookseller* entries at the time that public libraries ordered titles, and an (improbable) 100% hit rate at the time of cataloguing. We have no reliable recent information on *Bookseller* hit rates. The main disadvantage of a trade listing, in comparison with the national bibliography, is the more limited detail given in entries for each item, which provides less information for a reliable decision.

A second major trade source of information about books – new and 'old' – is the range of products issued by Book Data under the generic title *BookFind*, available on CD-ROM and the web. These are primarily targeted at the book trade, and are apparently little used by librarians, although they have a major advantage over all other sources in the generous information provided about titles on their databases; the details include BIC (Book Industry Communications) subject category indicators, a few lines summarizing each title, contents lists and an indication of readership (though as with most of the information this last item is provided by publishers and frequently over-claims).

The UK national bibliography – the *British National Bibliography (BNB)* – was scarcely mentioned as a selection source by public librarians in the 1998 survey. This is surprising, since its comprehensiveness (within certain limits) and the detail of its content make it an important tool. Butcher's lucid paper (Butcher 1988) described the three main functions of the *BNB*: as a national bibliographic reference service, as an aid to current book selection, and as a source of catalogue and file records. In most developed countries, national bibliographic records are available in machine-readable form – an important point, since in many libraries selection is part of an integrated approach which also includes acquisition and cataloguing, and the records are used for all these functions.

The *BNB* is available in a weekly printed version, a monthly CD-ROM, and on BLAISE – the British Library's automated information service, available through the web. BLAISE provides access to 21 databases, including – in addition to the *BNB* – *British Books in Print*, the Stationery Office database of government publications, data from the UK Centre for Serials, and bibliographic records for all books acquired by the United States Library of Congress. Nicholas and Boydell (1996) found that 73% of libraries (of various types) used BLAISE for interlibrary loan purposes, 68% for enquiries and 33% for acquisitions (though 'selection' was not specifically mentioned).

The *BNB* records give a good deal of information: author, title and subtitle, edition, publisher and place of publication, price, whether there are bibliographical references and an index, International Standard Book Numbers, subject headings and a classification number.

An important element of the *British National Bibliography* records is the UK Cataloguing-in-Publication programme (CIP), which since 1975 has provided pre-publication information for a proportion of the new titles, based upon information provided by the publishers. Since 1996, the CIP has been administered by Bibliographic Data Services Ltd, an independent company based in Dumfries, Scotland. CIP records appear in the printed *BNB* (and related products) between six and 12 weeks in advance of their publication date.

A common complaint about national bibliographies is that the high level of data content included in entries for the benefit of cataloguing records is achieved at the cost of timeliness. Where the *BNB* is concerned, there is consistent and reliable information available about the timeliness of records. Chapman[13] in 1998 described the BNBMARC Currency Survey, which since 1980 has monitored the availability of records in MARC format for titles awaiting cataloguing by UK libraries (and since 1989, for titles awaiting ordering). The information is based on random samples taken on a monthly basis from public and academic libraries in the UK. These 'hit rates' of records sought and found are fairly satisfactory and – at least when hits for November 1999 are compared with those for November 1998 (UKOLN, 2000) – improving:

Table 3.1 *Cataloguing and ordering survey*

	Cataloguing survey Hit rate	
	Nov 98	Nov 99
Academic libraries	79%	80%
Public libraries	84%	85%
	Ordering survey Hit rate	
	Nov 98	Nov 99
Academic libraries	78%	83%
Public libraries	82%	86%

Information from library suppliers

As the demand for 'on approval' copies of books decreases, some suppliers have responded by producing in-house CD-ROMs giving details of new titles (including titles not yet published), stock titles and (in some cases) audio items. Information on the CD-ROMs varies: there are bibliographical details of the kind given in *BNB* records (and sometimes actually taken from MARC records); often a brief description of the book; for some titles, a representation of the book jacket; and other details connected with supplier services, and ordering processes.

There is a need for a detailed investigation into the advantages and disadvantages of using supplier CD-ROMs for selection (compared with using trade databases such as those issued by Whitaker and Book Data). The main advantage is the easy interface for acquisition purposes. A major question mark concerns the coverage of supplier products: how far do they include the smaller, more specialized low-price publications which libraries need to stock but which are unprofitable for booksellers to supply?

For those using these products, a key point is that the detail provided is descriptive and never *evaluative*. In particular, there is no evaluation of titles listed against other titles on the same subject. It is for librarians to superimpose the evaluation process onto the descriptive information given about titles.

There is an exception to the point about evaluation: the most interesting recent development is the *Children's Romread* from Peters Library Service, which adds a short evaluation of each book included, made by qualified librarians on Peters' staff (see Chapter 13). This development provokes some interesting questions about the possibility of related services in future. Would this kind of service from the relatively restricted area of children's books be applicable across the whole range of, for instance, adult non-fiction? Would a short evaluation from one or more library suppliers be of value to librarians? How could the quality of such evaluations be monitored? Would evaluations include comparisons of a title with similar titles? What kind of evaluation would suppliers give to 'bad' books which do not warrant purchase at all?

Above all, perhaps, we may ask why librarians do not cooperate with each other, take the whole process out of the hands of the trade, and produce objective evaluations on a national basis which could help libraries to identify a wide range of 'the best' books for stock.

Some library authorities also require suppliers to produce stock revision lists, based upon profiles provided by the authority. This seems a particularly risky approach, given that suppliers can have only the most cursory knowledge of libraries' existing stock and user needs – not to mention the extensive investigation needed over a substantial time span to identify 'the best' titles in each aspect of a subject field.

The 1998 CPI survey[1] provided a detailed picture of the way that public librarians evaluated and selected books. (It is a pity that no comparable source is available for academic libraries.) The sources reported were split into three strata – arranged chronologically:

1 For pre-publication orders, the main sources used were the *Bookseller* seasonal *Buyers guides*, publishers catalogues' and suppliers' lists.
2 For on-publication orders, the main sources were approvals, although the *Bookseller*, suppliers' lists, visits to suppliers and reviews were also heavily used. Suppliers' CD-ROMs were also accessed by about a third of authorities, and the proportion using this source has almost certainly increased since 1998.
3 For retrospective selection, 'visits to suppliers' was by far the most commonly mentioned source (by about 70% of authorities), while Bookbank, profiled lists from suppliers, visits to stock-holding booksellers and publishers' cata-

logues were also mentioned by 25–40% of authorities.

A cursory examination of this information shows how responsibility for the key function of stocking materials for users is gradually being abdicated to the book trade, notwithstanding the trade's completely different (and entirely legitimate) aim – which is to make a profit. This point applies both to on-publication selection and to stock revision. The justification for the approach, summarized in the CPI report[1] is the 'shortage of time' available to librarians – a comment implying that time could more profitably be spent on other activities. Librarians who selected books apparently indicated that 80% of the titles selected were 'inescapable':

> . . . time spent on selecting them could no longer be justified and approaches that used the knowledge of suppliers to recommend what the library should buy, or supply within agreed selection and financial parameters, were worth consideration, if only to allow adequate time to be spent in the evaluation and selection of the other 20% of titles.

This statement is so full of holes that one must only hope it came from a trade source, and did not accurately represent what librarians had reported.

We must be clear that a supplier-dominated approach would damage user interests in several ways:

1 It would ignore what users want, because suppliers can have only the most superficial knowledge of library use, of what users want in a given library, and (most of all) of what is or is not on library shelves.
2 It would reduce the range and coverage of stock, because suppliers will inevitably soft-pedal on material which it is unprofitable for them to provide.
3 It would fail to distinguish quality stock from 'poor' stock, because suppliers are concerned with selling books, and not with stocking library shelves with 'the best' titles available.

Furthermore, any supplier-led system would require the most stringent and time-consuming checks to be conducted by librarians to verify that these points were being addressed. There is no evidence that such checks *are* being conducted – and in any case, if time is to be put into the provision process, why not use it on selecting rather than checking someone else's work.

Recent proposals from the public library sector have gone even further than 'selection from suppliers' lists' to explore selection by suppliers themselves. It is hard to believe that this is being seriously considered by a body which describes itself as 'professional'. A paper by Moira Arthur[14] – a qualified librarian working for a library supplier – strikes exactly the right note: willingness to do the work (at a cost) for her employers, together with barely concealed astonishment that her former profession may be willing to contract out its most important function.

Subject bibliography

A key element of the stock revision process is that libraries need to identify 'the best' books on the subject under revision. 'Best' is hard to define in this context, but it means something like 'the books generally agreed to be of highest quality, and which are appropriate for that particular library'. If stock revision is to be done properly, libraries need to use *selective* bibliographies – either those put together by librarians or (better still) those already compiled by an authority on the subject who has sifted through the literature and identified the most important items.

A good selective bibliography gives a bird's-eye view of a subject literature, and where a reliable source of this kind already exists, stock revision in that subject area is considerably simplified. Instead of needing to evaluate each item personally, librarians merely select from an already select list. What is mainly required then is to verify the authority and reliability of the lists, and to update their content by evaluating works which have appeared since their publication. Subject bibliographies are therefore the raw materials of stock revision, and librarians revising stock need to acquire a working knowledge of their existence and contents in the same way that a reference librarian is familiar with the major reference tools in the collection.

Benge (1963a), in a valuable discussion of select bibliographies, noted that this kind of listing offers various degrees of helpfulness to its user:

- lists in which items appearing are selected, and purport to be the most important works on the subject, but for which no annotation, evaluative or informative, is given
- lists where symbols are used to give informative or evaluative comment on the content of the titles
- lists in which an evaluative or informative annotation is given for each item
- critical reviewing agencies in which detailed individual evaluations are made of each title.

Subject bibliographies in book form have almost gone out of fashion, though The Library Association still publishes the occasional volume – notably, Walford's *Guide to reference material*. Beyond these, selectors need to hunt around for pamphlet bibliographies, or bibliographies within other vehicles. Some useful sources are:

- organizations concerned with the promotion of books, such as the Book Trust or the British Council
- official bodies, organizations and societies of all kinds which publish select bibliographies of their own field for the benefit of their members, including advisory bodies and quangos, consumer and welfare associations, professional institutions, hobby and interest societies
- libraries which specialize in one subject area
- reading lists and bibliographies in reference books and standard works
- reviews of progress appearing at intervals (often annually)
- bibliographies on the web, such as those on the *Encyclopaedia Britannica* website.

4
Evaluating electronic materials

In the past ten years there has been a big diversification in the range of electronic formats through which libraries offer information to their customers. These developments have moved – and are moving – so fast that it is difficult for librarians to anticipate at any one time which are the cost-effective formats to use, and which *will* be cost-effective in the near and medium-term future. But choices have to be made – between the different electronic formats, and combinations of these formats, and between electronic and/or print formats. We examine below the various criteria for evaluating electronic media – many of them similar to the criteria for print, but some very different – and try to relate these to cost. Library user attitudes are also referred to, reflected in actual use as well as in opinions. To date, many of the electronic sources are essentially material for reference and information purposes, and these are further discussed in Chapter 11. Electronic serials are separately considered in Chapter 10.

Online services

Online searching through hosts was the first form of electronic service to come onto the market, in the late 1960s. Databases are mounted on large computer systems and offered to users for a fee. The traditional ('supermarket') approach is for a large number of databases to be offered by commercial 'host' services (such as DIALOG), though databases are increasingly being made available through the web. The most common method of measuring online use – and thereby charging – is via 'connect hours', with discounts offered for high-volume use.

In higher education libraries, the early use of online hosts began to give way in the 1990s to the purchase of databases on CD-ROM. That continues, but in the period 1989–91 a new concept emerged: the central provision of online access for end-users, making use of JANET (the UK's Joint Academic Network) as a facilitator. This led to the establishment of the Bath Information and Data

Services (BIDS-ISI) in 1991, which gave 'free at the point of use' access to the Institute for Scientific Information databases, and subsequently to a number of others. Initially, standard annual subscriptions were payable by the higher education institutions for use of the BIDS service. At the time of writing the charging structure is being revised, so that fees are matched to the amounts of use in individual institutions. Under both arrangements, fees are a good deal less than institutions would pay for individual purchase of the same databases on CD-ROM. Though new databases are constantly being added to the BIDS menu, the total numbers made available in this way are still small when compared to the numbers offered through commercial hosts.

There have been several studies of BIDS-ISI use. In 1998 Ajibade and East[1] analysed over 3000 questionnaires from BIDS users over a three-week period. Use was divided evenly between undergraduate students (31%), postgraduate students (33%), and academic and research staff (31%). Some 11% of all users said they accessed the service daily, just over half weekly and 19% monthly. Significantly, only 23% of all users accessed BIDS from their institutions' libraries; 12% did so from a computer centre, 13% from their department, and 49% from their office or laboratory.

Two earlier surveys by the same authors, conducted in 1992–93[2] and 1995–96[3] respectively, analysed use by the number of 'sessions' conducted. (A session was defined as the period between logging on and logging off.) They found that there were 85% more sessions in the second survey period – but the information came from 97 sites in the second period as opposed to 67 sites in the first. The average length of a session was between 17 and 18 minutes in both surveys. In the 1995–96 survey, 47% of all use was in the natural and physical sciences, 12% in the clinical sciences, and 10% in engineering and technology; only 9% came in the social sciences and a mere 3% in the humanities.

Chris Batt's survey[4] found that in UK public libraries the use of online searching is diminishing rapidly, supplanted by CD-ROMs and the Internet: whereas over half of public library authorities used online hosts in 1991 and in 1993, only a third did so in 1997.

The most intensive use of online services in the UK is in workplace libraries. The 1998 survey *Libraries in the workplace* (see Appendix) gave details for nine workplace sectors. For instance, 95% of libraries in the finance sector used online services regularly, with three-quarters of them having recourse to three or more databases. Some 70% of energy libraries, 93% of pharmaceutical libraries, and 94% of management consultancy libraries, all used online services on a regular basis. In response to a question about trends, some sectors reported – as expected – that online searching was giving way to accessing databases on the Internet. On the other hand, use of online searching in financial and management consultancy libraries was increasing much more than it was decreasing. The message seems to be that each electronic medium finds its own level in appropriate sectors.

CD-ROMs

CD-ROM technology became increasingly prominent in the 1990s, particularly in academic libraries, and for material such as directories and newspapers it competed with the printed book. Though their initial price is high, CD-ROM products can, once bought, offer unlimited access at no extra charge, so that they constitute a predictable item in the library budget. Initially put to work on a PC with a CD-ROM drive, they are often developed further to run on a local network, opening up their contents to large numbers of users – with suppliers' prices adjusted upwards accordingly.

In higher education libraries networks soon became widespread, affording access over the whole university campus. Though centrally provided databases (such as the BIDS-ISI service) supplanted some databases formerly offered through ROM technology, CD-ROMs remain an important constituent of the information scene for higher education. Leach's 1996 survey[5] analysed provision in 34 universities and 11 HE colleges. The mean numbers of holdings per institution were: 39 titles in old universities, 47 in new universities, and 23 in HE colleges. The mean annual expenditure on CD-ROMs in 1995 was £52,000, rising by 25% to £65,000 in 1996. These figures covered a total of 317 different titles in 1995, and 535 titles in 1996. The list of the ten most common titles reported was entirely comprised of newspapers and citation indexes (Psyclit, MEDLINE, ERIC etc).

The CD-ROM medium is also well used in further education institutions. In institutions of further education, Wallace and Marden's 1996–97 survey (see Appendix) found that the numbers of CD-ROM terminals available to FE students was a median of 13 in small colleges, five in medium-sized colleges, and three in large colleges.

CD-ROM use in UK public libraries, though increasing, is much lower than in the academic sector. Batt's survey[4] found that in 1998, 88% of all authorities had CD-ROM for staff use, and 85% for public use – the latter representing a very big increase on the 1993 percentage. But only a quarter of all public library service points in the UK provided public access at that time. Newspapers and bibliographies were by far the most common forms of content found.

As many as 90% of UK school libraries had CD-ROM facilities in 1997,[6] with newspapers and encyclopaedias prominent amongst the types of content offered. Some of this CD-ROM use is recreational rather than educational.

Spreadbury's survey[7] found that whilst nearly half of year-7 pupils used CD-ROMs regularly (often for recreational purposes), only 21–22% of years 10–13 made regular use of them.

Most workplace libraries offer CD-ROM services either through a stand-alone system or through a networked service. Data for 1997–98 of the median numbers of CD-ROM titles held for different sectors, and the median numbers of searches made per year, are now available (Library and Information Statistics Unit, 1999b, 144–166): respectively, in government libraries, 14 titles and 470 searches a year; in professional association libraries, 10 titles and 200 searches; in legal, commercial and financial libraries, 10 titles and 375 searches; in energy and pharmaceutical libraries, six titles and 200 searches; and in management consultancy libraries, seven titles and 550 searches.

The Internet

No introduction is needed for the collection of interlinked computer networks known by the title of the Internet. Its enormous growth, in the UK as elsewhere, has essentially been concentrated in the 1990s. During this period the Internet has been transformed from an academic network into a widespread popular and com-mercial means of communication – accessed through organizations and libraries of all kinds, but also increasingly from terminals in people's homes. Such has been its impact that many databases traditionally offered through other media – CD-ROMs and online hosts – are now also available on the Internet.

Two of the important facilities offered by the Internet – the ability to exchange personal messages with individuals through e-mail, and to send mes-sages to a number of people through mailing or discussion lists – are largely outside the scope of this book. Our main interest is in the already vast amounts of information set up by individuals or institutions on the Internet's key infor-mation server tool, the world wide web – and in particular, the reference sources which currently constitute many of the sites on the web. They already cover many different types of information, of interest to libraries of all kinds:

- information about organizations and their services, from government bodies, societies, companies, universities and colleges, and many others
- the texts of standard reference works, including many previously offered (or still offered) in print form, such as the *Encyclopaedia Britannica*, the *Oxford English Dictionary*, and yearbooks and directories (see the discussion of this in Chapter 11 – in particular of the *KnowUK* service offered by Chadwyck-Healey Ltd)
- the full texts of material previously published in book form (such as *Litera-*

ture on-line, which will contain over 200,000 English and American works of literature)
- the texts of newspapers, from Britain and overseas
- information about employment opportunities
- government information (from government departments, local authorities, international organizations), including Acts and green and white papers
- current information on world events, sport, entertainment, the weather, transport and numerous other subjects
- catalogues of goods and services
- advice on legal, health and other citizenship matters
- electronic journals and current awareness services (see Chapter 10 for discussion of these)
- library catalogues
- the full text of research reports (often not available in print form).

Also of interest are three information networks for which content is currently being developed, and in the creation and use of which libraries will be heavily involved. The National Grid for Learning, described as 'a mosaic of interconnecting networks and online learning materials',[8] will be a way of finding and using online learning materials (see Chapter 13 for further discussion of this). The 'people's network'[9] will bring together public service information on legal, business, health and personal choice matters. For research libraries, the Joint Information Systems Committee (JISC) is supporting the development of the Distributed National Electronic Resource (DNER; see References), which aims to create a managed national collection of electronic information sources to support academic research (see Chapter 11).

Activities to develop these networks technically, and to train staff, will be supplemented by work on information content: the flagging up of existing Internet sites, the digitization of existing print resources, and the creation of new material specifically for the networks.

The main problems in using the Internet are well known. It contains great quantities of information, and because there is no editorial control, much of this is useless information. (This applies particularly to many of the personal websites.) The sheer size of the enterprise makes it more difficult to identify the material that *is* worthwhile. Some apparently useful sites – for instance, on health – contain dangerously misleading information. Because some sites have to sustain themselves commercially, there is a lot of intrusive advertising. The Internet is a dynamic resource from which sites disappear without warning. Rapid increases in the numbers of users often lead to difficulties and delays in obtaining access.

On the face of it, librarians have a simple question to address in relation to using the Internet for the 'selection' of materials: do they provide access to it, or not? And if they do, is it public access or merely access for staff? But in practice, introducing an Internet service into a library is a good deal more complicated than this. For instance, some types of material are more suitable for Internet access than others, and – when sites are produced on a commercial basis and only made available on payment of a subscription charge – some are more cost-effective than others. Serial contents may be available in print, online through hosts, on CD-ROM or on the Internet, or through various combinations of these options – and a choice has to be made between these options.

Once an Internet service *has* been made available, library users need guidance on how to get the best from it. The proliferation of material on the web has led to a variety of different subject search mechanisms being made available, and choices have to be made between them (see below). It is also helpful when libraries highlight quality sites which they judge to be suitable for their own users; this can be done by indexing and/or 'bookmarking' (or 'privileging') sites on the library's network, or by producing printed guides containing lists of recommended sites. A good deal of library activity along these lines is already taking place.

In many school libraries, the 'privileging' process is taken a stage further, with suitable sites downloaded and integrated with other electronic resources – so that the great bulk of Internet sites are *not* available in the school library. This solves the problem of information overload (and the problem of pupils' access to unsuitable material), but loses the main advantage of the Internet's comprehensive approach (see Chapter 13).

The Internet is now very widely available in UK higher education libraries. University-wide electronic information services often provide pointers to Internet sites or to external subject gateways. Internet access is also provided in many further education institutions, though the numbers of student-access terminals are relatively small: in a 1996–97 survey (see Appendix), the median numbers per 1,000 students (full-time equivalent) were five in small colleges, two in medium-sized colleges, and only one in large colleges. In school libraries, The Library Association's 1996–97 survey[6] found that 31% of all secondary school libraries had Internet access. Access is likely to increase rapidly in all these sectors.

In public libraries, Chris Batt's 1997 survey[4] found that 46% of authorities reported public access to the Internet, but that 95% of all service points remained without access. The figure of 40,000 terminals in public libraries by the year 2002, proposed by the Library and Information Commission's *New library* project,[9] shows how quickly new terminals are being put into place – but also how much work has still to be done. Project Earl was set up in the UK to enable public library authorities to share development experiences in this area.

The public's reaction to the prospect of Internet services in public libraries is – as might be expected – different for different age groups. Bromley's 1996 exit survey of library users[10] found that only 24% of all those users interviewed said they would 'definitely' make use of Internet access, whilst 56% said 'definitely not'; but 58% of the 15–19 age group said they would 'definitely' use, and only 16% 'definitely not'. New services such as the Internet need to be heavily promoted, to library users and non-users alike. Howkins's 1999 survey of non-users of a unitary authority (Howkins, 1999) found that only 40% of all non-users were aware of the existing Internet service – though a third of all non-users, on discovering its existence, said they were 'likely to use' it.

Two surveys of workplace libraries by Spiller and by Creaser and Spiller (see Appendix), shows the extent of Internet use in different sectors: in government institution libraries, 84% had access in 1997–98; in professional associations, 84%; in legal, commercial and financial organizations, 94%; in energy and pharmaceutical libraries, 92%; and in management consultancy libraries, 100%. These figures show big increases on percentages between 20% and 50% in 1994, and 30% and 60% in 1996. For all of these sectors, two of the most common forms of information used from the Internet were government data and company home pages; in addition, more than a third of government and energy libraries used university library catalogues; and a quarter of government and management consultancy libraries used catalogues of goods and services.

Subject searching on the Internet

Databases have to be evaluated before being purchased or (in the case of the Internet) privileged for library use. The various factors involved in evaluation are discussed separately below. In practice, decisions on which databases to use (or not to use) are often decided by one or two key features – rather than an exhaustive trawl through all their qualities.

A lot of the recent literature on evaluating databases refers to the Internet, though for the most part it is also relevant to databases in other formats. Alison Cooke's *A guide to finding quality information the Internet*[11] is especially helpful. Nisonger's chapter on the Internet[12] is also a good summary. Bertha's article[13] comparing the pricing structures of information on various electronic media is invaluable on the relationship between quality and costs. And Craig's article on UK agricultural websites[14] demonstrates an approach to evaluation in a single subject field. A valuable survey of the whole area is Michael Breaks's chapter on the management of electronic information.[15]

Not everyone searching for information on the Internet has access to a list of website addresses which can be accessed directly. Often, the enquirer needs to use search facilities to sift through the vast bulk of Internet sites and identify those most likely to give reliable information on their subject. Cooke[11] classified the different search facilities available into four groups, and the descriptions below are drawn from her outline of them.

Search engines (eg *Excite* and *AltaVista*)

The most commonly used method of finding information on the web, these provide *automatically generated* lists of sites. They have a very wide coverage, but the vast lists of sites resulting from a search are also their main limitation. Search engines do not evaluate the content of sites; the nearest they come to this are the so-called 'relevance rankings', which order (with mixed results) items by the frequency with which the searcher's keywords appear in the title and text of sites.

Subject catalogues and directories (eg *Yahoo* and *Galaxy*)

These are created by *people*, and generate far fewer items than search engines. Suggestions are submitted by the sites' authors. This approach scores more highly on identifying relevant sites, but does not compare sites for quality.

Rating and reviewing services

These *do* evaluate site quality, giving ratings for different features. For instance *Lycos* – one of the best known – gives three ratings (each out of 100) for content, design and usefulness. Inevitably, the coverage of any of these manually compiled services is limited, and the criteria used for evaluation tend to be impressionistic.

Subject-based gateway services (eg *BUBL Link* and *SOSIG*)

These are compiled by information professionals, and include high quality resources only, using explicit evaluation criteria and aiming at specific audience groups. But they cover relatively small quantities of resources, and are updated much less frequently than search engines.

Overview

In summary, it is no more possible to compile a comprehensive evaluation of Internet sites by subject than comprehensive subject bibliographies of books. In the case of the Internet, the speed of its development, and the volatile nature of sites, renders the mapping process even more problematic. But use of the various subject searching methods outlined above certainly facilitates the task.

Evaluation of sites/databases

We turn now to consider how to assess an individual site, once it has been located (with many of these points also applicable to databases accessed through other sources). A site's identification through one of the searching mechanisms described above may form part of the process. Also, many reviews of sites now appear in printed sources.

Personal assessment of some site features will be second nature to librarians accustomed to evaluating printed materials – for instance:

1 The *purpose* of the site, its coverage, and intended audience.
2 The *accuracy* of information – not easy to establish, unless it is possible to spot-check an area known to the person evaluating the site.
3 The *authority* of the site's issuing agency, which is the main guarantee of accuracy. This may be a society or institution which is a recognized authority in one subject area, or one of the many government bodies distributing information on the web. Alternatively, there may be a named 'author', whose authority can be checked via previous work on the subject (although many web authors have *not* 'published' previously).
4 *Cost*. Many sites issued by commercial agencies can only be fully accessed on subscription, or through some form of payment (though some information is often available gratis to encourage enquirers to take the payment step). A comparison of costings between Internet, CD-ROM and online sources is referred to below.

Other features to be evaluated are peculiar to the electronic environment:

1 The main technical consideration is the site's *accessibility*. There may be software limitations, with certain sites only available through specified browsers. The number of images on a site affects the speed with which it can be accessed. Some sites require users to be registered, via a password – usually in connection with charges for the information.

2 The *currency* of information on a site is more important for some subject areas than for others. Electronic sources are generally regarded as being more up-to-date than print, but are not always as current as they seem. Users will want to know when a site was issued and when it was last revised – the latter is sometimes indicated, sometimes not.

3 The *arrangement* of the site, and the ease with which users can move about it, is of secondary importance compared to content – though really poor presentation may eventually result in users going elsewhere.

Craig's survey of information available on UK agricultural websites[14] reflected the strengths and limitations of this kind of evaluation process, and demonstrated some additional ways of assessing content. In terms of continuity, of the 132 sites she examined in March 1998, all but two of them were still available six months later.

In terms of *content*, of the sites which were (or were equivalent to) organizational home pages, 70% included a mission statement, but only 40% gave bibliographical details of their organization's publications. One-third provided information on their organization's infrastructure, such as details of different departments. Only half of the sites gave any kind of contact information, for some or all of the staff.

Craig also noted the proportion of sites which contained more detailed information: the full text of new items, fact sheets or documents. The results were disappointing. Some 70% had a minimum of one item of detailed information – but one item was also the most common number of items. A quarter of the sites had none, while only 20% had a 'what's new' section.

In terms of currency, 46% of sites displayed a revision date, and most of these had been revised at least in the preceding year (a quarter in the preceding three months, and 13% in the same week). But 19% remained unchanged when checked six months after the first visit.

Craig also cross-checked the organizational websites against two printed sources: the *Aslib directory of information sources in the UK*, and the *Directory of rural organizations*. Both printed directories had more entries than the 132 websites; on the other hand, only 56 of the *Aslib directory* entries and 75 of the rural organizations directory entries were matched by websites. A similar situation was found in the detail of the entries in these sources: the websites were able to provide more information, but not all of them covered all the content provided in printed directories.

Craig concluded that there were enormous variations in the range of information found on different sites. Some had been very impressively put together, while others appeared to be rushed jobs. There were some useful starting points for exploring agricultural information, but no major UK gateway site existed; and there was a real need for a comprehensive list of agricultural websites. These are points which no doubt apply to many subject areas on the web.

Nicholas's 1999 article[16] on developing testing methods to determine the use of websites explored use measurement in relation to the newspaper industry.

Selecting between different formats

Developments in electronic services are making the business of 'providing materials for library users' increasingly complex. Some material is now available through at least three or four different sources: print, CD-ROM, the Internet or via online hosts. Librarians need an overarching policy for provision of all these media, but they also have to make hundreds of individual decisions about which medium (or media) should be used for any particular item of content. The items currently available in a large number of formats often come under the heading of 'reference material' (including large numbers of bibliographical databases); but format choice will increasingly affect teaching and research materials and monographs.

We consider immediately below the most important features to be considered; cost – probably the most important – is discussed separately.

Frequency of use

This means the frequency with which any particular item or database is likely to be used. Something which is likely to be a one-off request (*likely* to be, because no one can be sure) may be obtained via an online host (if in electronic format) or interlibrary loan (if in print). If use is considered likely to recur, the library is more likely to want to possess the item. The popularity of the CD-ROM format is in large part due to one feature: it permits repeated use with no additional charge (on an admittedly high original price). The point has also been true of BIDS databases, though the introduction of differential charging rates (according to use) may lead to some rethinking.

Number of users

This refers to the number of users wanting access to an item at any one time. There is a world of difference between (on the one hand) a standalone CD-ROM workstation offering access to a little or moderately used database and (on the other) a series of networked CD-ROM datasets which are expensive to maintain and require complex technical support – as well as periodic extra funding to upgrade the system.

Lancaster[17] envisaged for higher education libraries different levels of electronic access according to demand, with those in greatest demand permanently accessible through the campus network, down through remote access when needed (eg through the Internet), to multiple workstations and single workstations in the library for the least-popular material. Leach[5] predicted a move away from networked CD-ROMs towards services via the web and/or through commercial hosts. He commented (in 1996) that the majority of higher education institutions did not subscribe to host systems, but that those that did were satisfied with them, and there was a growing interest in the subject.

Searching facilities

Wherever material lends itself primarily to automated searching, electronic versions are likely to be preferred to print. This applies very clearly, for instance, to bibliographical and financial information; but there are also less obvious applications – such as researchers in 'language and linguistics' using the *Oxford English Dictionary* database. A small point is that some of the high-volume CD-ROM databases (eg MEDLINE) are so big that a year's output fills a disc (incurring more searching time).

Tied/untied availability

At present some print publications are only available electronically as an extra – that is, the purchaser must take the print version to receive the electronic version (for which a small additional charge is usually made). This is true of many of the electronic journals which derive from print. The situation is likely to change, but until it does purchasers will think twice about paying extra money for the same product; where there is advantage to having both, the amount of the extra charge will influence a decision on having the electronic version.

Archiving

There has been much discussion about the archiving of electronic materials. It affects libraries in two ways. Overall doubts about the durability of electronic materials over time are discussed in Chapter 11 (and there are also questions about what to do when the software used to run older material becomes obsolete). A more immediate question is about retrospective access to subscription services (such as BIDS or many CD-ROM licensing agreements) after libraries have cancelled their print versions; how to access backfiles of data, should BIDS or CD-ROM subscriptions be cancelled, or those services discontinued?

Printing out

The existing electronic sources are ideally used to obtain snippets of information: citations (from bibliographic databases), or names and addresses (from a directory-type database). These applications are highly suitable for material in electronic form. Where more substantial information is required (and as more of it appears in electronic form) there are problems about how users will 'take possession' of information from terminals – given that few people are willing to read long documents from screens. There appear to be two main options: either the library provides printing facilities (but this would transfer to the library budget a cost which in most public and academic libraries is currently carried by users, in the form of photocopies); or users download documents onto their own disks, and print elsewhere at their own expense. Until this problem is addressed – and users' views on it taken into account – it will continue to be an imponderable in acquisitions policies.

Nature of the subject area

Where library provision is for a single-discipline subject area, with use heavily concentrated on a relatively small amount of material, acquisition – for instance, in the form of print or CD-ROM items – may be preferred. Where the subject area is multidisciplinary, and use is heavily dispersed, access to remote services – for instance, through online hosts – may prove more cost-effective. (See Chapter 9 on the BIODOC experiment at Cranfield University.)

Cost comparisons of different media

Bertha's invaluable 1998 article[13] compared the pricing structures of different electronic media. She observed that two key elements in the pricing structure for electronic information are 'access versus ownership' and fixed as against variable fees. Direct comparisons between the different media are only partially valid, because of the different characteristics of each. Nevertheless she included an extremely helpful table which attempted to summarize the advantages and disadvantages of each medium under several headings. The main features recorded were:

Access through online hosts

1 There are no hardware or software costs, and database fees are variable.
2 Costs of system maintenance are low, and of training users medium to high.
3 In quality terms, access is limited, but both the currency and time coverage of databases are very good.
4 Users are limited to those who can pay the fees (unless the institution absorbs them).

CD-ROM single workstation

1 Hardware costs are low, and there are no software costs; database fees are fixed, in the medium range.
2 Costs of system maintenance are very low, and training users medium.
3 In quality terms, access is limited, the currency of databases is medium, and time coverage medium to bad.

CD-ROM local network

1 Hardware costs are high, and software costs medium; database fees are fixed, but high.
2 The costs of system maintenance are high, and of training users medium.
3 In quality terms, access is unlimited. The currency of databases is medium, and time coverage medium to bad.

The Internet

1 There are no hardware or software costs, and not usually any database fees.
2 The costs of system maintenance are very low, and of training users low to medium.
3 In quality terms, access is unlimited. Both currency and time coverage of databases are variable.

5
Stock logistics and stock revision

The quantitative framework

Books and other items for library stock have to be selected inside a *quantitative* framework, within which some important technical concerns are addressed – how many titles to stock on each subject, how to modify these numbers as policy or use changes, how to keep the stock in each subject relatively fresh and interesting, and so on. Such matters are sometimes referred to under the heading of stock logistics.

The logistic aspects of stock provision must be combined with considerations of library policy. The more subjects the library has to cover, the more complex logistics becomes. For instance, a university or school library essentially relates provision to subject areas for the curriculum, and/or for research – and registered use in these subjects then influences further stock acquisitions (particularly in university short-loan collections). Matters are less straightforward in public libraries, which are supposed to address the subject needs of entire communities – ie just about any subject under the sun. In their case 'use of stock', as a guide to acquisitions policy, must be balanced with the requirement to have at least some material available on the shelf from a very wide spread of subjects.

The quantitative (or logistic) factors apply to selecting newly published books, as well as older material acquired through stock revision. Libraries *have* to acquire some copies of new books as they are published; if they delay, the small imprints of new titles – now customary – can lead to out-of-print reports. Even so, the distribution of these 'new book' acquisitions within different subject areas should reflect the use of the existing stock (and library policy) – and not simply echo publication patterns.

But buying items new (ie in the year of publication) is only part of the story. Library stock needs to be subjected to a process of continuous subject revision, in which additional titles are added so that there is – as far as is reasonably possible – always material available *on the shelf* in each key subject area. In this process (described below), the items added are likely to contain a larger proportion of 'old' than 'new' titles.

We also discuss below the duplication of individual titles in response to demand, and the rotation of stock between service points – the latter to ensure a continuing *variety* of choice for users within subjects.

McClellan's logistic system for public libraries

Amongst the surprisingly few works by practising librarians on this subject, A W McClellan's is certainly the most comprehensive. He carried out his original experiments in logistics at Tottenham public libraries during the period 1950–65, but the results were not put in book form until *The logistics of a public library bookstock* appeared in 1978.[1] There had also been a summary of these ideas in an article.[2]

The basis of stock logistics is the subdivision of stock into categories of manageable size, within which decisions about the numbers of items to be added can be made more easily. McClellan called these 'interest categories', each one intended to represent a discrete field of user interest, with the size of the *shelf* stock at any service point no more (in his scheme) than 100 titles. Most of them corresponded to Dewey classes, or groups of Dewey classes.

Any library authority can devise its own list of interest categories along similar lines. One helpful approach would be to follow the standard subject categories recently developed by Book Industry Communications (see References), comprising 17 categories at 'level 1' and 115 at 'level 2'. An advantage of this for public librarians is that the BIC scheme collocates the subject areas concerned with practical interests (gardening, cookery etc) and hobbies, which together – according to a recent survey of acquisitions[3] – account for nearly a quarter of public library stock additions; and according to a survey of use,[4] for over half of all non-fiction borrowing.

Other subcategories can be assigned for material outside the non-fiction bookstock:

- for adult fiction, groupings which go beyond the traditional 'genres' (see Chapter 12)
- for recorded sound, formats (compact discs, cassettes), then music types (classical, jazz, popular etc)
- for videos, feature films (possibly further subdivided by subject matter and/or audience ratings) and documentaries (divided by subject).

The McClellan system estimated the desired size of stock on the shelves for each interest category. This was derived from periodic counts – from issue records – of the numbers of books on loan in each category. This is where a balance between library policy and use of stock is needed. If a simplistic approach were to be adopted, libraries would allocate shelf stock space in proportions which reflected exactly the use of each category. But this approach would ignore the awkward problem of representing minority interests. Use is never evenly distributed throughout a library's stock, and some categories are only borrowed by small numbers of users – users who nevertheless have the same appetite for material in their small category as the users of large interest categories. Some adjustment to formulas involving 'books on loan' is therefore necessary to give users in minority-interest categories a better deal. McClellan offered a rather crude mathematical solution, involving square roots. It is probably simpler, and just as effective, to introduce a rule-of-thumb bias in favour of the smaller interest categories.

Having worked out the optimum size for interest categories, McClellan then monitored the stock within them. His record cards, at that time produced manually, can now be replaced by automated systems. Their purpose was to reveal at a glance the condition and effectiveness of stock in each interest category, and to work out an 'annual replacement target' – ie the number of acquisitions for the category during the forthcoming year. This reflected three different types of depreciation affecting stock in the category:

- physical wear and tear
- obsolescence (as content became out of date)
- exhaustion of stock by its readers (ie stock had no 'unread' material to maintain individual readers' interest).

In a last stage, McClellan monitored and recorded all the factors bearing upon the need for stock revision. This took account of weaknesses and strengths inherent in the the stock from the previous years' acquisitions, and also indicated the need for weeding. Stock revision priorities – between different interest categories – were obtained by comparing these stock records.

McClellan's system had its limitations. He himself always stressed that the logistical approach only provided quantitative information about acquisitions, and could not inform librarians which titles to buy. He also acknowledged that the system was time-consuming to apply, but urged that good stock provision was the first priority of a good library authority.

Other criticisms are more difficult to rebut. For instance, it is hard to accept McClellan's assurance that the system was responsive, to an extent, to unsatisfied demand; it relied heavily upon the use of existing stock as a barometer, and most users do not make known unsatisfied demand through other mechanisms (such as the reservations service). Secondly, the interest categories used were fairly broad subdivisions. To divide them further could make record-keeping impossibly complicated; not to do so could lead to minor subjects being overlooked.

Thirdly, the system allowed little note to be taken of the level or approach of material in existing stock. For instance, as Smith observed in his valuable study of non-fiction management information,[5] 'there is much more demand for general books covering a whole subject than for books on particular aspects of a subject.' A purely quantitative approach ignores the make-up of stock on the shelves. (A user searching for an introduction to playing chess may find only *A history of the pawn throughout the ages*.)

It is hard to reach any definitive conclusions about the best way to absorb McClellan's ideas into library practice, decades after they were first publicized . With modern automation systems, it is relatively easy to muster detailed information about the stock in given subject categories (in the catalogue *and* on the shelf), the percentage of each category on loan, and the average annual loans of titles in each category. This sort of information is certainly useful and indicative, but needs to be followed up by judgement about other matters – notably, the make-up of existing stock in each category, its usefulness and its interchangeability. Judgement is also needed for fixing the desirable size of shelf stock in each of the interest categories.

Recent logistic work on public libraries

The only other substantial work on stock logistics from the UK has been Tony Houghton's *Bookstock management in public libraries*, published in 1985.[6] Unfortunately Houghton – a management analyst – adopted a highly simplistic approach, based on maximizing the numbers of issues per book in stock, and scarcely touching upon the need for subject coverage on the shelves. He commented:

> A lending library after all is only a means of delivering a commodity to consumers in pretty much the same sort of way as a supermarket. So it should be governed by the same economic laws of supply and demand.

This statement, whilst in one sense salutary, strikes a chilling note for those who believe in the public library's mandate to address all tastes. Despite this general criticism, Houghton's book contained (in Chapters 12 and 13) useful material on bookstock rotation and injecting fresh stock into a subject area.

Some other comments have appeared in articles in professional serials. Moore[7] described the progress made in a handful of progressive authorities. Betts and Hargrave[8] gave a detailed account of what was achieved in one county.

Kerr's 1998 article[9] described some logistic measures (not unlike McClellan's) adopted in a Scottish authority, which demonstrated what could be done with an automated system. Data for groups of class numbers, measuring 'the percentage of stock on shelves' and 'average use per stock area', were used to assign subjects to three categories: understocked, overstocked or 'on target'. For instance, less than 30% of stock on the shelves and high average use (not defined in the article) signified 'understocked'; whilst more than 75% of stock on shelves and low average use signified 'overstocked'. The aim was to bring most categories 'on target', to get stock working harder overall, and to achieve shelf availability for users. The automation system was used to produce tables and graphs for each category, and make comparisons between service points. A 're-stock model sheet' indicated how many items should be purchased for each subject area, and which areas should not be added to. Special funding was made available for the additional purchases – a pragmatic measure which probably contributed a lot to the success of the process.

One very revealing study was Ian Smith's analysis of non-fiction borrowing in the libraries of a London borough[5] – which also showed how much can be derived from management information. We have noted above that a 'making the stock work hard' approach – through a high average number of issues per book per year – has to be balanced with the need to cover minority interests, where lower issue rates are the norm. That said, Smith's findings suggested that too many titles fulfilled neither of these objectives. He noted that 30% of the authority's stock was not borrowed at all during a given year, whereas a third was borrowed six or more times a year. (Surprisingly, the breakdown of non-fiction issue patterns – 9% borrowed once a year, 28% 2–5 times a year, 20% 6–10 times etc – was not so very different from the breakdown of fiction issues.) The most-used 13% of non-fiction stock accounted for 44% of issues, and the least-used 38% for 2% of issues.[10]

Smith then broke down the non-fiction issues. He found that by far the most heavily used subject areas contained books of a practical nature – health, child care, do-it-yourself, cooking, photography and so on. Conversely, the least-used areas were academic in type – notably literature, nature and the environment. Even within the least-used subjects, the most-used parts of them had a practical orientation – for instance, books on essay and report writing within the literature section. The legal section consisted predominantly of popular material – writing wills, letting property and so on – and as such was one of the most heavily used. Use of the biography section was inconsistent, with high demand in the first year, then a sharp decline.

Two sets of data in given subject categories show the imbalance between 'use' and 'provision' (see Tables 5.1 and 5.2).

Table 5.1   *Percentage of subject stock on loan, related to average issues per item pa*

% on loan	issues per item	
computers	80	9.7
law	69	7.4
DIY	50	7.7
biography	24	6.0
nature	19	4.2
literature	23	2.7

Table 5.2   *Size of stock related to 'popularity of stock' (both rankings)*

	stock size	popularity
literature	1	36
travel	2	15
history	3	31
biography	4	26
computers	10	1
law	25	2

Two other figures brought home the lopsided provision even more clearly. On a given day – across 11 libraries in the authority – there were 600 books on the shelves on 'computers' and 9000 books on 'literature'.

This evidence tends to corroborate the accusation – sometimes levelled – that public librarians have predetermined views about non-fiction provision and take limited account of what users actually want or use. A similar analysis in other library authorities would probably produce figures that are comparable. A trend analysis of monograph acquisitions[3] in a large number of public library authorities singled out another instance of slow response to user demand. Over most of the period 1984–98, acquisitions of computer books fluctuated between 0.9% and 1.2% of all public library additions, rising during 1996–99 to 1.7%. The modest increase contrasted strangely with the intensive demand for computer books – not to mention their much heavier rate of acquisition in university libraries over the same period (2.4% of all additions in 1983, rising to 5% in 1998).

Stock rotation in public libraries

Two other logistic matters are worth special mention. The more important of these is the *rotation* of stock between service points. We have commented above on the public library's responsibility to cover minority interests as well as the most popular subject fields. The extraordinary range of these interests was spelt out in Timperley's survey of non-fiction lending[4] and also in Francis's list of several hundred specialized user interests reported in three 1993 surveys (Francis, 1996). Just as striking is the persistence with which users pursue these interests in their public library. Timperley found that 91% of all the non-fiction borrowers he interviewed intended to borrow again from the subject area they had cited.

Reborrowing within subjects on this scale – even more pronounced than might have been anticipated – creates a big problem in stock provision terms. In small-interest categories, the choice of stock offered at any one service point is bound to be restricted, despite any bias introduced into logistic formulas to increase the amount of stock available. This problem is particularly acute at small service points. Any small library that did acquire new stock often enough to keep a small number of readers continuously supplied with fresh material would have to purchase at an extremely wasteful level.

Part of the answer to this is to order from one central point, and locate copies of titles artfully around the authority, so that users at every service point get some insight into the variety of stock available; and to promote the resources of the whole authority at each service point, through the catalogue, the reservation service and any other available means. That said, it is well known that users normally visit one – or at most two – libraries in their authority, and that few use the reservation service. The number – and variety – of titles *on the shelf* in user interest categories is therefore of crucial importance.

The best – and most obvious – solution to this problem is the regular exchange (or rotation) of stock between service points in the same authority. There are two main ways to do this. One is to make direct exchanges between two service points. Kerr[9] described how this was done in West Lothian:

> Overstocked areas common to two branches are identified and around 50% of each one's stock is randomly selected to 'select lists' on the computer using specially written in-house programs.

This was a corrective measure to rectify original errors in provision, and give low-use stock a new lease of life in another library. West Lothian also arranged systematic exchanges between pairs of service points for the provision of fiction 'romances' – which were being under-used at most service points – and amended provision so that the pair received new romances only in alternate months. As a result, expenditure on romances was reduced by 50%, and all the items purchased issued approximately twice as often.

A second way of moving stock between service points is to set up circulating (or rotating) collections of stock in user interest categories; these are not allocated to any one service point, but move at regular intervals between locations. They can be created for any stock category where use is relatively small, or tails off after an initial burst. Valentine's article[11] made the point that to avoid duplication of titles in circulating collections, new stock should be allocated to stock circulation routes at the point of acquisition (see Chapter 7).

The Audit Commission report *Due for renewal*[12] singled out 'stock rotation' as an area of stock management which needed attention. The report showed a figure of acquisitions from Surrey County Libraries – where increases in issues across different stock categories followed the introduction of stock rotation. The largest increases were recorded in 'large print' and 'science fiction' categories (both double the 'average issues per annum' achieved before rotation), but use also expanded in the other three categories cited – 'thrillers', 'biography' and 'food'.

It is instructive to compare stock turn figures (average numbers of issues per book per year) for static service points with those of mobile libraries. Stock movements tend to be common practice in the latter – because of exchanges between service points, or rotating collections, or natural circulation as material borrowed at one mobile stop is returned at another. Lumb's study[13] found that in four UK authorities stock turn figures for mobile libraries were always 20% higher than for static service points, usually 75% higher, and in some cases 200–300% higher. Direct comparison is not possible, because mobile libraries invariably have much smaller shelf stocks – but their high turnover figures are nevertheless striking.

Administratively, rotating stock between service points is easier than it was, because of computer catalogues (though many of the smallest service points, which need stock rotation most, have yet to be automated). Stock exchanges have certainly increased in recent years, to an extent unknown – though the impression is that the West Lothian approach is the exception rather than the rule. More research is needed in this area – on the amount of rotation taking place, the most cost-effective methods, the user interest categories most appropriate for rotation, and the kinds of results (in terms of issue increases) achieved. Meanwhile, all the evidence suggests that rotation is an essential mechanism for increasing the cost-effectiveness of stock in any library system which has geographically distant service points.

Duplication of titles

Another logistic matter concerns titles which are so popular that they are constantly in circulation, and therefore rarely available on the shelves to constitute part of the choice available to users. In such cases, the 'rate of issue' factor should be linked to information about the quality of the title to determine the rate of *duplication*.

Demand for individual titles can be temporary or long-lasting. During the first year after a book's publication, issues are likely to be artificially exaggerated by demand. Libraries in fashionable areas, where it is fashionable to read books reviewed in the broadsheet newspapers, often come under a lot of pressure to satisfy reservation waiting lists quickly. The point applies particularly to fiction best-sellers, certain biographies and titles of any kind which happen to hit the best-seller lists. All the same, multiple copies of such titles are hard to justify. There is no particular merit in reading a new title soon after publication, and an overdose of duplicates, bought on publication, is likely to be found taking up space on the shelves a year later. Duplication during the first year after publication should therefore be exercised as sparingly as local politics will allow.

Smith's survey of non-fiction use[5] revealed that a completely different set of titles receive *long-term* demand. Over a single year, he found that about 7,500 non-fiction books were issued 16 times or more in the libraries of one authority. Of these titles, 20% were about 'computers' and 15% about 'the body' – whilst other subjects featuring prominently were law, language, the paranormal, business and do-it-yourself. He identified a number of principles which determined whether a book was likely to be popular over a long period of time: practical books which help to solve problems; general books covering a whole subject, rather than special aspects of a subject; A-level textbooks; 'standard and classic texts' in almost every subject; and so-called 'reference material' made available for loan. He commented: 'With very few exceptions (new biographies) the list does not contain the most recently published books.'

Smith observed that books which issue more than 16 times a year are likely to spend very little time on the library's shelves – and so will be unavailable to most users, unless they place reservations for them. In which case, should these titles be duplicated – and if so, to what extent? The answer must depend upon the quality of the title in demand, and the quality of other titles in print on the same subject. All things being equal, it is better to buy one copy each of two different titles, rather than two copies of the same title. But where only a limited range of quality titles is available on a subject, duplication is certainly justified. This is an area where stock revision is essential – to compare the quality of different titles, and settle on a hierarchy for duplication purposes.

Location of copies

Where there is centralized selection of titles for a whole authority – either of new titles or through stock revision – the choice of locations for titles is an important factor. Some consideration is normally given to spacing out orders geographically – throughout the whole system in a small authority, or throughout the regions in a large one. Many public library users are prepared to travel reasonable distances within an authority to obtain material that is important to them, and it is common for people regularly to use the nearest large library to their home as well as their local library.

Large public library authorities tend to establish 'levels' of service point – four to six levels is typical – with each level defining a different type of service provision. In stock provision terms, it is common for the 'lower' levels of service to concentrate on recreational reading, with 'serious' or purposive reading mainly to be found in the upper levels. A 1993 survey of Essex county users (England and Sumsion, 1995) demonstrated very clearly how use is apportioned in this way. The percentage of users visiting seven different size brackets of Essex libraries for 'browsing purposes' rose evenly from 45% in the largest bracket to 64% in the lowest; whilst the percentage visiting to 'find out information' fell evenly from 27% in the largest bracket to 7% in the smallest. The percentages seeking specific books, or specific subjects and authors, also fell as the size of library diminished.

All the same, it is counter-productive rigidly to allocate specialized material to large service points, and general material to small ones. Some carefully chosen specialized items placed in smaller service points give users some conception of the range of stock available in the system as a whole. And of course any particular local interests should be taken into account in the distribution of titles.

Stock logistics in academic libraries

We discussed in Chapter 1 the kinds of policy decisions facing academic librarians who have both teaching and research functions to support, and we noted the strong current bias in favour of research support. The bias tends to devalue any logistic analysis related to function in university libraries, since findings about disproportionate use (or non-use) of these elements of stock are rarely acted upon.

University libraries (particularly those in the US, but also in the UK) tend to accumulate very large amounts of material indeed. On the whole, these collections receive low amounts of use, particularly if loans from short-loan

collections are excluded from consideration. In fact, many of the books purchased by the big research libraries are not used at all. A study by Fussler and
Simon[14] reported that over half the monographs accessioned by the University
of Chicago Library during the years 1944–53 had not been borrowed during the
period 1953–58. A celebrated research project by Kent[15] looked at monographs
acquired by the University of Pittsburgh during the years 1969–75. Some 40%
(36,000 books) had not circulated, and any given book was reckoned to have a
one in two chance of being borrowed.

UK library studies are based upon smaller collections, but the rate of use,
where known, remains generally low. (Not surprisingly, many librarians are
reluctant to put figures of this kind into print.) For instance, in the 'old' (pre-
1991) universities, the average number of loans per book in stock per year in
1998 is 0.5 – a figure inflated by intensive issuing from the short-loan elements
of stock. The number of books in stock in these libraries is given as 65.2 million
(Library and Information Statistics Unit, 1999b, 139, 141).

The 1998 'loans per book' figure is slightly higher for the 'new' (post-1991)
university libraries, at 1.7 loans per book. In this case, the number of books in
stock is given as 17.6 million. This higher – though by no means impressive –
use figure reflects the emphasis on teaching rather than research in the former
polytechnics. A study in one of them (Payne and Willers, 1989) found that 11%
of the bookstock was in circulation, while in another (Brophy, 1985) two samples taken from law and the humanities revealed that three issues per volume
was the average use per year, and that two-thirds of the items were loaned in a
two-year period. It is perhaps a reflection of the overall scene in academic
libraries that these rates of use were deemed to be quite good. Arfield's 1993 article[16] described a weeding exercise at the University of Reading, where he found
that large proportions of the stock had not been borrowed in the preceding ten
years: 8% of management stock, 33% of the social sciences, 57% of religion and
49% of history.

There has been little UK-based research comparing expenditure and use for
research collections on the one hand and short loan collections on the other.
Sumsion's 1993 survey (see Appendix) found that issues from short-loan collections had increased by 30% in the previous five years – less than the 38%
increase for all loans from academic libraries. His conclusion was that short-
loan collections were not developing fast enough to meet demand. The
respondents were asked whether they would increase the extent of the short-
loan operation if they had more space, or staff. Of 147 respondents, 57% said
they would, with 'space' the main constraint cited. Apparently few of the
respondents considered that the space devoted to large, little-used research collections could be slimmed down to make way for better short-loan operations.

If few academic librarians have used stock logistics to change the balance of expenditure between research and short-loan collections, there have been some reports of logistics used to rationalize the distribution of funding between subject areas. Adrian Peasgood described work undertaken at the University of Sussex in 1986.[17] He noticed large variations in the loan rate of different subjects in the long-loan collection. Two measures were used: the percentage of additions loaned, and stock turnover (average loans per item per year). In some subjects, up to 90% of stock added was loaned in the first two years, whilst in others less than 40% was loaned; whilst for the same stock additions, the turnover range between subjects varied between 0.5 and 4.0 loans per volume over the two years. (In-house use was not included in the study.)

Peasgood therefore undertook to make extra provision for high-scoring subjects, and correspondingly lower provision for the lower scorers. The aim was 'substantially to reduce the factor by which use of the most used subjects exceeds that of the least used', with 'material attracting little or no immediate use being sacrificed to allow better provision of material in current demand'. The results were very positive: the proportion of long loans attributable to new books (across the whole stock) rose from 5.5% in 1982–83 to 7.4% in 1983–84. Loans in the period 1983–85 of stock added in 1982–83 were an average of 3.2 per item – an increase of 13% on the performance of the previous two years.

Peasgood observed that whereas some balance in *coverage* was being lost, balance in *access for readers* was being gained – and he felt that the latter was clearly more important. He was nevertheless concerned whether Sussex was failing to provide for future research needs, and another survey was undertaken to shed some light on the possibility. All 6000 books on loan to staff or to PhD students were listed in 50 subject groups. In a third of the subjects analysed, 20% or more of researchers' borrowing was of material available in short-loan collections. In half the subject areas, 20% or more of use was of items generating four or more issues per year. He felt that researchers were taking a higher proportion of popular stock than expected, and that they would probably benefit from the shift of resources from low-use to high-use stock (though there were sometimes particular circumstances where application of the general principles was not appropriate). In general, Peasgood felt that the exercise had maximized current use of the library, helped to justify the library's share of the university budget, and led to more satisfied users.

A later study by Mike Day and Don Revill in 1995[18] followed similar procedures to Peasgood's work. Again the two measures of 'stock turnover' and 'percentage of additions loaned' were used – and each measure confirmed the findings of the other. Again the findings were used to reallocate funds between subject areas. The results of these measures were described: in high-performing subjects, 80% of items added in one year were used, with an average use per item of 4–7 loans; in low-performing subjects, about 40% of items were used, with an average use per item of 0.5–1.5 loans.

Short loan collections in academic libraries

The most intensive use of books in academic libraries comes from short-loan collections. For several reasons, these are highly suited to logistic investigations: they are of manageable size, and subjected (for the most part) to the same type of use – use which can be manipulated through duplication and control of the loan period.

Short-loan collections have been common in the UK since the 1960s, and are designed primarily to meet the needs of taught-course students. The underlying principle is that material in high demand is separated from the main loan stock of the library, placed on closed or controlled access, and made available for shorter loan periods than the main collections. Quite often there are variable loan periods for different materials, to fit the intensity of demand; and sometimes more than one short-loan collection – the contents of each determined by the length of loan periods.

Neil Jacobs[19] described quite a complex two-tier arrangement at the University of Sussex. The 'short loan collection' had 50,000 items relevant to taught courses, mostly duplicate copies of texts in demand, or with anticipated demand. They were issued on a non-renewable loan of four days, and could not be reserved. This facility was backed up by a reserve collection – a 'safety net' which contained at any one time five to ten thousand titles in exceptionally high demand. These were available for one-day or half-day loans, and were reservable. The reserve also contained another element which is becoming common in short-loan collections: two to three thousand photocopied articles, copyright-cleared.

The Acorn project (see References) described short-loan collections at Loughborough University. In a resource of 12,000 items, 6500 were books and 5500 photocopied articles. There were 127,000 short loan issues in 1995–96, of which 12% were of articles; 82% of loans were to undergraduates. The 12,000 items represented only one-third of the items on reading lists.

Terry Wall[20] in 1994 identified two criteria for short-loan facilities: they should contain 'many of the titles required by potential users, and few of the titles not required', and should hold 'just enough copies of each title to satisfy the majority of demands, and make them available for just long enough to suit the convenience of most users'.

Academic libraries try to anticipate user demand by requesting from taught-course lecturers a list of recommended reading in advance of each academic year. In theory this greatly facilitates the whole process, because for most undergraduates the reading list contains all the material they are going to read. In practice, some libraries experience considerable difficulties in obtaining all the necessary reading lists, and obtaining them in time to have recommended texts in place at the beginning of the year. Yeadon and Cooper[21] asked academics at Imperial College London for lists of required reading, and felt that a 60% response was 'good'. A JISC survey[22] found that only one in six of lecturers routinely supplied their library with reading lists. Kingston[23] observed that about 60% of reading list items were repeated year by year, and noted the wide date spread of high-demand articles – spanning the years 1955–97.

The most important early work on short loan logistics was done in the 1970s by Michael Buckland,[24, 25] who observed that the librarian's capacity to determine official loan periods gave him 'a powerful and precise device for influencing the availability of books in his library', and concluded: 'The cardinal rule of library stock control is that both the loan period and the duplication policy should be related to the level of demand for the title and to each other.'

Unfortunately, very short loan periods are often a turn-off for would-be users. Jacobs[19] found at Sussex that the weekday 'due time' for one-day loans (10.30 am), coupled with high fines rates, made it difficult and expensive for students (particularly part-time students) to return books. This contributed to the image of the reserve collection as a 'small, intimidating and out-of-the-way collection'. A 1999 survey by Wall[26] confirmed that one-day loans were much less popular than one-week loans, and that in half the cases where a one-week loan copy was sought but not found, one-day loan copies were available but not used. Kingston, in her survey of short-loan users,[23] found that the greatest perceived difficulty about the collections was getting books back on time. In this instance the loan period was until 2.30 pm on the day following the issue – and 58% of respondents said it was too short. (On the other hand, 37% of respondents said they found no difficulties at all with the collection.) Kingston's survey of 70 non-users of short-loan collections also identified three main deterrents: inconvenient loan periods, fines and the difficulty of returning books on time.

Jacobs also found, in a book availability survey in the University of Sussex,[27] that many students were inept at searching for material in short-loan collections. Though 26% of books sought from short-loans were found to be 'already on loan', the very large proportion of 44% were found on the shelf. Following the survey, Sussex improved a number of administrative features – user education, signs and layout, the OPAC screen layout, and the reshelving procedures – and increased overall book availability figures from 63% to 72%.

Wall[20] carried out a survey of short-loan book use over 12 months during

1992–93, amongst two groups of undergraduate students – in optometry and pharmacy. He found that of the 643 titles used, 231 were used by two or more optometry students, and 141 by two or more pharmacy students. Of all the titles used by two or more students, he recorded that:

- the number of users per copy was 5.1 for optometry and 4.7 for pharmacy
- the number of issues of a title per user was 1.9 for optometry and 1.7 for pharmacy
- the mean number of copies available per user was 3.8 for optometry and 4.3 for pharmacy.

Wall found that there were never more than 65% of users borrowing any one title. Half to three-quarters of the titles (across the two subject areas) attracted very few users indeed, yet all the titles had been actively recommended. He concluded that the uneven distribution of use lay with the preferences of the users.

Because of the unpredictability of use, most writers on the subject recommend that duplication of titles in short-loan collections should be cautious to begin with, to be expanded as the pattern of demand became clearer. Yeadon and Cooper[21] reported on a well-ordered system for textbook provision at Imperial College, where all texts were allocated to one of four categories:

- essential text, which all students should buy (and the library did not buy)
- recommended text for a course, provided in multiple copies
- supplementary text, of which the library bought one copy
- background reading, of which the library also bought one copy.

The scale of provision for recommended texts was more generous than is customary: one copy for reference, plus one extra copy for 1–5 students, 2 copies for 6–10 students, 3 copies for 11–20 students, 4 copies for 21–30 students, and 5 copies for 31–50 students.

We have mentioned above that providing photocopies of articles is becoming standard practice for short loan collections. Paula Kingston's paper[23] described Project Acorn, one of several pieces of work to explore the digitization of articles on reading lists, with the aim of presenting them to students through an online demonstration system linked to the library OPAC. A number of difficulties were described, including the length of time taken to obtain digitization clearance from publishers (an average in 1997 of 66 days), and the complexity of the digitization process (about 30 minutes per article page). She expected the technical difficulties to become easier – though publishers' future reactions to digitization projects are still unpredictable. If the problems can be overcome, we might expect digitized articles to take over from article photocopies in short loan collections. It will be a good deal longer before digitized textbooks become the norm.

A 1997 JISC study[22] summarized work by Acorn and several other digitizing projects, and related this to existing 'print' short-loan collections. There were a number of conclusions:

- copyright clearance was the main barrier to progress
- there was a need to cut the costs of digitization by importing electronic material directly from publishers
- universities needed to cooperate in commissioning digitized text
- terminals had to be more widely provided (one survey found that 42% of students waited ten or more minutes to use a workstation)
- on-demand publishing had to be part of a general approach to appropriate technology, integrated into teaching/learning processes.

Stock revision

Libraries have to acquire some copies of books at or near their publication date – and in practice most libraries spend most of their book funds in this way. Even so, it remains an inefficient way of adding to library stock. Books are usually ordered 'new' before there is enough information to evaluate them properly (reviews of specialist material, for instance, often appear two years after publication); and without being compared against other (probably better) titles on the same subject.

Without any doubt, stock revision is the more systematic and cost-effective way of spending funds. It is focused – as stock logistics is – on individual areas within the stock. Selectors scrutinize existing stock on the subject, weed out titles which are out of date or unused, identify the most important works in print on the subject, and the most appropriate for their library, then select. By systematically studying use of the existing stock, revision ensures that the selected titles relate to demand. Surveying the whole subject literature at once ensures that the 'best' titles are selected (and undeserving titles not).

Stock revision is most necessary in libraries where users need to find some material relating to their subject interest *on the shelves* (as in public and school libraries) – or particular titles on the shelves (as in the short loan collections of academic libraries).

It is tempting to think that if acquisitions of 'new' books could be made more systematically – in ways which overcome the problems of new book selection raised above – then stock revision would be unnecessary. But in practice, deterioration of shelf stock over time inevitably sets in, because of a variety of factors:

- fluctuations in funding over a period of years
- fluctuations in demand, caused by changes in the constituency, or changes in their needs, or reading fashions
- fluctuations in the use of individual items
- poor control of withdrawals and replacements of stock.

Such deterioration requires library staff regularly to revisit the shelves, to make good deficiencies.

Dovetailing 'new' book selection and stock revision is inevitably a messy business. In one sense, new book selection can be seen as a way of filling in between stock revisions; but this assumes that the whole stock is revised, subject by subject, over a given time span – and that is rarely possible. Stock revision can be on a large scale – spanning, for instance, a substantial subject area over a whole public library authority – or small-scale, with one service point carrying out numerous mini-revisions in a continuous process of upgrading.

Several factors determine the sequence in which subject areas are revised. If stock logistics procedures are applied (as described above), priorities are determined by the quantitative information provided. The priorities of the library's parent institution are extremely important, and the length of time that has elapsed since the previous revision has an influence. Chance may also play a part – as when, for instance, selectors capitalize on the appearance of a good subject bibliography.

During the practical work of stock revision, three sources of information are especially important. First, existing stock on the library's shelves needs very thorough scrutiny. The whole point of the exercise is to improve what the user finds *on the shelf*. The strengths and weaknesses of the stock should be noted; the elements of the subject which are well covered, and the gaps; the types of material which are well (and poorly) used; the level of material, and the balance between general introductions and specialized aspects of the subject.

Secondly, internal management information about the stock should be analysed – not just for one service point, but for the system as a whole. Here the most interesting feature is the performance of individual titles – especially, perhaps, of titles in other service points within the authority. Levels of use should also be compared to those for other subject areas in the library/authority.

These two sources are internal, concentrating on titles (and information) already within the system. A third type of source is external – ie critical bibliographies (see Chapter 3), and reviews in the main reviewing serials. These give a new dimension of information independent of the existing library service – opinions about the quality of individual items, whether these are in stock or not, and comparisons between items.

If the preparatory work is done thoroughly, the final step of selecting material becomes reasonably straightforward. The one difficult area is judging the numbers of items necessary to achieve the desired shelf coverage, and the duplication (if any) of titles. A single order may not be enough for this – in which case the shelves should be revisited once new stock has been absorbed, so that topping up can take place. Revisiting and topping up is a more or less continuous process. In the last analysis, the amount of funding available determines how far it can be taken.

How much stock revision actually happens in UK libraries? In a 1992 survey of public and academic libraries by Book Industry Communication,[28] 86% of public library authorities and 77% of academic libraries gave the prompted option 'formal stock revision' as one of their 'factors in purchase decisions' – though it came only sixth in priority in a list of 13 options for public libraries, and 8th for academic libraries.

Other evidence suggests that libraries pay lip-service to stock revision without actually doing it – except in the most cursory manner. A trend analysis of library acquisitions[3] provided interesting data about the *timeliness* of public library acquisitions, by comparing their dates of publication with the dates of acquisition. It transpired that for most of the period 1984–98 the great majority of acquisitions – for instance, 84% in 1998 – were made when the books were 'new' (defined as 'acquired in the calendar year of publication or the following year'); and another 10% were acquired within two to three years of publication. In 1998, only 6.5% of all acquisitions were four or more years old. Presumably the bulk of these represented replacements of older titles which had worn out physically.

We may infer from these figures that very little stock revision is being done in UK public libraries – a depressing conclusion. Though it is more difficult and more time-consuming than the processes for selecting newly published books, stock revision is also a vital ingredient of overall stock provision and a much more cost-effective way of using a book fund. But it seems that many librarians are taking the easy options.

6
Stock evaluation and performance measures

Background

The days when it was enough for a library to have a collection, and to open its doors, have thankfully passed into history. Towards the end of the 20th century, governments of developed countries began to demand more from those in receipt of public funding: an indication that funds were being deployed efficiently, and to the satisfaction and benefit of their users. This 'proof' became increasingly necessary if libraries were to be guaranteed continued funding. Such pressures led librarians (along with many other occupations) to introduce more relevant management information, and to use it more creatively; and to devise various user surveys, to measure the parts that management information could not reach. Developments in automated library systems greatly facilitated all these processes, though the reach of such systems is still far from comprehensive. (In the case of UK public libraries, fewer than half the total service points had automated catalogues in 1998.)[1]

A second step was for the measures to be augmented by targets, attached from within the library system or from outside. The resulting performance indicators, incorporated into planning processes (generally requiring *improved* performance over a period of time), represented the aspirations of the library's managers and/or the outcomes required by the library's funders.

A third step was to use the measures to compare one library system's performance with that of others. Comparability was the catalyst for creating various standard user surveys, and for much work on improving the standard data sets of management information required from libraries of a particular type by their umbrella bodies. There were also projects to standardize sets of performance indicators applicable to different types of library. The term 'benchmarking' then became common to describe a library measuring its performance against that of other libraries, using comparable sets of management information or survey results. Benchmarking ensured that performance measurement was rooted in the real world, rather than – as tended to happen previously – judged against aspirational and theoretical targets published in library standards.

Amongst the many measures devised, those relating to the provision of materials are perhaps the most numerous, the most detailed and the most interesting. We look at them in more detail below. They cover collections and access to other collections (through electronic sources and interloans); the use of materials; and the impact of use upon the users.

Sources of management statistics

Much work has been done in the UK recently on identifying a set of management statistics which can be used by higher education libraries for the purposes of comparison. The most detailed data for universities are the SCONUL *Annual statistics* (see References), the questionnaire for which was recently revised. A separate publication is available for the higher education colleges (Higher Education Funding Council Colleges Learning Resources Group, annual).

Following recommendations in the Follett Report,[2] a consultative report was published in 1995 by the Joint Funding Councils' ad hoc group on performance indicators for libraries.[3] This report generated a large number of suggested measures and performance indicators – so many that a further report was commissioned to boil them down to a small set. Jane Barton and John Blagden[4] recommended just nine measures to enable funding bodies and university managers to compare library effectiveness across the higher education sector. The report is also a very readable summary of recent work on performance measurement in this sector.

For UK public libraries, the main annual source of management information is the Chartered Institute of Public Finance and Accountancy's *Public library statistics* (see References), for which the questionnaire was also revised quite recently (Sumsion, 1996). A list of recommended performance indicators appeared in the then Department of National Heritage report *Reading the future*.[5] Soon after this the renamed Government department dealing with libraries – the Department of Culture, Media and Sport – began to require public library authorities to submit annual library plans, including sets of performance indicators.

There are no annual data sets for UK further education or school libraries, but The Library Association's biennial surveys of these sectors[6, 7] will in future provide some time series for norms of performance. Similarly, little has been known about the different types of workplace library, but recent LISU/TFPL surveys (see Creaser and Spiller, and Spiller, et al in Appendix, and Library and Information Statistics Unit, 1999b, 144–66) have begun to provide some means of comparison with norms.

In a study which covered various types of library, the European Commission's 1995 report[8] contained valuable lists of the elements in its title, together with detailed instructions for collecting the information. Jakob Harnesk[9] described work in progress on the International Standards Organization standard on library performance indicators – ISO11620.

At the level of individual libraries, a 1992 report by Book Industry Communication[10] detailed survey responses from 99 public library authorities and 122 academic libraries. The authors commented that, overall, public libraries produced more information than academic libraries. A general observation was that management information was nearly always short-lived – ie rarely kept for further analysis over time. Another was that within the ball-park figures of, for instance, circulation, few libraries charted aspects such as the performance of certain kinds of books or the reading habits of certain kinds of users. One might expect most libraries to keep records of items which are never used, for relegation purposes; or league tables of highly used titles (particularly short-loan titles in academic libraries) to determine which should be duplicated. In practice, the specific figures given – albeit in 1992 – for the percentages of libraries which maintained certain kinds of issues analysis, were surprisingly low:

- user types: public 46%; academic 52%
- class numbers: public 29%; academic 38%
- individual books: public 18%; academic 30%
- year of acquisition: public 8%; academic 13%
- loan status: public 0%; academic 11%.

Ian Smith's work at Westminster is a valuable example of what can be done with automated management information – see studies on non-fiction,[11] fiction[12] and frequency of use.[13]

Key indicators

Between them, the publications referred to above propose a variety of performance indicators for the provision of materials, the majority of which are listed below (most of them as measures 'per year'). There was a reasonable consensus on the key indicators of each type, and those which recurred most frequently are marked with an asterisk:

Cost

- expenditure per capita on the provision of materials*
- materials provision expenditure as a percentage of total expenditure
- spend per document delivered.

Provision

- items added to stock per capita (often subdivided by type)*
- titles added to stock per capita
- age of items (subdivided by subject)
- use of expert checklists (see below).

Use

- number of loans per capita (often subdivided by type of material)*
- items on loan per capita*
- stock turnover – ie loans per item per annum (often subdivided by type of material)*
- percentage of items borrowed, or not borrowed (subdivided by subject/type)
- time taken to satisfy requests*
- proportion of interlibrary loans to total loans*
- ratio of interlibrary loans (ILLs) received to ILLs lent.

Satisfaction

- a 'needs-fill' measure on whether users find what they look for (obtained via surveys – see below)*
- a measure of user satisfaction with stock (obtained via surveys – see below).*

Further comment on these measures is made below.

Measures of cost and expenditure

Though it is not recommended in all the studies, 'the percentage of materials provision costs to total library costs' seems a crucial measure. Most users visit their library to borrow materials or use them on the premises, not to consult staff or admire the building. Yet in most libraries, the percentage of expenditure on materials provision is falling. In public libraries it fell from 18% in 1987–88 to 15% in 1997–98, following a similar drop in the preceding decade (Library and Information Statistics Unit, 1999b, 17). In higher education libraries the picture is different, because most costs are excluded from the expenditure figures, and it is hard to differentiate between 'materials provision' and 'infrastructure' in the much-increased automation expenditure. All the same, expenditure on printed materials (books and periodicals) fell in the 'old' universities from 35% to 28% of total expenditure in the 10-year period, and in the 'new' universities from 31% to 26% (Library and Information Statistics Unit, 1999b, 111, 113).

'Spend per document delivered' is the kind of measure used in a 'budgeting by function' approach, where managers benefit from knowing how much is spent on (for instance) lending books, or lending videos, or reference services; and then how much on each transaction – a book loan, a video loan, a reference enquiry. The measure lends itself to internal comparisons over time, more than external comparisons – for which comparable data are difficult to pin down exactly. Though often recommended by Government bodies, the approach has yet to find general favour in UK libraries. An example for public libraries is set out in the recent Audit Commission report.[14]

'Expenditure per capita on provision of materials', when compared year on year, must be related to price indexes of materials costs, to reflect changes in real terms.

Measures of provision

'Items added to stock' is an unavoidable general parameter, if not a very significant one – unless mere size of stock is considered to be valuable. There is discussion of the size issue, in relation to academic libraries, in Chapter 8.

More interesting is 'titles added to stock', intended to reflect the *variety* of acquisitions. It is of particular interest in a public library authority, where heavy duplication between service points can restrict the overall range of titles available – especially as relatively few public library users request, through interlending systems, items which are not already in the library catalogue. The subject has received little attention since the UK government's *Bourdillon report* (Department of Education and Science, 1962). Bourdillon's view was that of the 24,000 titles (19,000 non-fiction) in the *British National Bibliography* for that year, 5000–6000 of these were suitable for inclusion in the lending section of any small or middle-sized public library, whilst the largest service points should be expected to include about 17,000 titles. Without further work on the subject, we cannot know how these proportions have been affected by the vastly increased numbers of published titles (105,000 in the UK alone in 1998), the increased number of interlending options, and the development of electronic services.

Of the few practical investigations into the matter of 'stock variety', Bryant (1983) noted the number of selections made by seven public and academic libraries in eight weeks of the *British National Bibliography* (BNB) in 1982. Out of a total of 7300 BNB entries, the libraries ordered an average of 627 titles (9% of those published), with a range between 280 and 1204. Another study (Spiller and Creaser, 1999) showed that in 1995–96 – when some 95,000 new titles were published – five UK public library authorities acquired an average of 17,900 titles (19%), with a range between 13,869 and 24,132. (The higher average percentage, compared to the Bryant enquiry, is probably due in part to the inclusion in the count of replacements and stock revision titles.) The measure of 'new titles acquired' has recently been included in the CIPFA statistics (see References), so the information will in future be available for all UK authorities.

Automated housekeeping systems allow detailed subanalysis of items added to stock (or in stock), and more use can be made of this facility. 'Age of items' is the example given in the list above. For instance, a library can verify how much of the stock on 'computers' has been published in the previous three years (at least 50% would seem a reasonable target), or how many of the additions for that year had been published in the previous three years. The findings of a recent survey of acquisitions in public and academic libraries suggest that these features do need monitoring – see Chapter 5.

It is also possible to measure stock and/or additions in given subject fields, relating these to use. Studies by Peasgood[15] and by Day and Revill[16] showed how subject additions were proportionally related to use in academic libraries (see Chapter 5), and Smith[11] analysed non-fiction stock in a public library.

One measure in the list above which is *not* linked to automation systems is 'the use of expert checklists'. This is a tool for stock revision purposes, to ensure that key titles in each subject area are in the library's stock and/or on the shelves. Managers might also use a related measure: a list of subject areas for which at least some titles should be *on the library shelves* at any given moment. More comment is made on both these measures in Chapter 5 on 'stock revision'.

Mention should be made of 'collection profiling' – a formal process for gathering quantitative and qualitative information about library collections, generally in the academic area. Most examples are based upon an American approach called Conspectus, described by Wood (1996), amongst others. A rare instance of its take-up by a UK academic library was described by Russell (1999).

Measures of use

The most widely applied measures of library use are those of circulation (or loans, or issues). Most libraries keep a record of issues, analysing them to shed light upon the use of stock, and to diagnose changes required in their acquisitions policies. There are some exceptions. A survey of independent school libraries[17] showed that 20% of the respondents did not maintain issue records. In some workplace libraries, lending material is a minor function compared to electronic services, reference work and other activities. For instance, in legal, financial, energy, pharmaceutical and management consultancy libraries, median issues scarcely amount to more than one a day (see Spiller et al in Appendix).

There are some obvious limitations to circulation records. They provide only a partial analysis of library use, because they do not include in-house use. And of course, a book loaned is not necessarily a book read, and a book read has not necessarily given its readers what they wanted from it. More research is needed in this area, though some has been done in public libraries: Goodall,[18] summarizing several surveys, found that between 71% to 80% of users had read all of the fiction books they had borrowed; Timperley[19] found that nearly all those who borrowed non-fiction books made some use of them (cover-to-cover reading of non-fiction often being inappropriate), that the average length of time spent reading each book was nearly six hours, and that 23% of the books borrowed had been used by someone else in addition to the borrower.

Common applications of circulation analysis are:

- increasing or reducing the provision of individual titles, or books in particular subject areas
- changing the location of individual items within the library
- reducing the loan period of items in high demand.

These logistic elements of stock provision are discussed further in chapter 5.

The widespread use of automation systems has enormously increased what can be done in the way of circulation analysis. All the same, most issue systems require loaned books to carry a record of past loans on their date labels. This humble piece of evidence – the date stamp – should not be undervalued, since a loan history on the book may be correlated during stock revision with other factors (physical condition, the content of other shelf stock) in a way that cannot be achieved through the automation system.

The Barton–Blagden project[4] on academic library indicators included both 'number of loans per capita' *and* 'items on loan per capita' as two of its nine measures. The authors argued that for the purposes of comparing one library with another, 'number of loans' data are too easily manipulated by changes in the loan period; the number of items *on loan* at a given date (or the average of several dates) is more reliable, and also gives an indication of the range and depth of use.

It is a pity that the measure 'percentage of items borrowed over a given time period' (or, just as significant, 'not borrowed') is not used more widely. We must accept that many libraries need to achieve coverage in their priority subject areas, including coverage of minority interests – and therefore that some items issue more frequently than others. That said, far too many items in libraries do not issue at all, yet are allowed to remain on the shelf; worse still, unless acquisition policies are adjusted accordingly, items of a similar type continue to be bought. Unused stock is a serious problem in higher education libraries, but Smith[13] also draws attention to it in a public library setting (see Chapter 5).

'Stock turnover' (or 'stock turn') is a widely used measure consisting of 'loans per item per year'. Overall levels of stock turn are of interest, but the measure becomes even more significant when there is subanalysis of relevant features. For instance, in academic libraries, short-loan material must be analysed separately from research collections. In public or school libraries, fiction analysis is separated from non-fiction. In most types of library, subanalysis of non-fiction, if detailed enough, gives valuable information for acquisitions expenditure subject by subject.

Other measures included under 'use' are a clutch concerned with explicit demand, where users reserve items not on the shelves, or not in stock at all – in which case they may (or may not) be borrowed via interlending systems. This is a complex area, for which indicators need to be very carefully thought through. For instance, 'time taken to satisfy requests' is often used, though in public libraries which receive multiple requests for new best-sellers, speed of supply can only be achieved through overduplication of copies.

'The ratio of interlibrary loans received to those lent' is also common, with 'larger numbers borrowed' generally felt to be less favourable than 'larger numbers lent'. This *may* be the case if a library has not achieved a good balance between buying and borrowing, or between retaining and discarding; but it is not always a useful indicator for benchmarking against other libraries, since so much depends upon the relative size, the budgets, and the functions of library collections.

Measures of in-house use

Circulation statistics considerably under-represent the overall use of library stock, because they take no account of unrecorded use inside the library itself. Obviously, measurement of in-house use is important for material which is not loaned – notably, serials and reference books – but it is also important for material which *is* loaned.

Any such measure must first define what degree of exposure to a document in the library counts as 'a use'. Borrowing a book at least signifies an intent to use, whereas flicking through one removed from library shelves may presage a decision *not* to use. The main methods for recording in-house use are described by Baker and Lancaster,[20] Ford[21] and Lancaster:[22]

- counts of books left on tables
- slips placed in books which users are asked to complete
- user questionnaires
- interviews
- unobtrusive observation.

Each of these has its advantages and disadvantages. Table counts considerably underestimate the amount of use (studies suggesting that only 25–50% of use is recorded), and yield no information about the users themselves. The slip method is unreliable. Questionnaires and interviews do give user information, though interviewing is comparatively expensive. Observation – see a survey of periodical use (Wenger and Childress, 1977) – can measure precisely the amount of time that a book is scrutinized, but does not give specific information about items consulted, or allow the observers to say which of the consulted items were also checked out of the library.

Research leaves no doubt that a lot of in-house use takes place. The University of Pittsburgh study[23] found that it largely correlated with circulation patterns, but increased the total 'transactions' by about 2.75 times. Rubin,[24] using the table count method, found that the average ratio of items used in the library to those circulating was 0.5 to 1.0. A substantial proportion of patrons – between 47% and 63% – used materials in-house, and whereas most visitors spent less than half an hour in the library, the in-house users spent half an hour or more. Harris[25] reported a survey at Newcastle Polytechnic library in which 8500 items (10% of the stock) were studied for 19 months: 50% received no use of any kind in that period, whilst 55% had no issues and 80% had no in-house use. An American project studied both circulation and in-house use over seven years at the University of California.[26] More than 30% of the monographs and 25% of the serial volumes had one kind of use but not the other; weeding based on circulation data alone would have eliminated, from the stock of one million volumes, at least 112,000 volumes which had been used quite recently.

There are numerous other pieces of research, but those referred to above are diverse enough in their findings to draw attention to a characteristic problem of in-house use studies: the wide variations in results. Ford[21] summarized his section on this subject by observing that the ratio of books consulted in-house to books borrowed has been reported as a range from 0.4:1 to 11.2:1. He drew three conclusions:

- short-term study of in-house use cannot safely predict long-term patterns
- a study in one library cannot safely predict patterns in another
- even within one library, there is a wide difference between patterns of use from one subject to another.

Availability studies

Neither circulation nor in-house use studies reveal anything about 'availability' – which Baker and Lancaster,[20] in their review of the literature, define as 'the probability that an item sought by a user will be on the shelves'. Availability is also often referred to as the 'needs-fill rate'. Some of the early work in this area was done in the 1970s by Schofield,[27] who used a simple system of asking users to complete a slip of paper for each 'failure' to locate an item on the shelf. He found the failure rate to be 37%, and identified the 500 titles (out of a shelf stock of half a million) which were most often unavailable.

Most studies employ questionnaires, either self-completed by users, or used as the basis for interviews. Van House[28] has examples of questionnaires for availability studies. Kantor's work on this subject in the US is the best-known.[29] He has developed five main categories of non-availability:

- title not acquired
- catalogue error
- title in circulation
- library error (title missing or misplaced on shelves)
- user error in searching.

To these might be added 'binding', which in the case of journals is often the most common reason for non-availability.

A number of other availability studies have been carried out. Mansbridge[30] and Ford[21] summarize some of them, and Line[31] has written on the subject in the UK.

Kantor had estimated that in large academic lending libraries the probability that specific works will be found when needed is 0.57 (0.66 in a reference library). Revill[32, 33] reported availability of 0.69 and 0.74 in a UK polytechnic library.

Availability studies are not carried out purely to satisfy librarians' curiosity. They are used to improve user success in finding material over a period of time – either by duplicating titles found to be in high demand, or by improving housekeeping to make it easier for users to find material which is already in stock. Jacobs[34] described two availability studies carried out at a UK university library. As soon as users delivered completed questionnaires, library staff checked for the books listed – on the library OPAC, in the collections, and again in the collections the following morning, after reshelving. In the first study the availability rate was 63%. Of the 1500 searches which failed, about half were because books were on loan already. Where the library had single long-loan copies, 79% of the books sought were on loan already; but where there were short-loan or reserve copies, only 26% were on loan and 44% were *on the shelf*. Following the survey, managers made a number of administrative changes: improving signs and layout in the library, and reshelving procedures; revising the layout of the OPAC screen; and carrying out more user education, in different ways. In a second study, undertaken after these measures, the availability rate had improved to 72%.

Much of the work on availability has been done in academic libraries, as the projects described above demonstrate. But some of the most interesting questions relate to demand in public libraries. Since 1992, the CIPFA PLUS standard user survey for public libraries[35] has included a needs-fill question. Results of the 1997 PLUS surveys, covering 23 UK authorities, are summarized in *Perspectives 2*.[36] Overall, 55% of users found specific books they had sought. The questions went a stage further, to investigate the types of specific books sought. Of all the responses, 24% were sought by author, 29% by title and 32% by subject – with 15% unspecified. We may expect these percentages to be very different for adult fiction (primarily sought by author/title) and non-fiction (primarily sought by subject). In 1999, the PLUS group revised the needs-fill questionnaire so as to clarify the subanalysis of findings.

Spreadbury[37] made an approach to needs-fill in secondary school libraries. Some 18% of pupils in four schools said they 'always' found subject books related to their curriculum in the school library, 56% 'most of the time', 21% 'sometimes', and 4% 'not very often'. The percentages were less good for 'popular books'.

Non-availability studies have their critics. Schofield[27] pointed out that failures to find are naturally in proportion to the number of successes – one person's success being another's failure. Much depends upon the efficiency of a library's housekeeping, as the Jacobs survey[34] demonstrated. Also, surveys of this kind do not show up users who omit to check the shelves at all, because of low expectation of success. And some critics have suggested that making improvements to services improves performance only temporarily, since higher expectations increase user demand, and drag success rates back towards a constant.

User surveys

In addition to in-house use and availability surveys, many other types of user survey have been carried out in the past 30 years, most of them shedding some light on users' views of library stock. There are surveys from a variety of sources: individual libraries (only a fraction of which are published), academic departments of library and information science, commercial consultants, and student dissertations. Some of these are easier to locate than others. For practitioners, the more generally applicable findings may be used for planning and decision-making in their own libraries, or at the very least the methodologies used can be adapted as a basis for further research locally.

From a very substantial literature, there is only space to mention a handful of the more recent or more influential surveys. Ford[21] summarized surveys from different library types under a variety of 'factors associated with book use', though his book is now in need of revision. In academic libraries, Erens's 1989 and 1995 surveys of the library needs of academics (see Appendix) were well reported. Pickering et al[38] prioritized 91 different aspects of service for a variety of academic library users. Two international conferences on performance measurement in libraries, organized by the University of Northumbria at Newcastle, have generated books of proceedings[39, 40] – with many of the contributions covering academic libraries.

A surprising feature in universities is the lack of investigation into serial use – especially in view of the high proportion of materials budgets spent on serials. There is further discussion of this in Chapter 10.

In public libraries, Luckham's 1971 survey (see Appendix) was one of the first major studies. Craghill (see Appendix) summarized public library surveys up to 1988. Goodall[18] summarized a number of user surveys concerned with browsing. The Aslib *Review of the public library service in England and Wales* (see Appendix), published in 1995, contained the most wide-ranging user (and non-user) research on UK public libraries in the past decade. CIPFA PLUS[35] is a standard user satisfaction survey, introduced in 1992, to which a majority of UK public library authorities now subscribe. Two publications by the Library and Information Statistics Unit – England and Sumsion's *Perspectives* and Bohme and Spiller's *Perspectives 2* (see Appendix) – summarized surveys from a variety of sources during the last decade. There has been a series of valuable surveys from Book Marketing Ltd, notably the 1998 *Household library use survey* (see Appendix).

Naturally, the findings of local surveys are not often publicized beyond the area they refer to. Elizabeth Barron's 1999 dissertation (see Appendix) investigated the methods that public library authorities were employing for user consultation. Of 134 authorities that responded, 108 (81%) had carried out user satisfaction surveys. The aspects of service most commonly targeted by these were: audiovisual services (18 authorities); children (17); mobile library users (15); housebound users (14). There had been ten surveys on 'stock satisfaction'.

Surveys can reveal different types of information about the provision of material for users. For instance, the CIPFA PLUS survey has a straightforward question about user activities: which services people use when they visit the library, or which types of book (or video, or music recording) they prefer. This information is helpful for allocating resources to different services, especially for services (such as electronic resources) where there is no regular information to reveal use. Another approach is to seek users' opinions – especially helpful for managers trying to plan future service developments. For instance, Bromley's Exit survey[41] asked for user reactions to various proposals for new, IT-based services in the authority. The most common type of survey is certainly the 'satisfaction' survey, where a graded set of responses indicates the degree of satisfaction with existing services, yielding clues about which need improvement.

A much quoted article by Orr[42] in 1973 provided a good summary of the problems faced by libraries trying to establish any form of *benefit* obtained by users from their services. Despite an extensive literature on this subject, little can be found by way of surveys which explore the *impact* of services upon users – though such information, once obtained, can be used for advocacy of the library, as well as for service development. One recent example is Patrick Timperley's survey[19] on the impact of non-fiction lending in public libraries.

An effective way to use surveys is to repeat them over a period of years, so that lessons learned can be applied, and satisfaction remeasured. Hilary Johnson[43] described surveys carried out annually over five years in a college of higher education. In 1993, 70% of students found 'availability of texts' poor, and less than 10% good; four years later, 25–30% of students found availability 'good' – a slightly larger proportion than found it 'poor'. This change was the result of better liaison with faculty members, and a realignment of stock to courses.

One problem of satisfaction surveys is that most library users tend to rate services highly – perhaps more highly than they often deserve. All the more worrying, then, that in the great majority of surveys there are critical findings on 'the availability of books', or 'the range of books on shelves', or 'the numbers of new books'. One cannot but believe that such results have to do with the diminishing resources allocated to materials, and the diminishing time spent on getting materials provision right.

For those needing 'how to do it' material on surveys, Line's valuable book *Library surveys: an introduction to their use, planning, procedure and presentation*[44] is, regrettably, out of print. A seminal American text by Van House[28] gives examples of different kinds of user survey. Ford[21] summarizes data collection methods. A recent UK publication described how a number of academic librarians carried out surveys in practice. It included a paper by Hayden[45] on Libra software, produced by Priority Search, which is widely used in UK higher education libraries for prioritizing the views of users on different library services.

Measures of electronic services

Few of the existing sets of management information, or standard user surveys, have satisfactory measures of electronic services, though work is being done to develop them. Measures of electronic *provision* are to be found in some data sets – numbers of public access terminals, numbers of terminals with the Internet, numbers of terminals with CD-ROMs, numbers of CD-ROMs held, and so on. But measures of access for remotely held materials, and measures of use, are still being considered.

Lancaster's paper[46] discusses the difficulties of evaluating electronic services when provision is organized at a number of different levels – from, for instance, high-demand materials available throughout a university campus network, to low-demand materials available from a single workstation located in the library. Traditional measures such as 'the number of items in stock' or 'shelf availability' have little meaning in these circumstances. 'Circulation' is replaced by 'items accessed' as a quantitative measure. But Lancaster observed that if the actions of users can be monitored via a form of transaction logging, we may be able to develop measures which are better than those currently in use for print – for instance, by registering *how much* text is accessed.

The best-known UK work in this area has been done by Peter Brophy and colleagues, and was summarized in 1997 by Brophy and Wynn.[47] Brophy abandoned attempts to measure the 'number of documents delivered', because 'in an electronic environment not only is it virtually impossible to define "a document" but the key issue for users is not the *number* of documents they can download but the *range* and *depth* of resources which are available to them.'

His key type of measurement was therefore 'resource discovery', and the key measure proposed under this heading was 'sessions per service per month' – which measured each time a user 'tries to do something'. This was supported by a measure of the user's satisfaction with the service results. Under a second heading of 'resource delivery', Brophy recommended 'items downloaded per service per month' (which is not good for web searches) or 'the number of hits per service per month'.

Other proposed measures included under a heading for 'infrastructure provision' were:

- queuing times for access to workstations
- downtime (as a % of total time) per month
- availability (as a % of attempted accesses) per month
- pages of print per month.

It may be a while longer before generally accepted measures in these areas are incorporated into data sets.

Nicholas[48] in 1999 explored the possibilities and pitfalls of measuring use of one type of electronic resource.

Benchmarking

When reliable data about library provision of materials are available for a number of libraries, benchmarking becomes possible. A single library – or library authority – compares its data about services and use with those of a number of other authorities. This is most commonly done with management information (though it is also possible using data derived from standard user surveys). It is possible for a library to do its own analysis, using data from CIPFA (for public libraries) or SCONUL (for higher education libraries), but much easier to put the work in the hands of a statistician, using databases which already hold data for similar libraries, over a period of time.

In the UK, CIPFA – or their commercial arm, the Institute of Public Finance (IPF) – currently do some basic benchmarking for the Department of Culture, Media and Sport, when sending out annual guidance to public library authorities for preparing library plans. But instead of being based upon a standard package of measures, the process is best used by individual librarians specifying measures which relate to their own circumstances – and particularly to areas of service which they suspect to be potential weaknesses. Such measures should anticipate a set of performance indicators incorporated into library plans, which aim to improve performance over a period of time.

The Library and Information Statistics Unit (LISU) in Loughborough has two large databases, of public and higher education library data, both spanning a number of years, and carrying data from CIPFA and SCONUL respectively which has been 'cleaned up' – ie comprehensively edited – and with tables completed with interpolated estimates. LISU undertakes benchmarking for individual academic libraries and public library authorities.

The benchmarking process was described in a recent article[49] which gave examples of the kinds of graphs used. The golden rules are for libraries to compare their performance with similar libraries (for instance, a pre-1992 university with other pre-1992 universities) over a period of time; and measures used should be based upon ratios, rather than upon raw data. Examples relating to library materials are (for 'books' can be added 'videos', 'compact discs' and so on):

- expenditure on books per capita pa
- total book additions per capita pa
- book issues per capita pa
- bookstock turnover (average issues per book in stock pa)
- books on loan per capita (on a given date)
- percentage book replenishment rate (the number of years to replace entire stock at current rate of acquisition).

One rarely gets a sight of such benchmarking exercises, which are generally confidential to the commissioning authority. However, this is an extremely powerful tool for informing library managers about what is right – and wrong – with their services. For instance, a public library authority which spends well above average per capita on materials, but registers use per capita which is well below average, will want to review its policy for provision, promotional activity and a number of other factors.

In the example described above, one library's performance is compared with that of another library. Benchmarking can also be used to compare the performance of one library within a system with that of others, as long as the rule of comparing 'like with like' is adhered to.

7
Managing the provision of materials

We have discussed elsewhere in this book some key overall requirements for stock provision: fitting provision to users' needs; getting a good subject coverage on the library shelves; making the widest possible variety of material available. The challenge of *managing* provision is to fulfil these requirements with maximum effectiveness and efficiency across all the service points which make up the library system. The larger the system, the better the opportunity to maximize resources – but the more complex the process.

The key element is the way that staff are organized to handle provision, and we look in detail below at approaches involving subject specialization and centralized/decentralized provision, in both public and academic libraries. We also append a short list of essential components for a cost-effective management system.

Formal stock provision plans are discussed in Chapter 1, without a conclusion as to whether or not they are desirable. The importance of budgeting as a tool for reinforcing management priorities is discussed below, and in Chapter 2.

Whether or not written guidelines to provision are used, there should be a continuous internal programme of staff training, to ensure that staff take on board management priorities for provision. Some of this occurs as in-service training – for instance, in the course of book meetings – but other points are best addressed at separate training events. This is important because the approach to provision differs so much between systems, and because the practicalities of provision are scantly addressed in the professional literature, or at schools of library and information studies. Also, provision involves making hundreds (or thousands) of individual decisions, so that making sure all colleagues are on the same wavelength is a good deal easier than continuously monitoring work – though some spot-checking is also necessary. The difficulties of monitoring are doubly acute when subject specialists are involved, or when large-scale stock provision is in progress.

Success, in provision terms, is slow to take effect and hard to measure – much harder, for instance, than in enquiry work. Managers should put into place good performance measures for provision (see Chapter 6), and see that statistics relating to them are regularly monitored, and successes recognized – particularly if they are the result of trying out new approaches.

Managers must also ensure that the provision process gets what it needs in terms of staff time – and is not squeezed by other, apparently more pressing, but actually less fundamental activities. Little reliable information exists about the time spent on library stock provision, but there is an impression that less and less attention is devoted to it. A comment by a public librarian in a recent survey of selection procedures[1] may apply to a good many libraries: 'It takes such a small amount of our time. It appalls me every time I think of it. It should be taking most of our time but it doesn't.' Notably sparse is the time given to stock revision, for which there *are* some figures. Sumsion's 1994 survey of higher education libraries (see Appendix) found that on average approximately 354 hours a year of professional staff time were spent on stock revision and weeding. A 1998 survey of public libraries[2] found that 57% of authorities used 10 or fewer people to select books for stock revision (with a range of one to 60 people involved).

Though managing the provision process is usually a matter of managing library staff, in some libraries users also come into the picture. The Sumsion survey noted that academics spent a small amount of time advising on provision. In workplace libraries, users are a fundamental component of the process: CAPP's 1995 survey (see Appendix) noted that in 38% of workplace libraries books were selected by staff, in 35% by users, and in 27% by both staff and users.

Managing *electronic* materials is – almost by definition – a matter of centralized provision for networked systems. That said, several aspects of electronic provision can benefit from an 'all staff' managed approach – for instance, privileging Internet sites for users, and surveying user needs and satisfaction with services. The training requirement for staff is perhaps even more important in this area.

Organization of public library provision

Amongst the most useful items in a small subject literature are the 1998 CPI survey[2] and Sue Valentine's paper on the Hertfordshire experience.[3] Chambers and Stoll's 1996 publication[1] is valuable for its impressionistic report on selection in six authorities.

Before UK local government reorganization in 1972, book provision in many of the (then quite small) local authorities was often operated by the chief librarian and/or the deputy. Some authorities gave a lot of responsibility for the provision function to specialist posts – usually called 'stock editors'.

Post-1972, in much larger authorities, different systems had to develop to cover large numbers of service points – from 15 to 70 (or even more) in one authority. There is no comprehensive information about the organization of materials provision in these authorities, but a basic pattern emerges. Responsibility for provision normally resides with a bibliographical services unit, which provides centralized services of acquisitions, cataloguing and interlending, as well as for the provision of books and other materials. Some of these departments have on the payroll a stock editor, who works exclusively on stock.

The way that librarians in service points interact with the bibliographical services department varies a good deal. A crucial point is whether provision is coordinated centrally, or left mainly to individual libraries. The CPI report[2] found that in 1998 decisions about the selection of new adult books were made by service points in 28% of authorities, at an area or group level in 48%, and for the whole service in 59%. (Many authorities reported both local and central arrangements, so the figures do not add up to 100%.) For children's books the figures were 25% by local libraries, 44% at area level, and 50% for the whole service. There was further information about the *management* of selection decisions: these were centrally coordinated in 86% of authorities, whilst in 69% the final decision was made centrally.

Stock revision selection decisions were less centralized. The report found that for adult books 47% were made at service points, 49% at area level and 41% for the whole service. For children's books 42% were made at service points, 43% by areas and 38% for the whole service.

A particular 'provision' problem is posed by large city library collections, where the central reference collections are usually divided up on a subject basis. We do not have any information about how these are coordinated with lending provision in these authorities.

The Chambers and Stoll survey[1] shed some light upon the different cultures of centralized and decentralized selection:

Centralised authorities tend to treat their stock as a single entity. This means that they treat book selection in the light of adding a title to the authority's stock. Deciding which branch or branches should carry the title is important, but at times a secondary issue . . . The drawbacks with the system are that decision-making is to some extent removed from the branch and that responsibility is concentrated in the hands of relatively few librarians.

Decentralised authorities tend to treat each branch library as having its own, separate stock holding. Selection is ultimately the concern of branch librarians . . . There are a number of concerns arising from the operation of decentralised systems. These include a tendency for branch librarians to be proprietorial and possessive of their collections and at times to be idiosyncratic in their choices. On the whole, selection at branch library level tends to produce more conservative selection . . .

Sue Valentine's revealing paper[3] described how the county of Hertfordshire moved from a decentralized to a centralized provision system. The management team had identified several limitations in the decentralized system:

- a fragmented view of stock as a county-wide resource
- conflicting priorities, and no county-wide system
- not enough high-level stock fed into the system
- staff time diverted away from stock matters
- an expensive way of acquiring stock, involving much duplication of effort (for instance, 50 separate orders placed for a best-seller).

Hertfordshire worked with five 'bands' of library service – from the five large libraries with issues of more than 500,000 in the first band, down to mobile libraries in the fifth. All staff were involved in the provision process; librarians at one service point worked in teams, with colleagues in their area, but also with staff across the five bands of libraries. The teams were responsible for selecting all new stock across the authority – an approach described not as centralized selection but as 'cooperative purchase'. The minimum requirements for each band of service were defined quite precisely: for instance, the percentage of fiction and non-fiction in libraries of each band (in large libraries, 30% fiction and 70% non-fiction); and the minimum turnover figure for stock.

Stock circulation was an important component of the overall approach. With the decentralized selection system, Hertfordshire had found that the circulation procedures too often involved rotating the same titles. (This was partly a function of using approvals collections, which were abandoned during the project.) Valentine made the crucial point that cooperation must take place *at the point of selection*, and not later in the cycle. In the revised Hertfordshire system, most new stock is allocated to stock circulation routes at the point of acquisition.

The handling of the budget was another key element. New stock budgets were not devolved to service points; on the other hand, each library was given a stock editing budget.

With the new system in place, the Hertfordshire management team felt that their initial objective to provide stock more cost-effectively had been achieved.

In terms of books on the shelves, the system afforded less duplication, fewer missed titles, and more scope for experimentation. But making the change was not easy. The new system needed a sustained effort, and involved more work than had initially been estimated – particularly in managing the documentation. Some of the county's staff needed 'a good deal of convincing'.

In summarizing the discussion about centralized versus decentralized provision, this writer comes down heavily in favour of the former: a decentralized approach appears to be a form of madness at a time when budgets are increasingly stretched and Government (rightly) requires authorities to demonstrate that they are adopting cost-effective approaches. The arguments (summarized above) in favour of Hertfordshire's change of system are highly pertinent: on the one hand, the cost-effective use of staff time; on the other the cost-effective use of the materials fund, on a stock with a much richer variety and less duplication. Centralized budgeting for (and selection of) 'new' books is absolutely essential to the good health of an authority's stock. Decentralized allocations for stock revision are a pragmatic move, intended to ensure that service points do the necessary work to ensure on-shelf availability in core subject areas – though one must ask whether authority-wide stock revision lists in core subject areas would not also be more cost-effective than a completely decentralized approach to stock revision.

The main obstacle to change is often the traditional attitude of service point staff, who feel that they need to 'own' the stock at their library. This has to be overcome, by taking extra time to involve all staff in a system-wide approach – time well spent on *the* core library management function.

A footnote is needed on the system of subject specialization operated by McClellan in Tottenham in the 1950s.[4] Essentially the system now widely used in academic libraries (see below), it is virtually defunct on the public library scene. Were he alive today, McClellan would no doubt observe that his system's intended strengths – staff knowledge of materials, and personal service to users – have been pre-empted as librarians become bogged down in a heavy burden of administrative routine.

Organization of academic library provision

The management of stock provision in academic libraries is complicated by several factors:

1 **The number of library sites**. Though many institutions have their library services concentrated on one site, others are physically split into a number of departmental services – especially when there is no main campus, or when

certain departments are physically located off-campus. Sometimes departmental libraries operate along with a 'central library', with the latter handling certain defined functions (such as short-loan collections).

2 The involvement of academic staff in the provision of materials, either in decisions about budgeting (see pages 11–15) and/or decisions on the selection of individual titles.

3 The organization of library staff, either by function and/or by using subject specialists (who enact all the functions in their subject areas).

Departmental libraries can be a function of academic politics as well as of physical location. Some universities have 50 or more separate libraries. Where this happens, there may be a need for some form of coordination, though such evidence as we have is not conclusive. Hindle's 1997 survey at the University of Lancaster[5] found that in one year a total of 17 departmental libraries had acquired books on the subject of 'operational research' – two of these ordering more titles than the operational research department itself. On the other hand, another survey (Urquhart and Schofield, 1972) looked at the overlap of acquisitions in the libraries of the University of London – an institution with large and geographically scattered subject collections, where a divide and rule approach was inevitable. It found that duplication was in fact relatively small: an examination of the catalogue entries for 20,000 titles ordered during one six-month period for 49 different libraries found no more than 1.85 entries per title.

In the past, various permutations have been used involving librarians and academics for selecting stock – some giving almost total control to the librarians, and others dividing up the bookfund on a departmental basis and leaving library staff only a minimal allocation to balance up departmental orders. Neither extreme is satisfactory. The input of lecturers and researchers is essential, for research and (even more so) for teaching materials. (Lecturers' lists of recommended reading are the crucial indicator for the acquisition of undergraduate texts.) At the same time, a system which relies entirely upon departmental selection is bound to lack balance. Some lecturers are more enthusiastic than others about building up library collections (or more knowledgeable about their subject literatures). A form of central coordination is needed to balance inequality of treatment between subjects, to select interdisciplinary material, and to be a long-stop for titles which have been missed.

Most academic libraries now opt for a system involving all those who have a contribution to make. Librarians normally retain control of the ordering process, and sometimes of the book fund. Alternatively, departments have an allocation, while the library retains a generous contingency fund. Librarians bring items to the attention of lecturers, and suggestions from departments are automatically ordered (unless funds are running out). Sumsion's 1994 survey (see Appendix) found that on average 10% of the time of professional staff in the library went on 'academic liaison' (including provision). Behind the executive structure is the library committee, to which any problems may be put. For instance, some librarians consult it (or a subcommittee) about new periodical titles – often quite a controversial matter, since they can cut across different subject fields.

The way that these organizational arrangements work out are again often a matter of personalities and university politics as much as anything else. Norman Higham's book[6] has a discussion of the various permutations, together with some advice from experience.

Evans (1970) suggested in one academic study that books selected by librarians circulated more freely than those selected by academic staff. There is no evidence to suggest that this is generally true.

Finally, there is the question of how academic libraries are organized internally. Many of them have appointed to their staffs subject specialists, with qualifications and experience in a subject as well as in library and information science. In the 'pure' model of subject specialization, specialists are responsible for all professional activities (selection, classification, information service, academic liaison etc) in their subjects. A 1982 survey (Woodhead and Martin, 1982) found that 40 of the responding university libraries used subject specialists in this way. Higginbottom (1987) suggested that most UK polytechnics also used the subject librarian approach – despite problems caused by multisite operations and multidisciplinary courses.

Martin's 1995 follow-up survey[7] of 59 universities (excluding the former polytechnics) noted a considerable shift in management structures. He identified five categories:

1 **Functional.** All functions were performed on a centralized (non-subject) basis (reported by five libraries).
2 **Dual.** Some staff carried out certain functions, subdivided by subject, whilst others carried out functions on a central basis (reported by 29 libraries).
3 **Hybrid.** Some or all staff carried out certain functions by subject, but were also responsible for at least one centralized function (reported by four libraries).
4 **Three-tier.** Most senior staff carried out subject functions, whilst middle or junior level staff carried out centralized functions (reported by two libraries).
5 **Subject divisional.** Subject teams consisting of both senior and supporting staff were responsible for a physically separate portion of the library collection (reported by three libraries).

Martin noted, in conclusion, a big reduction in the numbers of staff doing all their work on a subject basis – though belief in some form of subject specialization appeared to be undiminished. The main change since the 1981 survey was that the 'dual' model had become dominant.

Minimum system requirements

The following are suggested as minimum requirements for a book provision system for most kinds of library:

1 If a book provision policy or code of practice exists, the points included should be detailed and specific, and made known to all members of staff.
2 Management allocates the budget to specific types of materials, and monitors acquisitions to ensure that allocations are spent as directed.
3 Allocations are made for stock revision and maintenance, and spending of these is monitored.
4 Acquisitions are evenly paced throughout the year.
5 Where a library (or system) has multiple sites, decisions about what material to buy and what to discard are made centrally, and not by individual service points. Where sites are devoted to different subject areas (as with departmental libraries in a university), provision should be centrally coordinated rather than directed.
6 Where there is stock rotation between sites, material is allocated to exchange routes at the point of acquisition.
7 The selection of newly published material is linked to a single base source of information.
8 A specified minimum amount of staff time is allocated to materials provision, and monitored.
9 All professional staff are involved in materials provision across all library sites.
10 There are regular staff training programmes for materials provision.
11 Performance indicators are developed for materials provision and use, with targets for the future over several years.
12 Detailed management information is maintained about materials and their use, and regularly analysed and made known to staff.
13 User surveys are carried out to obtain information about the use of materials, when this is not obtainable from management information.

8
Weeding

Terms relating to weeding and related activities are not always used in precisely the same way, in the literature or in library practice. 'Weeding' normally describes the removal of stock from library shelves – either from the open shelves, or from reserve stock or remote storage. 'Reserve stock' normally describes a closed-access section of stock located in or near the same building as the open access sections. 'Remote storage' describes a closed access building located some distance from the main library; it often has rudimentary heating, lighting and shelving, permitting a considerable reduction in the costs of housing stock, whilst sacrificing the facility for immediate access.

'Disposal' normally means the complete removal of library material, followed by pulping, sale or transfer to another library. 'Discard' or 'withdrawal' sometimes mean the same as 'disposal', but can mean removing stock from open shelves to be redistributed elsewhere in the same library. 'Relegation' always means removal of stock from open to closed access.

Sorting through stock on library shelves often involves other activities not strictly covered by the term 'weeding', such as identifying books for binding, replacement (by the same or a later edition), cleaning or repair.

Reasons for weeding

Weeding usually occurs for one of two reasons. By far the most common of these is to clear space on the shelves to make room for new stock. Whatever the desirable size of a library's stock, its actual size is in practice dictated by the size of the library building; one with full shelves has to be weeded at a rate consistent with the rate of new additions. It is a fact of life.

There is always – in theory at least – the option of a new and larger library building, although the chances of realizing this solution to full shelves are in the hands of luck and local politics. In university libraries it was this factor which led to the publication of the Atkinson Report (see below) – itself a political solution.

As more material appears in digitized form, research libraries (in particular) may be able to make space savings by discarding print versions (for instance, of runs of serials) and keeping them in electronic form (see Chapters 4 and 10). Some evidence of this trend is already apparent in workplace libraries. A recent survey by Spiller (see Appendix) found that 23% of 285 libraries had reduced their collections in the previous five years – reductions ranging from 8% in the voluntary sector to 33% amongst management consultants.

The second main reason for weeding is the desire to increase the *use* of stock – either by improving its appearance, or by providing easier access to the 'live' elements by removing the dead wood. The use motive is more common in public and school libraries, where providing an up-to-date stock of attractive appearance is more important than in other sectors; the rate of use in public and school libraries is generally higher, so that the condition of stock declines more quickly.

Slote, in the standard American work on the subject,[1] claims that weeding stock always increases circulation. It is likely that weeding does usually increase use – if properly conducted – but the point is hard to prove, since so many other factors bear upon circulation. Williams[2] described the weeding of 20,000 volumes from a stock of 90,000 in a British academic library; circulation increased by 13% in the year following the weeding (compared to 2% in the preceding year) and by 16% in the year after that (though other factors may have influenced this).

Reasons for not weeding

Plausible reasons can usually be found for avoiding weeding:

- it is a labour-intensive process, likely to lead to embarrassing blunders if badly done
- the possibility that books may be needed at some future date encourages a defensive strategy of retention
- library procedures are generally designed to facilitate the addition of books rather than their withdrawal
- in university libraries, storage costs, though real enough, are not charged to the library's budget.

Buckland[3] discussed some of these factors in detail.

A major barrier to weeding in many large research libraries is the sense amongst their custodians that 'big is good'. Sara Williams's comments,[2] in her chapter on stock relegation in US academic libraries, probably hold good for many of their UK counterparts:

> Academic and research libraries regard the size and comprehensiveness of their collections with great pride . . . any action to reduce the size of collections, however necessary it may seem from an intellectual or managerial viewpoint, is essentially distasteful to the librarians who have built them.

Another barrier is lack of staff time (the polite description) or inertia (the impolite description) or the low priority given to weeding compared to other library activities (the politically correct description). Henry Heaney, speaking on retention policies in UK academic libraries,[4] commented (disapprovingly, rather than defensively):

> To select and process items for withdrawal, or even relocation, requires effort and few of us are so well staffed today that we will accord high priority to such tidying up operations unless pressurized by space shortages to do so.

Arfield[5] found that in a weeding exercise at the University of Reading, each relegated book took up eight minutes of professional staff time and 12 minutes of a library assistant's time.

'Shortage of time', as a reason for not disposing of stock, can equally be described as 'cost', and the costs of weeding are rarely built into the library budget. Of course, retaining material on library shelves also costs money, in a sense – though one may argue that it costs nothing to fill up shelf space which is empty.

In practice, UK university librarians have tended to identify the types of material which are *cheapest* to relegate or dispose of – especially when their location can be moved without major alterations to catalogue records. This is, unashamedly, a policy of relegating by expediency rather than by any stated objectives. Taylor and Urquhart[6] found that the cost of relegating periodicals was about 13 times lower than for monographs. Ford (1980) commented that other early candidates for relegation were special collections, books published before a certain date, and material in certain formats (such as pamphlets). In all these cases, catalogues can be amended simply by a general notice explaining that the groups of materials have been moved to remote storage. Gilder's literature survey (Gilder, 1980) contained a useful summary on the costs of relegation.

Capital Planning Information's 1994 survey[7] provided many valuable data about disposal practice in academic, public and workplace libraries (see Table 8.1).

Table 8.1 *The mean number of staff hours allocated to disposal, based on responses from 150 libraries*

	prof. staff	non-prof.	clerical
public	99	208	92
academic	25	42	48
workplace	12	32	16

The survey also had information on the mean numbers of items disposed of annually. In public library authorities, these were: 38,000 fiction, 29,000 non-fiction, and 28,000 children's books. The variation between authorities was enormous: for instance, non-fiction disposals ranged from 350 volumes in one authority to 160,000 in another.

As one would expect, academic libraries disposed of much less material. The mean numbers of disposals per year were 5000 textbooks and 5700 other non-fiction. Fifteen of the 49 responding academic libraries providing information 'never' routinely disposed of stock; on the other hand, three libraries regularly discarded stock (initially relegating, to check on demand). Relegation was generally preferred to disposal. The book categories most commonly disposed of were outdated textbooks and reference works, and duplicates.

Disposals were also modest in workplace libraries, with a mean of about 3500 volumes a year – though this information came from only a handful of libraries, of differing sizes.

Chapman and Spiller's survey[8] of academic and public library acquisitions between 1984 and 1999 reinforced the picture of variations in practice. Five UK public library authorities were asked what percentages of bibliographical samples submitted in earlier years were still in stock. Of samples submitted in the years 1981–84, a mean of 55% of the titles were still represented in stock (by at least one volume) in 1999 – at least 15 years later. The range between the five authorities was 32% to 88%. From similar samples submitted much later, in the years 1995–98, the percentages still in stock were naturally much higher: a mean of 93%, with a range from 85% (a sample submitted in 1995–96) to 100%.

Unsurprisingly, in the academic library samples the proportions of titles retained years later were much higher. Of samples submitted in the years 1980–82, a mean of 88% were still represented in stock, with a range from 79% to 98%. From the later samples submitted in the years 1988–89 (ie still at least ten years earlier) the mean was 91%, with a range from 83% to 97%.

Library automation systems can provide extensive background information about the need for weeding (if it is assumed that 'non-use' is the crucial indicator). In Chapter 6 we suggest the adoption of the performance measure 'the percentage of items borrowed (or not borrowed) over a given time period'. Some examples of non-use from the academic sector are given in the section immediately below. Smith's analysis[9] of public library management statistics in a London borough found that in one year 24% of fiction and 31% of non-fiction was not borrowed at all; and 40% of the non-fiction stock generated only 2% of the issues.

Academic library size and the Atkinson Report

The weeding of academic libraries was intensively discussed in the 1970s. UK university libraries tend to accumulate very large amounts of material (and US libraries even more). The generally low use of these collections is referred to in Chapter 5. Heaney (1987) put the case for the defence of large, little-used collections. Articles by Gore (1976) and Cronin (1988) were rare examples of the critical approach. The most concerted attack upon the monolithic principle was the 1976 report of the UK University Grants Commission (UGC) – the Atkinson report.[10] Atkinson demanded for universities a 'self-renewing library of limited growth' (or 'steady-state library'), which meant that beyond a certain point in size a library's acquisitions should largely be offset by the discarding of obsolete material. The self-renewing concept arose because the UGC was unwilling to provide the capital funding to extend university library buildings during the 1980s. They also reasoned that the costs of maintaining access to very large collections would erode funds available for new acquisitions.

Atkinson further recommended that universities should not hold large stocks in remote storage; as much as 85% of the materials should be on open access, and stock relegated to store should remain there for a trial period of five years before being returned to the main library, or transferred to a permanent back-up collection such as the British Library. The report offered a norm for establishing a library's notional entitlement to space, achieved by multiplying the figure of 1.25 square metres by the planned number of full-time students.

At the time, Atkinson caused much disgruntlement amongst university librarians, of which Steele's book[11] contained some representative examples. Critics said that the report had advocated crude measures to deal with a complex problem, and that not enough was known about the patterns of library use, the effects of borrowing, literature obsolescence or other factors, to put the future of university libraries at risk by wholesale withdrawals from stock; that it was extremely difficult to predict a useful book in research terms, and that retaining only titles which were in current demand would create serious problems for future researchers. They also complained that fundamentally different subject areas, such as the sciences and the humanities, were being treated in the same way.

Nearly a quarter of a century later Atkinson might claim, at best, to have had a very modest effect. Many of the questions which the report posed have yet to be addressed. There has been some interest in the size of collections, and much more in access to them by users. But writing in 1987, Ford (1988) could not identify any British universities conforming to the Atkinson mode. He observed that few libraries had developed a comprehensive approach to stock management and that, on average, university librarians were acquiring eight times as many materials as they discarded.

No real change in these patterns is observable at the end of the century. The total stock of all HE libraries in the UK in 1997–98 (89.7 million volumes) was 17% higher than the stock for 1993–94 (Library and Information Statistics Unit, 1999b, 139), signifying that the trend of accumulation is continuing. Reports of extensive weeding programmes are rare. Arfield[5] wrote about one at the University of Reading in 1989. Douglas's 1986 article[12] described a programme at Swinburne library in Australia, where the use of the monograph collection was analysed for a six-year period. From a constant-size open access collection of 113,000 volumes, 8% per year was removed – to the stack or for discard. During that period, the number of loans from open access remained reasonably constant. There were about six calls per year for each 100 titles removed to stack – with a small number of titles used consistently year on year, but 70% only used once. The total calls per title in stack varied between 0.042 and 0.075 over the six years.

Criteria for weeding

Chapter 5 discusses the indicators which reveal *when* sections of the stock need revision. A separate matter, examined below, is how to decide *which* titles should be withdrawn from any one section of stock.

In practice, the criterion used for weeding collections has often been 'the librarian's own judgement'. In a library which does not have specialist staff – or even in one which does – this puts a heavy burden of responsibility on the individual. It is unlikely that one person called upon to weed many subjects on the basis of judgement alone will consistently make 'correct' decisions; with more than one person involved, the chance of consistency is further reduced. Judgement has to be part of the weeding process, but practitioners have sought to augment it with reliable weeding criteria which can be applied scientifically.

The Capital Planning and Information survey[7] reported the 'reasons for disposal' in 150 public, academic and workplace libraries. For public libraries these were (in declining order of importance): poor condition, lack of use, age, lack of space, duplicate copies. For academic libraries: lack of use, poor condition, duplicate copies, lack of space, age. For workplace libraries: poor condition, lack of use, age, lack of space, duplicate copies.

A basic assumption of the weeding process is that the value of a book to library members can be estimated from the amount of use made of it. The disposal of less frequently used stock (or its relegation to a remote store) should increase the overall relevance of stock to users' needs – assuming that the books which replace weeded material circulate more often.

Much of the controversy in the literature of weeding is over the most effective method of predicting the future use of items in a collection. One school of thought says that 'use of the existing items' is the best indicator; another that 'imprint date' is just as accurate, and easier to apply. Hart (1986) provided a useful summary of the literature up to 1986.

Fussler and Simon[13] decided that 'past use over a sufficiently long period is an excellent and by far best predictor of future use' – although they observed 'the confidence limits of prediction vary significantly from one subject to another'. Trueswell[14] and Slote[1] also supported the 'past use' theory. Their work on weeding began from the premise that the open access areas of the library should house the 'core collection', defined by Slote as the materials 'most likely to be used by clients', and that the core collection can be accurately predicted by studying use of the existing collection. The library retains a 'core' collection which satisfies a predetermined amount of future use – for instance, 95% of existing demands. However, the full method for working this out, as described by Slote, is probably too complex for most purposes.

Slote's approach is based upon analysis of the 'shelf time period' – ie the length of time a book remains upon the shelf between successive uses. He claimed that the last shelf time period recorded upon books is highly predictive of future use, and described a simple method by which such information is analysed to provide a basis for stock weeding. He also noted alternative methods for libraries which did not record issues on date labels.

An important criticism of the approach followed by Slote and others was put forward by Taylor and Urquhart[6] in their 1976 research study. They claimed that the main predictor of future use in research collections was not the frequency of past use but the 'imprint date' of items in the collection. They observed that, for the great majority of research materials, use of an item declined rapidly about three years after publication, so that after this period any book had an equally low chance of being used. They had some disparaging comments to make about 'use' as a predictor for weeding purposes:

Monograph relegation based on date labels is highly suspect. If it is known that a group of books is little used then the borrowing record of items from that group is a nil predictor of future use . . . unfortunately the satisfying ritual of checking date labels gives the illusion that all is well and seems to be scientifically ennobled. The relegating acolyte does not realise that after a certain date nearly every book is as good or as bad a case as another.

This criticism of the 'past use' method – and the substitution of imprint date as the criterion for weeding – begs some questions. Without doubt, weeding of research collections by imprint date is *cheaper* than weeding by past circulation – a point also established by Raffell and Shishko (1969). But there is no certainty that it is a more accurate method. The overall use of research collections is known to decline with age, but the rate of decline within different disciplines shows considerable variations. And there are works in every subject area which resist the 'standard' rate of decline for their subjects. Taylor and Urquhart[6] conceded that such works may comprise as much as 10% of the total, and suggested that when the 'date of imprint' method was used for weeding, the 10% must be identified in some other way. But no other way was suggested, and that is not good enough; one might argue that the whole point of weeding scrupulously is to identify that 10% and preserve them for users.

On the question of use, it would obviously be helpful to those weeding library stock if there were some general rules for the diminution of use over time – a concept referred to as 'obsolescence'. This subject has generated much literature, most of it based on citation studies – that is, studies showing the number of times that individual books or serial articles are cited in the lists of references given at the end of a piece of research.

It is known that all forms of research literature do obsolesce, and that there are big differences between the pattern of obsolescence in different subject areas. Unfortunately an extensive survey of obsolescence studies by Line and Sandison[15] concluded that librarians can make little practical use of the concept of obsolescence. The authors observed that at the time of writing most obsolescence studies had been characterized by a superficial approach to what was a highly complex situation of interlocking factors. The relationship between citation and use was particularly complicated, and it was not yet known what factors determined which items in a collection would be read or cited, and the relative importance of age between them. They concluded:

Variations between individual titles, of serials as well as monographs, are likely to be so great that substantial data must be collected for each individual title, perhaps in each library (certainly in each type of library) if weeding is to be done on a rational basis.

Whichever is the main determinant used – 'past use' or 'imprint date' – those doing the weeding have to bear in mind the big variations in the rate of use between different subject areas, and different titles within them. An obvious example is that in public libraries fiction stock invariably issues more frequently overall than non-fiction stock; if weeding is based upon 'the number of years for which an item has not circulated', different thresholds are obviously needed for these two broad categories. In practice, a great many different thresholds are needed, particularly in sectors (such as public libraries) where a basic coverage of all subject areas is required on the shelves. Some subject areas of non-fiction stock generally circulate more than others (for instance, books on computers more than those on French history); and some fiction stock circulates more than others (for instance, best-selling thrillers more than a first novel, or a European novel in translation). Nevertheless, all these examples – and many more – need some representation in library stock, despite the variations in use.

There is a further complication. Within these subject categories – however minutely they are defined – some types of books may be expected to circulate much more frequently than others: for instance, in a public library general books on a subject usually circulate more frequently than works on one aspect; practical books generally circulate more than theoretical works in the same subject area.

All these complexities suggest that in the last analysis librarians do have to use their judgement for individual cases, though judgment should be backed by the general criteria discussed above.

In some library sectors, staff may be more rigorous in weeding than in others. For instance, librarians in schools are perhaps the most likely to withdraw books which have out-of-date content – even though they are still circulating well. The same point applies, to an extent, in public libraries, and even to undergraduate student texts. This has to do with librarians taking on more direct responsibility for customers when they feel that customers' judgement of stock may be faulty.

All the discussion above refers exclusively to circulation data, and not to in-house use – though this also affects weeding decisions.

One other main criterion for weeding is generally applied in conjunction with 'use' and 'date'. The physical condition of stock is important, especially in libraries where stock is heavily used, and likely to wear out before its content becomes out of date. Public and school library service points generally aim for a minimum standard of appearance in their stock, though it is inevitably determined in part by the size of the materials fund. This physical standard can only really be evaluated by library staff through a direct inspection of the book.

Use is more commonly the cause of physical dilapidation than longevity.

Reuben and Spiller[16] provided some evidence on this, and also developed a table of criteria for judging the condition of books on library shelves. Estimates of the numbers of issues that can be anticipated from books on public library shelves are reported in Chapter 2.

Duckett[17] observed that the relegation to stack of public library material was often determined by 'category of material' – the most commonly relegated being local publications, documentary and source material (such as government publications), classics, 'books or subjects not well covered by other stock', profusely illustrated works, literary texts and 'heavy' biographies.

Recent literature on 'preservation' is partially relevant to discussion of weeding. Preservation has been defined as 'actions taken to maximize the useful life of all library materials' – and being about making items available in *usable* condition as and when required.

Finally, a crucial point is that librarians' decisions on the disposal of titles are greatly influenced by their knowledge of interlending facilities available in their country. For instance, in the UK the main source of interloans (the British Library Document Supply Centre) does not handle fiction – which makes UK public library authorities cautious about withdrawing the last copies of important fiction titles. This is not just a matter of what is available through interlending systems in theory, but also what other libraries are in practice willing to lend. These matters are fully discussed in Chapter 9.

Disposal of stock

The Capital Planning Information report of 1995[7] investigated the *destination* of stock which had been disposed of, by requesting respondents to rank seven options in order of importance, namely: sale to the public, sale to the book trade, donation to other libraries, donation to book aid organizations, offers to Book Net (see below), offers on exchange, and pulping. The reported rankings (in diminishing order of importance) for the three library sectors surveyed were:

- public libraries: sale to public; pulping; sale to trade and donation to other libraries; offers to Book Net; donations to book aid; offers on exchange
- academic libraries: sale to public; donations to book aid; sale to trade; pulping; offers to Book Net; donation to other libraries; offers on exchange
- workplace libraries: donation to other libraries; offers to Book Net; donations to book aid; pulping; sale to trade; sale to public; offers on exchange.

The Book Net service is operated by the British Library at Boston Spa. Donated material is collected and offered to other libraries on a non-profit-making basis.

At the time of the report the service handled 60,000 titles a year, and 900 libraries received the Book Net lists.

The mean annual income reported from disposal (in 1994) was £24,000 for public library authorities, £1000 for academic libraries, and £5000 for workplace libraries.

In the public library sector in particular, book sales have become a major activity – a bizarre development, since sales convey a jumble-sale atmosphere in organizations which covet the image of an up-to-date information service. It must be very doubtful whether book sales are cost-effective, especially when compared to pulping, which is by far the cheapest method of disposal; in fact, five public library authorities in the survey commented that staff time spent on disposal was rarely recouped. A 1997 survey of 18 UK public library authorities (Spiller and Creaser, 1999) found that the mean percentage of 'miscellaneous revenue from the public' obtained from book sales was 30%; but the 'miscellaneous revenue' figure itself was only 19% of total revenue income for the same authorities.

Stocktaking

'Stocktaking' (or 'stock audit') refers to a physical check to identify items which are recorded in the library catalogue but missing from stock. Until the 1980s it was common for public and academic libraries to carry out regular checks of their entire stock in this way. More recently, stocktaking has become unfashionable, and many libraries check their stock rarely or not at all – despite the opportunities for more streamlined stocktaking offered by library automation systems. The last major UK investigation into this was carried out in 1992 by Burrows and Cooper[18] on behalf of the Home Office Police Department. There were responses from 727 libraries. Of these, 32% had carried out full physical inventories (though about half did this only once every five years); 41% carried out 'counts' of stock (annually in seven out of ten cases), though these did not provide any information on the missing titles; and 28% carried out neither inventories nor counts. The incidence of both has probably declined further since 1992.

The Home Office survey found that annual loss rates were 4.2% in public libraries, 1.8% in academic libraries, and 2.2% in workplace libraries. The average overall loss was 3.3 books for every thousand loans. Non-return of issued books accounted for 29% of all losses. Preventive measures recommended included – in addition to better stocktaking – reducing the numbers of loans allowed at any one time, employing book recovery officers, amnesties and security systems. Some 36% of the respondents had security systems, four out of five of these installed in the 1990s; all felt that this measure had reduced losses, but only a few had checked up on it. The authors felt that the higher incidence of security systems in academic libraries (87% had a system) accounted for their lower loss rates. Foster (1996) estimated that a security system pays for itself within the first year of installation.

Policies not to stocktake are adopted because of staff shortages, but also on the premise that stock-taking is a waste of time because it does not bring back the missing books; and any item which is really important will be requested on reservation (though this is not so when a central reservation system is used).

The uncomfortable reality is that a lack of stocktaking over a number of years leads to inefficient book provision systems and inadequate stock. Losses and thefts from stock normally affect books which are most in demand. Only a fraction of readers make regular use of the reservations service; the remainder are affected by the absence from the shelves of a large number of important titles. Librarians continue to base selection and stock revision programmes upon catalogue records which are no longer accurate, and waste time searching for books which are no longer in circulation.

Binding

Publishers' casings are not designed for library use, and if subjected to multiple issues they can become damaged within a couple of years of purchase. Librarians must then decide whether to bind or discard. The bound book is (by definition) less up-to-date than a new book on the same subject, and less attractive than a new book in its original dust jacket (though there are always some users who prefer library bindings).

The main reasons to opt for binding – rather than a new book on the same subject, or a new copy of the same book – are likely to be:

* where past use suggests that there is still a strong demand for this particular title
* where it is cost-effective to bind rather than replace
* to keep an out-of-print title in circulation.

In research collections the 'attractiveness' of stock is a much less important factor; moreover, most research materials are retained in stock indefinitely, so where condition has deteriorated, the tendency is to bind rather than to discard.

Library suppliers produce 'library editions' of new fiction (and some non-fiction) by buying up sets of book sheets from the publishers, adding double-strength reinforcing, and laminating the dust jackets onto their own boards – the results having far greater durability than publishers' casings. But large-scale prepublication ordering of titles in this format, though widely practised, is open to criticism (see Chapter 3).

Public library expenditure on binding declined by 22% during the period 1988–98 (Library and Information Statistics Unit, 1999b, 17) – *before* the effects of increased costs are calculated. At a time of extreme pressure on book funds this is very surprising, and there is a strong case for re-examining the cost-effectiveness of binding in the provision of library materials. Expenditure in the pre-1992 university libraries has also declined: from 2.6% of total library expenditure in 1987–88 to 1.6% in 1997–98 (Library and Information Statistics Unit, 1999b, 111). In the case of universities, their lower use rates make it less of a surprise that the binding budget has been reduced in the face of overall budget pressures.

9
Holdings versus access

There is intensive discussion about how far libraries should 'acquire and own' material as against obtaining it from remote sources on request – an issue often described as one of 'holdings versus access'. Several factors make this of fundamental concern at the present time: more and more items (of all kinds) are being published; library funding continues to diminish; there is wider availability of secondary sources (especially electronic sources), leading to greater demand; and above all, the availability of some kinds of material through electronic media facilitates an 'access' approach.

The extent to which 'access' solutions are favoured depends very much upon types of libraries and types of materials. At one end of the scale, most school libraries lean almost entirely upon acquired stock, with little if any borrowing through interlending systems. 'Holdings' are also still paramount in UK public libraries, with only 0.1% of all book loans in 1997–98 coming from interlending (Library and Information Statistics Unit, 1999b, 62, 88), and very few photocopies of periodical articles. It is in academic and special libraries, where research materials are in demand, that an 'access' approach is more pronounced. Parry[1] reported that, in 1993, 2.3% of all academic issues were derived from interlibrary loans. A specialized research library recently reported (Chambers, 1999) that 55% of all documents required by users were obtained externally.

In a considerable literature, Sykes's chapter[2] on document delivery strategies is particularly good on electronic access, as is the section on document delivery in Rowley's *The electronic library*.[3] Finnie[4] provides an overview of practice. Parry's 1997 report *Why requests fail*[1] has much background detail about interlending. Morris and Blagg[5] report on two recent surveys. Finally, Line's 1996 article on access v ownership[6] trenchantly dispels myths and raises pertinent questions.

The current situation

Rowley[3] lists several types of document delivery service which are currently used by libraries:

Library networks and consortia

These systems are usually based upon union catalogues of holdings, often mounted on the web. The most prominent network is that of eight regional library systems in England and Wales, which coordinate most of the interlending between member libraries (public, university and college) in their areas. The regions are themselves coordinated by CONARLS: the Circle of Officers of National and Regional Library Systems. The regional systems handle a large amount of book traffic. A relatively recent service – London and Manchester document access (LAMDA) – is a distributed service for the exchange of serial articles between universities; in May 1998, ten sites were serving a total of 53 universities.

CD-ROM suppliers

These include suppliers of both full-text and secondary databases.

Document delivery services

These are primarily commercial services, operating from databases announcing their holdings, and largely concentrated on journal articles and conference reports. Examples are:

- UnCover, based on contents tables from 18,000 journals
- a British Medical Association service, for medical material only
- OCLC First Search, giving access to more than 60 databases and 1.5 million full-text articles.

British Library Document Supply Centre (BLDSC)

As the largest document delivery service in the world, BLDSC warrants separate mention. In 1998–99 it stocked 261,000 serials and 3.1 million monographs, and handled just over three million requests from the UK, and a further 1.2 million from overseas (Library and Information Statistics Unit,

1999b, 174–6). It dominates the UK interlending scene; Parry[1] reported that in 1995–96 BLDSC supplied 73% of items processed through the UK regional systems, and 92% of the serial requests. Morris and Blagg[5] found that all UK academic libraries used BLDSC – most of them on a daily basis.

Library suppliers and subscription agents

These handle electronic ordering of both print and electronic documents (serials and/or books).

Electronic journal suppliers

These include some commercial publishers, providing access through CD-ROM or online sources.

The traditional (print-based) form of document supply for public and academic libraries – which Morris found to be used in 90% of cases – is still dominated by BLDSC and the regional systems. (We discuss workplace libraries separately below.) Parry reported that amongst the eight regions, 66–84% of requests were satisfied from BLDSC (except in the London and South Eastern Region (LASER), where is was 36%); and 5–21% were satisfied from regional library members (except in LASER, where it was 55%). Parry also reported the percentage of traffic taken by each source in one region, for public and academic libraries:

Table 9.1 *Percentage of traffic in the Northern region (1995–96)*

	public	academic
BLDSC	60%	93%
others libs in N region	21%	–
libraries outside N region	19%	7%

Parry observed that most university libraries rationed requests – often by precluding undergraduates and/or by limiting (through the use of quotas) the numbers from postgraduates. Clinton (1999) found that of 120 respondents, 65% charged for interlibrary loans; £5 was the amount most often charged, with £1 and £2 also common. Respondents said that demand invariably fell after the introduction of charges.

Parry also observed (disconcertingly) that only six of 15 academic libraries used bibliographical tools to verify requests *before* sending them to BLDSC – and that a significant proportion of requests returned from BLDSC for more information were abandoned without further checking.

In public libraries, the level of initial checking was found to be more thorough, though variable. Some authorities accepted no requests for fiction. Many charged for interlibrary loans, amounts varying between £0.50 and £2.00. Parry also commented:

> There is a general feeling among public libraries that due to pressures on bookfunds they are requesting more things on inter-library loan that libraries would previously have purchased themselves.

Parry scrutinized the reasons for request failure. About twice as many were abandoned in public libraries as in academic and workplace libraries. Of all failed UK requests (from public and academic libraries), 39% were found to be for material 'up to two years old', and a further 14% 'three to four years old'. This suggested that about half of all interlibrary loan requests were purchasable, but requesting libraries had chosen not to buy. The percentages of failed requests reported by category were: serials 2.8%; non-fiction monographs 9.2%; fiction in English 14.9%.

Three main reasons for 'site failure' – ie libraries were asked to lend but declined – were:

1 'Library does not lend this material (reference or special collections)': 14% for public libraries, 28% for academic libraries.
2 'Title on loan or in heavy demand': 37% for public libraries, 14% for academic.
3 'Not in stock, or cannot trace': 22% for public libraries, 25% for academic.

The figures are revealing: for over half of public library titles, and 42% of academic library titles, libraries had the books in stock but were not willing to lend. One may speculate that a large proportion of the 'not for loan' reports concerned material published within the previous few years, and still in print. The message is that requesting libraries must consider not only whether there are existing locations for an item they want to borrow, but also whether those locations will be willing to lend.

The point was re-emphasized in a survey of 2392 ILL requests for monographs at the University of Dundee, conducted by Roberts and Cameron[7] in 1980–81. They found that 12% of all requests made were for material in its first year of publication; 39% for material two to five years old; 19% 6–10 years old;

23% 11–30 years old; and only 7% for monographs 30 or more years old. Larger proportions of the older monographs were in the arts and humanities, and of recent material in the sciences. The authors commented that much of the material requested was recent, and frequently low-priced and purchasable – and that in many cases the cost of borrowing was on a par with the cost of purchasing.

The patterns of borrowing for workplace libraries are substantially different from those in academic and public library sectors. In the first place, quite large numbers of workplace libraries do not use interlending or document supply services at all. Secondly, there is much more use of direct borrowing between peer organizations. And thirdly there is more diverse use of smaller, specialized document supply agencies in addition to the service of BLDSC. There are also big variations between sectors, and between practices for books and serials (see Table 9.2).

Table 9.2   *The percentages of libraries reported to be using different sources in Spiller's 1998 Libraries in the workplace survey (see Appendix)*

For books (percentages of organizations)

	no ILLs	peer orgs	regions	BLDSC	agencies
govt orgs	25	43	9	70	30
charities	79	13	–	17	4
prof assocs	44	30	8	54	4
legal orgs	36	50	5	50	9
financial orgs	38	25	–	50	13
energy orgs	13	38	19	88	22
pharmaceutics	6	9	9	91	31
mgt consults	61	6	6	24	15

For serials (%s of orgs)

	no ILLs	peer orgs	regions	BLDSC	agencies
govt orgs	23	48	9	68	27
charities	38	25	4	17	38
prof assocs	26	45	4	57	15
legal orgs	9	74	–	48	43
financial orgs	22	35	–	43	39
energy orgs	6	42	10	90	32
pharmaceutics	9	22	13	91	41
mgt consults	41	16	16	31	19

User views

What would library users have to say about the 'access versus ownership' discussion? The first point to make is that an 'access' approach largely precludes browsing. Line[6] observed that 'browsing is almost universally practised and is much appreciated by users', and that this applied even in the hard sciences, where 24–60% of scientists' reading was in the form of browsing. Erens concluded, from his survey of university academics (see Appendix), that there was an overwhelming desire amongst academics to see improvements to their own institutions' collections. Electronic browsing is a possible alternative, but Line felt that the screen page, as currently constituted, was too small for comfortable browsing; the browsing process was much slower, and scanning screens for long periods was hard on the eyes. Scanning the contents pages of serials services was useful, but only a partial answer.

McClellan[8] identified a 'scale of accessibility' for users in public libraries – though his comments apply to most kinds of library. Any user seeking an individual (print) document at a library is offered one of three different levels of service:

- immediate supply from stock
- supply from within the library system but not from the particular service point
- supply from an external location.

In terms of delays in supply, this stratification is decreasingly satisfactory to the user – hence the emphasis in Chapter 5 on stock revision, and the need to have subject coverage *on the shelves* in public and school libraries, and in the short-loan sections of academic libraries. A mitigating circumstance is that few library users restrict themselves to one source; Luckham's survey of public library use (see Appendix) observed that only 24% of users obtained all their needs from a single public library service point.

A survey by Houghton and Prosser (1974) somewhat surprisingly found that delays were not a major problem for research workers borrowing copies of periodical articles through the interlending system. This was just as well, since White's informative 1985 survey *Interlending in the UK* (White, 1986) found that the percentage of UK requests satisfied within a period of seven days (from all sources) had declined from 50% in 1977 to 32% in 1985. Matters improved in the 1990s. Morris's report of 1996 and 1997 surveys of document delivery practice in UK academic libraries[5] noted the percentages given in Table 9.3.

Table 9.3 *Percentages of requests fulfilled within one- and two-week thresholds,
subdivided by source*

Supplier	in 1 week	in 2 weeks
BLDSC	57%	79%
BIDS	98%	
Uncover	89%	97%
Anbar	94%	100%
Local/regional	51%	79%

Some services now provide material very quickly; supply within 48 hours was achieved – by BIDS, UnCover and Anbar – in 59%, 68% and 64% of cases respectively. On the debit side, Parry[1] reported that 20% of all UK requests were abandoned because they did not come through quickly enough.

Electronic access

McClellan's comments on a 'scale of accessibility' (see above) were made in 1962 (and re-published in 1973), but the principle of immediate access or remote access also applies to electronic sources. UK university libraries currently have access to a reasonable number of databases, by purchasing CD-ROMs or subscribing to centralized online services such as BIDS-ISI, but these are only a fraction of the databases generally available; requests for materials from databases which are not directly accessible must be handled through the traditional interlending systems, through online hosts or through the new agencies providing electronic document supply services. Elsewhere in this book (for instance, in Chapters 4, 11 and 12) we report speculations on the various possible permutations for future electronic forms of supply.

Sykes[2] commented (in 1999) that traditional interlending services were still flourishing, but that electronic methods for requesting and supplying material were developing fast, with library consortia, subscription agents, publishers and software suppliers all playing a part. She distinguished between Electronic (Document Delivery) – E(DD) – in which the original document was in print, and was scanned and transmitted electronically; and Electronic Document (Delivery) – ED(D) – where material electronic at source was transmitted electronically. The first of these is currently much more common, but the second may develop more quickly.

Sykes summarized by anticipating a three-pronged approach for the future of document delivery:

1 Libraries would be encouraged to open up their collections to researchers to a greater extent than is currently practised.
2 Advances in electronic services would mean users would be able to view more resources directly on their personal computers, irrespective of the location of the original documents.
3 Document delivery would increasingly be achieved by electronic transmission of the materials, once their existence and whereabouts had been discovered by users.

These developments would form part of the Distributed National Electronic Resource (see Chapter 11).

Rowley[3] posed some critical questions for librarians considering a switch from print to electronic access:

• Will electronic access cost more or less than print?
• What are the licensing terms, and who negotiates them?
• When is the right moment to make a switch to electronic?
• If a switch is made, should print versions be discontinued?
• Which electronic journals service will give the library a critical mass of titles?
• Does the library need to use more than one service?
• Can journal titles be selected, or will they be bundled together by the vendor?

Serials

Since about half of the interlending traffic in academic libraries is for serial articles, electronic serials handling is of particular interest. Sykes[2] commented on the new kinds of document delivery agencies which have established databases of core journals, usually by digitizing print originals, and provide access to them for a fee. But such services currently cover 100–500 serial titles, or up to 1000 at most – relatively small numbers compared to the serials available from BLDSC. Libraries which subscribe to the print versions of core titles in their fields of interest are likely to obtain articles from fringe journals via traditional interlending sources.

There is an alternative approach: the one adopted by the University of Cranfield in the well documented BIODOC experiment. Bevan[9] reported on three full years of the project so far. BIODOC aimed to evaluate the cost-effectiveness of a wholly access-based approach to information. Journal subscriptions for all titles serving the biotechnology departments at Cranfield were cancelled, and replaced by a combination of electronic current-awareness services and fast document delivery.

The immediate result of this approach was a very big increase in document delivery, as wider access to information fuelled demand. But as the numbers of requests settled down, staff observed a major change: a big increase in the numbers of different journal titles from which articles were requested (see Table 9.4).

Table 9.4 *The pattern of document delivery resulting from the BIODOC experiment*

	pre-BIODOC	1st yr	2nd yr	3rd yr
no of requests	1849	4849	3244	4102
no of journal titles	556	1189	1143	1169

Another change was that the majority of requests – post-BIODOC – were received in the *current* year, whereas previously document delivery requests had been received for articles published in the preceding year.

BIODOC carried out two impact studies on the project. They found that 25% of the articles obtained had been read fully, whilst 70% had been read partially; 77% of the articles had 'fully met' the need for which they had been requested, whilst 80% had provided 'new knowledge'.

The project also compared the actual costs of the document delivery services with the putative costs of subscriptions previously held, and found that the huge inflation in serial costs between years 2 and 3 of the project had rendered BIODOC's approach more economical than print subscriptions (see Table 9.5).

Table 9.5 *Cost (in £1000s) of BIODOC document delivery in comparison to equivalent serial costs*

	pre-BIO	yr 1	yr2	yr3
original model (subs + ILLs)	19	20	23	24
BIODOC	–	26	14	19

Bevan concluded that it would not have been economic for Cranfield to subscribe to any of the individual cancelled journals in any of the three years. Overall, BIODOC was both more economical than the print subscriptions approach, and had yielded clear benefits in enhanced current awareness and a wider access to serial titles. Staff and students found BIODOC 'infinitely preferable' to the preceding service, and no one wanted to revert to print.

The BIODOC experiment is rooted in a multidisciplinary field to which it is highly suited. A more discrete science discipline with a smaller number of core journals might require a different approach: some print subscriptions, supplemented by document delivery services for the remainder. That said, arts and humanities subjects are likely to be even more highly suited to a BIODOC system. Unfortunately there are few comparable examples. Prowse (1999) summarized the initial results of a follow-up project – MANDOC – in a school of management. Crump and Freund (1995) reported on a US university library which had cancelled 1377 journals; only 2% of subsequent interlibrary loans were for articles in the cancelled titles. Line[6] felt that serials were highly suited to an access approach because they were 'copiable'. He thought it 'extraordinary that most academic libraries keep periodical subscriptions going as long as they can at the expense of monograph publications', and concluded that they were obliged by their faculty to act irrationally.

Costs of access v ownership

Leaving aside the question of shelf space, and the advantages of browsing, the obvious question arises: what amount of use justifies print material being purchased for library stock rather than being borrowed through the interlending network? This cannot be precisely quantified, but several writers have had a stab at a formula. The stimulating article 'Some library costs and options' by Brown[10] (an economist) concluded: 'It seems worth acquiring and providing storage for books likely to be wanted more often than once in about 1.7 years over a long period.' Line (1983) took a very different approach, estimating the average cost of an interlibrary borrowing to a requesting library in the UK to be in the region of £4, and the average price of a book to be £10, plus £7–8 for acquisition and processing, and therefore deducing it to be cheaper to make five borrowings of a title before purchase.

Sykes[2] cited several studies which shed light upon cost calculations. Kingma (1997) estimated that if there were fewer than 35 uses of a journal in its lifetime, it was cheaper to rely upon document supply than to subscribe. Gossen and Irving (1995) estimated that if a journal volume was used less than five times per year, it was cheaper to use document supply services. Kohl (1997) reported that the total costs of the average interlibrary loan – including costs to both libraries – was around $30.

Of course, any costings of 'access versus ownership' cannot take into account the unquantifiable advantages of purchase – in particular, the possibility (which borrowing precludes) that purchased materials may be used several times, through either borrowing or in house use. This point leads back into the discussion about browsing.

Cooperative acquisition

One approach to an access system is where a group of libraries cooperate on the *acquisition* of materials, because of a factor they hold in common – usually their subject field or their geographical location. There have been numerous attempts to make cooperative acquisition work, but few successes. In the US, the well-publicized Farmington Plan operated from 1948 to 1972, this being a voluntary agreement between 60 American libraries to acquire at least one copy of each new foreign publication that might reasonably be expected to interest researchers. Also initiated in 1948 was the Mid-West Interlibrary Center (MILC) – then the Center for Research Libraries – in which a group of the major university libraries of the American Mid-West shared the purchase of little-used research items; in this case, all purchased items were centralized on a site at the University of Chicago, rather than scattered amongst the participating libraries. There have been various public library collaborations in the UK, including a subject specialization scheme operated at one time by the regional library bureaux, and a fiction scheme run by the Joint Metropolitan Fiction Reserve in London.

Perhaps the most attractive option for collaborative acquisition is between geographically adjacent libraries – for instance, between school, public and/or college libraries in an area. But a 1974 study (Wilson and Masterson, 1974) found that the scope for savings through cooperative acquisition locally was in fact small. The duplication of titles amongst the different types of institution studied in Sheffield was found to be very low. Given that central purchasing agencies tend to delay the ordering process, the report recommended against its introduction – though felt it was worth coordinating the acquisition of reference works and serials.

The title of Line's 1997 article – 'Cooperation: the triumph of hope over experience?' – trails his point of view on this theme. He felt that, though cooperation was usually assumed to 'a good thing', its purpose was rarely identified clearly. There were a great variety of cooperative schemes, but some (or perhaps many) of them were of dubious value. Of the many cooperative acquisition schemes tried, few had succeeded, and many had been abandoned – especially because libraries were expected to follow the unnatural course of buying items which *they* did not need but others might. 'Grace and favour' arrangements were now giving way to commercial systems. Line concluded: 'No amount of cooperative or other joint activity, and no currently conceivable developments in electronic technology, can serve as a full substitute for adequate local libraries.'

Line was, however, very positive about the need for cooperative *retention* policies – something which few countries have developed. In the UK, decisions about retention are made by individual libraries or authorities, and there is no coordination of the process.

Conclusions

Given the many and rapid developments in this area, it is extraordinarily difficult to make a sensible summary of the 'access versus ownership' issue – and, more to the point, difficult for individual librarians to pitch local policies effectively.

The numerous electronic initiatives in this field are initially likely to impact upon serials provision. The BIODOC experiment showed that using electronic contents lists in combination with rapid document delivery systems was found advantageous by almost all its users. Faculties permitting, we may expect more academic libraries to move towards the BIODOC approach – though in some subject areas they may adopt a combination of core journals in print form and peripheral titles through document supply. No one can currently predict what form will be taken by electronic delivery of serial contents; an article-by-article (rather than serial-by-serial) approach would be ideal, particularly if it could be managed by the institutions themselves – to reduce the ludicrous commercial pricing.

Where monographs and textbooks are concerned, electronic solutions are for the most part some way off, and librarians must continue to strike a balance between buying and borrowing. Users still want to browse in monograph collections. There is one key point: librarians must aim to acquire for stock the materials which are most likely to be used. (Since university libraries, for instance, make numerous ILL requests for 'in print' material, and numerous purchases of monographs which do not get used, there is clearly much to be done in this respect.) Where there are multisite systems – as with all public library authorities – acquisition *must* be centrally coordinated so that the widest possible variety of titles is made available within the system. Decisions not to purchase titles should bear in mind their likely availability through document supply systems (including the possibility that some existing locations may be unwilling to lend). Arrangements for retaining titles should be carefully coordinated within library systems – and, ideally, also on a national basis.

Where document supply systems are used, libraries will choose their suppliers on the basis of factors such as cost, reliability, administrative convenience (ie cheapness) and speed of supply.

10
Serials

ISO standard 329 defines a serial as a publication 'issued in successive parts, usually having numerical or chronological designations, and intended to be continued indefinitely'. The 1997 edition of *Ulrich's international periodicals directory* has data on 215,000 serials and newspapers from 200 countries worldwide. The British Library Document Supply Centre – the largest collection of serials in the world – has an annual intake of 58,000 current titles (Library and Information Statistics Unit, 1999b, 175).

The serial's frequency of appearance – typically daily, weekly, monthly, quarterly or annually – allows it to include content that is more up-to-date than the content of books. This defining feature of *currency* permits serials to engage in two main functions: acting as the first record for research findings, and reporting news for practitioners engaged in a very wide range of activities. The 'research' and 'news' functions frequently overlap – as in the *British Medical Journal* and the *Lancet*, where brief reports of recent research are a key updating source for medical practitioners and researchers. The main sources of these types of serials are learned societies and professional associations, and commercial publishers.

Serials (or journals or periodicals) are big business, especially in academic and workplace libraries. In the UK, university and other higher education libraries spent some 57 million pounds on printed serials in 1997–98 (Library and Information Statistics Unit, 1999a). This purchased a total of 407,000 current periodicals in the old (pre-1992) universities, 120,000 in the new (post-1992) universities, and 34,000 in higher education colleges (Library and Information Statistics Unit, 1999b, 140). In that year, print serials took 17% of the old university libraries' budgets, with nearly half taken by wages and 11% by books; the 21% taken by 'other' expenditure was dominated by electronic materials, which also included a substantial proportion on serials. In the new university libraries, serials took a more modest 12% of the library budget, with books accounting for 14% and wages again for 49% (Library and Information Statistics Unit, 1999b, 143).

The other sector with large holdings of serials is that of workplace libraries. Spiller's survey of these for the year 1996–97 (see Appendix) estimated a total expenditure of 118 million pounds on printed serials for the library sectors of government, professional associations, law, finance, pharmaceutics, energy and management consultancy. Sectoral holdings were estimated at a total of 74,000 titles in professional associations, 490,000 in government libraries, 172,000 in law libraries, and 55,000 in financial libraries. The median numbers of titles taken per library in selected sectors were: government agencies 225, professional associations 150, law 174, finance 100, energy 100, and pharmaceutics 120. Only in the voluntary and management consultancy sectors were serial holdings relatively small (medians of 25 and 12 respectively). Though the numbers of print serials taken were decreasing in government and energy sectors, they were on the increase in professional associations, law and finance libraries, and stable in pharmaceutics.

At the time of the workplace survey (1996–97), print was still the medium used for the majority of serials, ranging from 80% in the pharmaceutical sector to 95% in voluntary organizations. But electronic serials were becoming more common: for instance, in pharmaceutical libraries 12% of serials were accessed via CD-ROM, and 9% through online sources; amongst management consultants, 15% were accessed through online sources.

Outside the academic and workplace library sectors, there are much smaller holdings of serials in public and school libraries; these are mostly of the more popular journals and magazines which are mainly aimed at the personal market, and are discussed separately below.

Use of research serials

Comment on research serials is complicated by a serious lack of data about use (or non-use). It seems probable – though without research, we cannot be sure – that many of the serials held in academic libraries are poorly used. The size of these collections relates more to the prestige of the academics who publish in them than to their use and impact.

There have been cancellations of subscriptions in the past two decades, but large serials collections continue to be the norm; and they persist despite some extraordinary price increases imposed by serial publishers – increases which have squeezed other elements of library budgets over a long period. The onset of electronic serials appears to offer an alternative approach, but has so far complicated the situation without providing real solutions. That said, electronic journals are – in the opinion of most experts – the shape of the future. Another possibility, facilitated by electronic delivery, is for libraries to replace holdings and/or electronic subscriptions by access on demand. All these points are discussed below.

The use of serials takes two main forms: first, current-awareness use of the latest issues, to keep researchers and academics up to date in their subject areas; secondly, reference to specific articles from serial back-runs – normally located separately from the recent issues. Much of this use takes place in-house, so that methods for measuring it cannot rely (as they often do with other materials) upon issue figures. Amongst the measuring approaches that have been devised are:

- counting serial issues left lying on reading tables, on the assumption that they were taken from the shelf for consultation (sometimes called the 'sweep' method)
- attaching slips to current issues, and requesting users to tick them after each use
- removing serials from the open shelf sequence and counting the subsequent enquiries for them
- interviewing users to ask which serials they habitually consult (Horwill[1] described an extension of this method in the University of Sussex, where all potential users were asked to vote for titles they rated as important)
- observing serial display shelves over a period of time, and recording all consultations made (Wenger and Childress (1977) described this approach as applied to an American research library).

Of these methods, the first three are bound to lead to substantial shortfalls on the actual numbers of consultations, whilst the fourth is likely to overestimate use. The last (observation) method gives by far the most accurate picture of use, as long as the survey is carried out over a decent length of time (and serials are returned to shelves immediately after use). It means employing observers over a period of time, but this can be inexpensively done by contracting students to do the surveying. Surprisingly, the observation method seems to be little used in UK libraries.

Kent's celebrated 1979 study at the University of Pittsburgh[2] included a section on serials. In general, the survey found that the use of serials collections was low, and that large collections tended to have a greater proportion of low-use serials than smaller ones. Use was mainly of current journals, through browsing – whilst use of older material was largely derived from references and citations.

Serials use was studied for 39 hours in four departmental collections (in life sciences, chemistry, computers and mathematics), for 81 hours in engineering, and for 120 hours in physics. Across five of the subject areas during these periods, 86% to 93% of the collections received no use, while in physics 63% received no use. The numbers of uses per hour were: in physics 3.7, life sciences 5.4, engineering 2.1, chemistry 4.1, computers 0.6, and mathematics 0.8. Some 90% of all the use was of serials published in the preceding 15 years (except in the field of mathematics); in all subjects, at least two-thirds of use was of serials from the previous five years. Students – especially post-graduates – were the main users of serials; use by staff was relatively low, and largely of current issues.

A rare investigation into the use of serials by undergraduates was undertaken by Harris[3] at Newcastle Polytechnic in 1973. In four subject areas – physics, chemistry, sociology, and history – use of journal back issues ranged between 0 and 0.01 uses per student per week, and of current issues between 0 and 0.07. Only in one of the five subject areas explored – marketing – was use more substantial: 0.87 uses per student per week for back issues, and 0.4 for current issues. Harris observed that marketing was the only one of these subject areas where lecturers encouraged students to used the serials collection. The use of back issues was concentrated in the more recent years of the publication: 63% of serials published in the year 1970 and later; 27% of serials from 1965–69; and only 11% of serials from 1964 and preceding years.

Evaluation of research serials

Given the number of serials published, and the amounts of money spent upon them, there is a sparse literature on evaluation of their quality. In a way, this is not surprising. The key titles in any field are well known to academics and other experts in the subject; in research terms they are the refereed serials, particularly those which have built up a reputation over a number of years. (New titles carry much lower status – which is one of the problems now faced by electronic serials.)

A 1994 survey of *contributors* to journals[4] analysed 371 responses to questionnaires that asked about factors influencing quality in journals. Two key factors were highlighted as important: 'originality', which held good for both academic and practitioner contributors; and 'practicality', in the sense of material indicating a positive path of action. The factor ranked third in importance by the majority of contributors was 'clarity': serials where authors were known for using a logical sequence of argument, and for writing material which was easy to read.

Lancaster[5] has a valuable chapter on serials. It is mainly concerned with evaluating quality so as to *cancel* the least-used serials. He listed six main ways of doing this:

- from use data collected by the library itself
- from use data collected by other libraries

- from opinions collected from potential users, particularly within the faculty
- from citation studies
- from 'impact data', relating citation studies to the numbers of articles published in journals
- from cost-effectiveness studies which relate use to the costs of individual serials.

Lancaster observed that wherever possible any cancellations should be based upon combinations of these factors; also important was the correlation between the subject matter of serials and the subject interests of the institutions' departments.

Much of the literature on this subject is on 'bibliometric' analysis – the term used to describe the quantitative analysis of behaviour patterns of authors and users. Citation analysis, a particularly prominent bibliometric technique, is about analysing the lists of citations which appear at the end of scholarly papers. The assumption is that the most frequently cited papers are the most important, and that the serial titles containing the most frequently cited papers can be ranked as the most important in their subject area. The method can reasonably claim to give some indication of important serials in a subject literature, though citation of an article is no guarantee that it has been read; Scales[6] suggested that citation analysis is not a very accurate guide to use.

Another way of ranking serial titles is by analysing the interlending (or photocopying) records of a large lending library. The approach tends to highlight most of the serials which are commonly agreed to be important in their field, though at first sight this seems curious – since 'borrowing' libraries might be expected to hold the core serials in their own stock and borrow peripheral titles.

The British Library Document Supply Centre (BLDSC) is an obvious example of a library with records that are worth analysing, and it has carried out several surveys – including a major one in 1980, reported by Clarke.[7] He found that from the library's total holdings of 54,000 serials, 45% of all requests for articles could be satisfied by 2000 titles, and 80% by 7500 titles. However, a subsequent article by Kefford and Line[8] reported considerable variations between the 1980 survey and another survey carried out in 1976.

More question marks were raised, again by Line,[9] in an article comparing the consistency, over similar periods of time, between rank lists produced from interlending data with those from citation analysis. It showed striking differences, with citation-based lists holding up much better; for instance, the overlap in the top 100 titles of the citation-based analysis was 95% at its most extreme (cf 57% for the interlending-based surveys), and 78% at its least extreme (cf 56%).

In 1998 Kushkowski[10] outlined 'A method for building core journal lists in interdisciplinary subject areas' – a quantitative approach using multiple electronic indexes.

None of these studies appear to provide any definitive guidance for serials selectors (and deselectors). Lancaster's conclusions[5] broadly concur with those of an earlier (1978) article by Line[11] that no external data (whether from analysis of citations or the use of other libraries) are of much value in predicting use in one's own library, that such data may produce similar rankings of serials at the top of the register (where little help is needed), but that at the bottom (where help *is* needed, for cancellation purposes), results are not reliable. Unreliability is caused by the relatively low rates of citation (or interlending) for the least significant serials. Another problem is that serials used mainly for 'news alerting' purposes – rather than as a research record – are unlikely to be widely covered in citation analysis studies.

An important article published in 1998 by Alston and Nicholson[12] approached the 'quality' issue by following up the recent interest in the *impact* of collections – impact being linked in this case to research assessment exercise (RAE) findings. The survey explored how far 1996–97 expenditure on serials in academic libraries correlated first with research volume (represented by the numbers of category A research staff) and secondly with RAE gradings for 1996. Not surprisingly, they found a fairly close correlation between expenditure and staff numbers: the total serials expenditure per researcher – across 10 subjects – ranged between £665 and £1600, with the bulk of responses falling between £900 and £1300, and an average of £1171.

But correlation between expenditure on serials and RAE grades was not at all consistent. It was closest for sci-tech subjects, with a 'very strong positive' correlation for chemistry, mathematics and engineering, and 'medium positive' for biological and social sciences. But there were 'medium negative' correlations for psychology and English language/literature, and 'weak negative' for physics, law and education.

Cancellations of research serials

In recent years the price increases in scholarly serials have been astronomical. Fishwick[13] observed that average prices in 1996 were three times those in 1985 – a rise double that of the general retail price index over the same period. Over the period 1989 to 1999, prices have risen for UK and US serials by 162% and 161% respectively (Library and Information Statistics Unit, 1999b, 194). Several observers have commented that serials publishers have responded to cancellations of serial subscriptions by raising prices accordingly. There have been some very pertinent suggestions that universities – which provide many of the authors and the referees for the serials business – should get together and take over the whole enterprise, pricing the products sensibly in the process. Some pertinent comments on serials from the publisher's point of view are to be found in Graham's book *As I was saying*.[14]

Over the past 20 years the sharp rises in serial prices, coupled with reductions in library funding, have meant that academic and workplace librarians have found an increasing proportion of their budgets absorbed by serial subscriptions – to a point where cancellations became inevitable. For most academic librarians, cuts on this scale were initially a new experience. Blake and Meadows (1984), reporting on a survey carried out in 1983, described how it affected 33 UK academic librarians. An average number of 358 titles per university were discontinued during the period 1980–83. Decisions on cuts were largely taken by academic staff, though the process was often orchestrated by librarians. The most commonly cited characteristics of the journals discontinued were high price, large price increases, and foreign language content. (Others, cited in a survey by Woodward (1978), were: duplicate titles, titles for which a second subscription was held in a neighbouring institution, titles where the content was too general or too specialized, or where the content overlapped with that of other serials in stock.) A third of the libraries in the Blake and Meadows survey said that 'other things being equal' they would cancel serials from commercial publishers before those issued by learned societies.

The reasons most commonly given for retaining serials were frequent use, high academic value, and high relevance to teaching and research in the university. Half the respondents said that – other things being equal – they would retain journals with longer back-runs in the library.

Sumsion's 1994 survey (see Appendix) found that, in 1991–92, academic libraries had on average taken out 71 new paid subscriptions and discontinued 64. The main reasons given for new subscriptions were: new subjects taught (by 43% of respondents), newly launched titles (34%), and new subjects being researched (19%). The main reasons given for cancelling subscriptions were: funding shortages (by 59% of respondents), titles no longer relevant (33%), titles no longer value for money (16%), standard of title had declined (6%), and title had become available electronically (6%).

Erens's article 'How recent developments in university libraries affect research' (see Appendix) reported two major satisfaction surveys of academics carried out in 1989 and 1995. The percentage of academics who felt that the 'cancellation of serials' had become a significant problem had risen from 17% in 1989 to 36% in 1995. Similarly, 'not taking out important new subscriptions' was reported as a significant problem by 39% of academics in 1989, rising to 58% in

1995. Asked about the effects of these (and other) changes, 27% agreed with the statement that they had 'less awareness of their subject' (though 40% disagreed), 16% agreed that their 'research was less rigorous' (though 50% disagreed), and 25% agreed that 'research takes more time' (though 43% disagreed). Asked which two improvements to their university library would most benefit their area of research, 53% gave 'improved journal collection' as their first choice, and 22% their second choice; this compared to 18% giving 'improved book collection' as first choice, and 11% 'improved access to external databases'.

Linked to the need for cancellation of serial subscriptions are decisions on the relegation of serial back-runs to remote storage. Buckland[15] discussed the need to observe use of the entire run of each journal in stock so as to estimate the benefit of investment in continued retention, and compare this with remote storage costs. He also commented on the timing of periodical binding in relation to patterns of use (an apparently minor problem which in practice can cause a good deal of irritation). Fussler and Simon[16] found that 'the use of volumes within the same serial is closer than the amount of use of volumes chosen randomly from other serials'.

Taylor and Urquhart[17] noted that the cheapest way of identifying serial titles for relegation was to use data taken from BLDSC records on little-used material – which for scientific journals (but not for medical) compared well with other methods.

Line and Sandison,[18] in their review of obsolescence studies, concluded that it was probably more cost-effective to discard whole runs of less-used serials than to discard the older volumes of all serials taken (thus supporting Fussler and Simon's findings). They recommended that libraries discarding or relegating back-runs of serials should identify:

- serials which are dead (not now taken, or ceased publication)
- serials which receive little use of current issues
- serials for which use falls off dramatically after three years (a normal pattern, especially in scientific journals).

Where shortage of space is the main reason for discarding serial runs, some libraries have microfilmed the originals before discarding.

Electronic serials

At the time of writing, electronic serials are at a very early stage in their development. But the possibilities they offer for a low-cost, easy-access vehicle for research findings and current information have already encouraged a good deal of speculation about their future. A good summary of their development is given by Breaks.[19] Also informative are the contributions by JISC[20] (one of several publications on this subject from the Joint Information System Committee), and Johnston.[21]

Most commercial publishers are still experimenting with the new format, and the response of libraries has also been largely experimental. In 1995 the UK Higher Education funding bodies established the Pilot Site Licence Initiative (PSLI) with four major publishers. The project's aims, over a period of three years, were to explore issues of access to a critical mass of electronic full-text journals between higher education institutions and publishers, and to secure discounts for libraries on existing subscriptions. The project led to some relaxation of copyright restrictions on electronic serials with the four publishers concerned, but copyright remained a major problem. The libraries also found a need to increase IT spending, and user support, and there were technical difficulties (for instance, in loading the special software needed to read the serials). The licensing problems involved imposed a substantial management overhead on the libraries, with varying terms needed for different publishers, and the need to issue passwords individually to users (though this was eventually overcome with some publishers). During the three-year pilot, no libraries cancelled any print versions of serials.

The PSLI project came to an end in 1998, and was replaced by a new experiment – the National Electronic Site Licence Initiative (NESLI), which publishers intended to operate on a full cost-recovery basis.

The range of non-commercial electronic journals is increasing; these are often available free of charge, but are also often restricted to the latest issues only. The variety of different access methods makes it time-consuming to consult them individually. Some organizations – particularly subscription agents, anticipating future demand – are establishing journal aggregation services, which provide simplified, integrated access through a single source. Examples are Blackwell's Electronic Journals Navigator and Swets Net. Breaks[19] commented that most libraries were waiting for the market to mature, and for one leader to emerge, before subscribing.

Despite all the discussion of electronic serials, their immediate future is by no means clear. Fishwick[13] found (in 1998) that 22 of 50 learned societies consulted – mostly the smaller societies – had at that time no plans to provide any form of electronic access to their journals (partly because of fears of losing revenue from institutional subscribers). Only 10 of the 50 expected electronic delivery to predominate for the majority of their journals five years into the future.

Several potential advantages of electronic serials are discussed in the publications cited above:

Ease of access

In theory, an electronic format for serials gives instant and continuous access. Users are not impeded – as they may be with print – by someone else using the volume, or by finding it has been sent to binding. And the serials can be accessed from office or laboratory, as well as from the library. That said, there remains 'a widespread desire to avoid reading complex material online',[20] so that the problem of printing off articles has still to be tackled. And as an early user satisfaction survey found,[22] in these initial stages the procedures for accessing electronic serials (particularly those from commercial publishers) were far from user-friendly.

Space savings

Bound volumes of serials over several decades take up a lot of shelf space. King and Griffiths (1995) estimated that additional costs of administration and storage of a serial costing $120 were 50% or more. Clearly, electronic serials could save space, and related costs – *as long as* doubts about electronic archiving can be resolved (see Chapter 11).

Quicker publication

The JISC publication cited above[20] discussed speed of publication in detail. In disciplines which date quickly, the current delays in publishing research findings are excessive. ('Physics' was reported to be the discipline quickest to get research findings into print, at 9–12 months, whilst 'modern languages' could take up to three years.) Electronic serials could obviously speed up this process by dispensing with printing and distribution. But there is also a need for an accelerated refereeing process (see below).

Economy

The outrageous prices of scholarly journals in print have been discussed above. The electronic format appears to offer a path to lower prices, since it pre-empts print and distribution costs – although the problem of charging arrangements for 'printing out' has still to be addressed. Many of the 'original electronic serials (ie those not available in other formats) can be printed out free of charge. But most commercial publishers are currently providing electronic access at a price that is similar to, or more than, the print equivalent (Kibby and White, 1999). The customary arrangement is for the electronic version to be offered as an add-on to the print version, usually at a small additional charge. One possible route to more economical arrangements, suggested by Fishwick[13] amongst other observers, is for publishers to scrap serials as such and offer access to individual articles. 'Pay as you view' transactions of this kind would be much more efficient, but the transition to such systems from the present situation is fraught with difficulties.

Multimedia links

The electronic format offers possibilities for interactive access that are not provided by print. The JISC survey[20] found that this was of only passing interest to the majority of disciplines, but of intrinsic interest to half a dozen subject areas, including chemistry and archaeology.

An article by McKnight[22] reported user satisfaction with electronic serials amongst groups of Masters students from six disciplines, in 1996–97. They found problems of access with commercial journals (rarely with free ones), with students complaining of lengthy downloading times and systems that were not user-friendly. Legibility was rated as the least satisfactory feature of electronic serials, and there were the customary complaints about reading on screen. Browsing was found to be slower electronically than from print.

These grouses apart, there were a number of positive features reported: 80% of the articles were rated with a score of 3–5 for 'relevance' (with 5 signifying most relevant on a scale of 0–5), and students liked the good searching capabilities and the ready availability of the electronic format. The report concluded that the free journals were much less problematic than the commercial journals, that commercial publishers appeared to be driven by technological rather than human factors, and were at that time 'more interested in pursuing their own learning curve than in assisting their customers'.

Fishwick's 1998 report[13] presented a radical and lucid approach to the subject. He observed that demand for academic journals mainly came not from users but from *authors*, eager to get their work published for reasons of status, and to register points in the research assessment exercise. For this reason, the academic journals market did not follow the normal features of supply and demand. He cited an article by Noll and Steinmueller (1992), which characterized this unusual market: highly specialized journals aimed at small minorities of academics; low circulation and high price; large numbers of secondary serials, tending to publish many unimportant articles and the occasional useful one; and pressure from academics for libraries to pay a high price for a relatively small number of useful articles.

Fishwick concluded that because published articles were mainly a vehicle for the advancement of the authors, those authors should make a financial contribution to refereeing; this would also speed up the refereeing process, which is currently on an unpaid basis. Authors would then recoup some money by receiving a payment (as a type of royalty) for electronic use. He envisaged libraries paying for electronic serials through a combination of subscriptions and 'pay as you go' charges.

These proposals foreshadow a move from holdings to access which has been much discussed in the professional literature – in both print and electronic contexts. There is discussion of this in Chapter 9, and in particular of the BIODOC experiment at Cranfield, where all print holdings of serials were cancelled and replaced by electronic current contents notification and document supply systems – with results that were largely found satisfactory by the library's users.

Popular journals

The provision of serials in public libraries is very different – in scale and type – from that in academic and workplace libraries. In 1997–98, some 6% of all expenditure on materials went on newspapers and journals (a slight increase on 5% ten years earlier) (Library and Information Statistics Unit, 1999b, 17). This rate of expenditure may be rather too modest, given the steady use of serials in public libraries – including use by many people who do not borrow books. Luckham observed in 1971 (see Appendix) that 11% of all respondents in a general public library survey consulted newspapers, and 12% periodicals. Book Marketing Ltd's *Household use survey* for 1998 (see Appendix) found that just over 10% of the population visited their libraries to use serials. The figure was 13% in the CIPFA PLUS surveys for 1997,[23] and 11% in research for the Aslib review (see Appendix) in 1995.

Rare examples of published surveys into serials use in public libraries have been those by Oldman and Davinson[24] in 1975, Hillingdon libraries in 1993,[25] and Matchett[26] in 1997. Findings in these three surveys about types of use were consistent. Oldman and Davinson observed a relatively heavy use of local and national newspapers, journals on hobbies and subjects of practical interest, and trade and technical journals, and that this use was fairly constant despite local variations in provision. Most of this use was current; 66% of users did not consult back numbers of periodicals; 35% of the users were not members of their public library, and 68% claimed to consult certain titles on a regular basis.

The Hillingdon survey analysed use by age and gender of respondents. Categories of serial where preferences increased with age were found to be local newspapers, gardening, holidays and finance; and categories for younger users were music, home and fashion, science and video. Serials more likely to be read by male users were those on current affairs, finance, transport, politics and science; and by female users home and fashion, gardening, holidays and childcare.

The Matchett survey found that about one-third of the serials used in the three libraries studied was accounted for by newspapers, and that – in two of the three libraries – about one-third of users came specifically to consult the serials. Use was analysed by subject area, with a percentage of the use of each serials collection allocated to subjects, viz: hobbies/leisure, 25–30%, business and work-related 15%, 10% and 10%, study 7%, 7%, and 10%, and job advertisements 13%, 10% and 5%.

Though it is difficult to tell without further research, this seems to be an area where more surveying of user needs is required. In Barron's 1996 survey of 134 authorities (see Appendix), none had surveyed serial use (though a list of 23 other survey themes was given). The Hillingdon exercise mentioned the need for regular surveys, to adjust holdings to changing user demand. Oldman and Davinson commented on the lack of policy definition for serials and the poor definition of user needs.

Surveys of serial use should try to discover the subject areas which are in most demand, and within these the individual titles sought – in both cases, anticipating changes in provision to meet demand. There should be differentiation between titles widely acquired in people's homes and those not generally to be found on newsagents' shelves (and therefore perhaps not known to many users). It would also be helpful to try and gauge the importance to users of serials vis-à-vis other materials (though relating these findings to expenditure is bound to involve a value judgement). Surveys should also be a promotional tool, to ensure that users who normally use other library services are fully aware of what is available in the periodicals section.

Matchett's survey identified a crude 'core list' of titles which were available in the central libraries of all three authorities surveyed – a total of 80 titles in all. This approach would warrant further research.

A 1998 survey by Brunskill and others[27] investigated electronic serials in public libraries. Of the 129 authorities which responded, 61% had some electronic serials, but the numbers were extremely modest – an average of six per authority, usually only held in the main library. Most of the titles were newspapers, and in 96% of cases they were held on CD-ROM. Only three authorities had provided access to multi-title services, and three had taken out subscriptions to Internet-based services. Moreover, few authorities had plans to extend provision, via CD-ROM or the Internet.

Nevertheless, some Internet serial resources may prove of interest to public libraries. For instance, Neilson and Willett (1999) located some 40 UK regional newspapers on the web in 1999, and noted that these were attracting different audiences from the print versions, notably school children.

11
Reference and research materials

Reference materials

Reference materials provide the basis for one of the most important library services – in all library sectors. They are made available in a variety of formats. Many enquiries are answerable by short, specific items of information which can be quickly identified from databases through electronic searching, and retrieved without the need for extensive reading from a screen or printing out – features which put reference works amongst the first types of library materials to be transformed by ICT. Chapter 4 discusses the evaluation of electronic materials in general. The linked area of research materials is briefly reported at the end of this chapter.

Almost any library material can serve as a 'reference' tool, and lending from stock remains a common way of satisfying reference enquiries. (Smith's public library survey[1] also found that many books often thought of by librarians as reference material are heavily borrowed if made available.) That said, there are certain categories of print and electronic materials – dictionaries, directories etc – generally regarded as reference materials, and acquired by reference libraries as the basis of their collections. Nolan[2] suggested that their key features are to be authoritative and current, to give unique coverage, to appear in a reference format, and to be frequently used. Stacey[3] in an elegant and informative article commented on characteristics of quality, accuracy, completeness, currency, presentation and 'suitability'.

Library expenditure on these works in their print format is relatively modest. In public libraries, the 4.8% of total additions taken by reference books (Library and Information Statistics Unit, 1999b, 52–3) has been relatively constant over the past decade. In higher education libraries, a comparable 4.1% of all acquisitions was absorbed by reference materials in 1998.[4] (However, all 'reference book' statistics should be interpreted with caution, because of ambiguities in classification – particularly of annuals, which are an important component.)

Enquirers have their preferences in terms of formats for receiving information, and electronic sources are gradually forcing their way into the list. Print, in a variety of guises, is still very important. A 1994 survey by Bevis, reported by England and Sumsion (see Appendix), found that the 'main sources' used for answering enquiries in a group of public and workplace libraries were: print publications (ranging from 23% to 57% of all enquiries, with a mean percentage of 41%); library staff knowledge (3% to 33%, with a mean of 11%); leaflets (0% to 27%, with a mean of 13%); electronic sources (9% to 39%, with a mean of 19%); and referrals to another library (4% to 22%, with a mean of 12%).

Marcella and Baxter's 1997 survey[5] of nearly 1300 'enquirers' (at public libraries, citizens' advice bureaux and other types of information service) asked about enquirers' 'preferred methods of obtaining information', and ranked their first, second and third choices by means of a points system. The results were: talking face to face with someone, 1023 points; reading a book, 848; looking through a collection without help from staff, 827; reading a newspaper, 679; talking on the telephone to someone, 518; listening to the radio, 426; watching television, 411; reading a leaflet/pamphlet, 312; using a computer, 275.

A 1998 observation survey of a public reference library (Loughborough University, 1998) noted which types of materials or services were used by 600 visitors. The most significant were: reference books, by 44% of visitors; newspapers, 34%; periodicals, 13%; photocopier, 8%; leaflets, 7%; the Internet, 5%; microform, 3%; and CD-ROM, 2%.

The map of electronic resources is changing so rapidly that it is only possible to take a snapshot at this moment, and guess at possible future trends. Without doubt the rapid development of the Internet – and of reference sources on the world wide web – is the major catalyst for changing the way that libraries (and individuals) search for information. Where such information is freely available many people will search from their homes or places of work, although libraries may continue to play a big part in bringing useful sites to the attention of their users (see Chapter 4). Where information derives from a subscriber service, most users will probably continue to access through libraries for the foreseeable future.

It is already clear that the web is an invaluable repository for information about institutions, societies, associations and companies; in the year 2000, there are few significant UK organizations which do not have a website giving details of their aims and activities, events and publications. Government organization websites are prominent amongst these, and are already widely used by libraries of all kinds.

Recently, many traditional reference works, previously only available in print, have become available on the web. Some of these are on individual sites representing a single work. For instance, the *Encyclopaedia Britannica*, which went online on a subscriber basis in the mid-1990s, launched a free web service in 1999, funded by advertising and e-commerce. The *Oxford English Dictionary* announced a website launch for March 2000, funded on a subscriber basis (with individual subscriptions likely to be cheaper than institutional). Both these major reference works will be revised online, and the future of their printed versions is uncertain.

The major source of traditional UK reference works currently on the web is Chadwyck-Healey's *KnowUK* product. Since this highlights both the advantages and the problems of the switch to electronic reference materials, we examine it below in some detail. Launched in 1998, *KnowUK* already covers 65 publications, including celebrated works such as *Who's Who*, *Municipal Year Book*, *Statesman's Yearbook* and the *Which?* guides. The basic subscription was £3,495 as of February 2000, but there are flexible pricing models for larger customer groups; for example, for larger public library authorities, pricing is based on the size of the population within that authority. The KnowUK website (see References) lists current subscribers, which in January 2000 included 26 library authorities (covering 540 service points), seven university libraries, 13 government offices and one school. (An abridged and more modestly priced version – *KnowUK Schools Edition* – was launched for the school market in December 1999.)

Reports from public library authorities which already subscribe to *KnowUK* suggest that it is particularly valuable in smaller service points, which cannot afford all the print versions – though there is a major training implication for the support staff who usually run these branches. Search strategies need careful thought to find the right balance between speed and information recall; different results can be obtained from the 'search all directories' mode and the advanced search modes, which isolate one directory or a combination of like directories. (Searching of what are, in print, multivolume directories – such as *Which?* or *Who Was Who?* – is much easier online.)

At the time of writing, most of the larger libraries continue to run their print versions of the *KnowUK* directories concurrently with the online version. Despite this, it seems possible that in the long run online services will eventually replace the printed directory format in most circumstances – simply because of the close match of format and content.

Because of their multiple outlets, public library authorities are the most obvious customers for services such as *KnowUK*, particularly when the Internet becomes available at all service points. Amongst academic libraries, multisite operations are more likely to find the facility immediately attractive. That said, one possible development is a user authentication system, which might afford free access (through PIN numbers) to members of subscribing libraries. This would have great appeal to academic libraries, as an addition to existing campus-wide networks accessed from offices and laboratories, as well as the library; and some forward-looking public libraries are already discussing an option which would allow their members to access library services from home.

Librarians contemplating subscriptions to services such as *KnowUK* – and to similar services such as the Chadwyck-Healey counterpart, *KnowEurope* – need to weigh several key considerations:

- the relevance of the component databases to their users' needs
- the cost of a subscription (and add-ons) compared to the cost of print versions
- the number (and size) of service points in the system, and the possibility of having information available at all service points more cheaply
- the response times for the different methods of searching, linked to the success rates for each of those methods
- staff time saved from searching multivolume publications via single online searches
- the speed with which staff can be trained to absorb the new approach
- the facility to have online databases updated more frequently than the 'once a year' that is characteristic for many print reference books (though this is not yet a prominent feature in the *KnowUK* service).

Complementary to reference material developed on the web are a variety of products made available on CD-ROM. These are usually more cost-effective than Internet access when content does not need frequent updating and is subject to intensive use. Examples are dictionaries, encyclopaedias, maps and atlases, newspaper and journal back-files, and many training and self-learning materials.

Rapid developments in ICT, combined with corporate initiatives, are enabling reference materials to be made available in many other ways. Chapter 4 describes the central purchasing of bibliographic databases for higher education libraries through the BIDS-ISI service, funded by the Joint Information Systems Committee (JISC). We may shortly expect public library authorities to seek a comparable central buying system, following the establishment of the 'People's Network' (see Chapter 4).

Another widespread development, particularly in commercial company libraries, has been the *intranet* – a computer network using Internet technology which is used as an organization's internal communication system. Rowley (1998), amongst many others, outlines the technology and its applications. When the network is extended to include some authorized external users, it is sometimes referred to as an *extranet*. Most reference material included on these systems is generated within the organization, such as newsletters, staff director-ies, policy manuals and – on interactive Intranets – training packages and online enquiry services. Some intranets also include news alerting services, designed by external information service providers according to the organiza-tions' profiles. The organizations' librarians are often (but by no means always) involved in the selection and/or creation of intranet content.

A recent survey (Library and Information Statistics Unit, 1999b, 156) inves-tigated the use of intranets in workplace libraries in 1997–98, for both in-house data and news-alerting services. Table 11.1 gives the percentages of libraries in each sector which had these facilities.

Table 11.1 *Percentage of workplace libraries providing in-house data and news-alerting services*

	in-house data	news alerting services
government orgs	75%	21%
professional assocs	47%	20%
legal/financial	72%	28%
energy/pharmaceutics	84%	40%
management consult	82%	–

Research materials

The major repository for research findings remains the serial, and Chapter 10 discusses serials in both print and electronic formats. Research materials are increasingly available on the web (see Chapter 4). But some overarching issues concerning research provision remain (especially those which relate to digital preservation), and these are briefly referred to here. Most of them concern aca-demic research findings. Meadows[6] provides a valuable overview of the whole subject.

A publication by LINC in 1997[7] contained a number of papers summarizing current concerns about provision for research and suggesting courses of action. Anderson[8] summarized the overall strategy of the Working Group on National and Regional Strategies for Library Provision for Researchers, which originated in concerns expressed by the Follett Committee.[9] Two strategies considered but rejected as unworkable were relying on remote and electronic delivery, and shifting core provision to a national network of hyperlibraries. The model finally adopted aimed to 'seek to create structures that further facilitate access . . . by researchers from one HEI to the specialist collections of other HEIs and other libraries with particular strengths in their fields' and 'to encourage extensions of collaborative acquisition and retention policies'. The long-term aim was a nationwide network of distributed national collections. Heaney's paper in the same publication lamented the slow progress being made towards these aims. Further comments on cooperative acquisition and the whole area of 'access' are in Chapter 9.

Although a complete reliance upon electronic delivery was rejected by the Working Group, the new possibilities facilitated by ICT are already affecting research provision. A five-year strategy for the Distributed National Electronic Resource (DNER), funded by the JISC, is described on the DNER website (see References). Love and Feather,[10] describing special collections on the world wide web, identified two distinct types of site: those with access information for research visitors, mainly involving collection description; and those which aimed to create a virtual research resource by summarizing the content of items in the collections. But when the article was written (1998), most sites were at very early stages in their development.

Feeny's document on digital culture,[11] published in 1999, is a synthesis of studies (funded by JISC and the National Preservation Office) on the preservation of electronic research materials. It identified extensive creation of digital materials by research-oriented agencies, libraries and archives, and publishers, but also noted several threats to its long-term survival: damage to the medium on which the information rested; loss of information describing how to access it; and loss of the computing environment on which access depends. The report observed that researchers needed to improve their prediction of future information needs, and their selection of this material, since none of the existing electronic archives could accept all the material offered. It recommended the development of a strategy for a preservation centre (or network of centres) for scholarly data, and more research into technical aspects of preservation.

Parry's ground-clearing study[12] summarized digitizing activity in local authority libraries and archives up to 1997, and what was planned in the way of new projects. Of 146 authorities which replied, 34% had no digitization projects and none planned, 5% had completed projects, 19% were currently engaged in them, and 27% had planned projects but had not started them. Material from local studies collections was easily the most popular subject for digitization, offered through local or wide-area networks or, increasingly, through the Internet.

Of 146 future projects planned, 56% concerned local newspapers, 47% photographs, 40% historic maps or plans, 36% manuscript diaries or letters, and 29% indexes to special collections. A recurring concern – in addition to conservation – was the need to make material of local and national importance more widely available.

12
Reading for pleasure

This chapter covers public library provision of books which are read primarily for pleasure rather than for some specific purpose. In addition to the main focus on fiction, there are also references to biography and other types of non-fiction.

Fiction reading

Fiction provision is a major role in UK public libraries. In 1997–98, fiction comprised 37% of the total active lending stock, and 38% of the total annual additions. In loan terms that year, it accounted for 51% of public library issues, and 37% of all stock on loan on a particular date (Library and Information Statistics Unit, 1999b, 65, 77). These figures are echoed by the loan records from the Registrar of Public Lending Right for the same year (Library and Information Statistics Unit, 1999a), when fiction accounted for 52% of all loans recorded.

According to most surveys, women borrow more fiction than men, in a ratio of roughly 60:40. Book Marketing Ltd's *Household library use survey* for 1998 (see Appendix) found that 38% of all women and 22% of all men in the UK had borrowed fiction from their public library during that year.

Fiction may be heavily used in public libraries, but its use is diminishing. Over the ten years from 1987–88 to 1997–98, UK fiction issues fell from 358 million to 246 million – a reduction of 31%. This compared to much smaller falls of 12% in adult non-fiction issues and 3% in children's issues. The contrast with non-fiction use is even less favourable if we look at the percentage of fiction items *on loan* on a particular date: this has fallen from 45% to 37% over the same period, whilst non-fiction stock on loan – around the 25% mark – has actually risen slightly. Similarly, the stock turn rate for fiction (the average number of loans per book per year) has fallen from 8.0 to 7.3, whilst for non-fiction it has risen from 2.7 to 3.5.

These figures prompt some questions about the management of fiction stock in public libraries. Are libraries losing custom to a more competitive performance by Dillons, Waterstones, and other 'rivals' in the book trade? Before they were discontinued, the Euromonitor surveys (Euromonitor Publications, 1989) supported this hypothesis, indicating that more people were buying the books they were reading than were borrowing them. There is another question about the allocation of library budgets. Since fiction issues have fallen so much more steeply than non-fiction issues in the past ten years, why have fiction additions to public libraries not been adjusted downwards accordingly? (In practice, the reductions in additions have been a mere 8% for fiction, and only slightly less – 6% – for non-fiction.) Or to put this another way: if the balance between fiction and non-fiction additions, relative to use, was right in 1987, can it be right in 1997?

A breakdown of fiction lending into genres (or themes) is made available annually by the Registrar of Public Lending Right (Library and Information Statistics Unit, 1999a). In the figures for 1997–98, 52% of all loans were fiction, with the main subgroups being 'mystery and detection' (13%), 'light romance' (11%), then historical fiction (3%). Other fiction genres accounted for no more than 4% altogether. 'General fiction' took 22% of issues.

The past 20 years have seen some interest in fiction provision in the professional literature. Dixon[1] and Kinnell[2] related use surveys to stock management. Smith[3] undertook a revealing study of management information for fiction titles. Goodall's invaluable *Browsing in public libraries*[4] summarized the findings of a number of fiction use surveys, including her own, plus work by Sear and Jennings,[5] Spiller,[6] Turner,[7] and Spenceley.[8] Finally, John Sumsion, the former Registrar of Public Lending Right, published detailed tables of his organization's statistics,[9] which reported fiction use in a large number of libraries.

As well as revealing what people read, surveys have also discovered a good deal about the way they choose fiction from libraries. Most user strategies for finding fiction revolve around *browsing* on the one hand, and discovering *authors* whose works they like on the other. Goodall[4] summarized several surveys which studied the success rate of these two approaches.

A majority of the novels borrowed are read in their entirety – between 73% and 86% in five surveys which explored this aspect. But the way that books were found appeared to affect whether they were enjoyed. In surveys by Goodall,[4] and by Sear and Jennings,[5] 81% and 70% respectively of books were enjoyed when sought by 'the author's name', and 59% and 58% were enjoyed when the reader 'browsed and recognized the author's name'. On the other hand, 68% and 36% were enjoyed when the reader 'browsed and thought the book looked interesting'. So in the Goodall survey the different approaches did not appear to make much difference to enjoyment, whereas in Sear and Jennings the author approach was much more effective than browsing. Both surveys analysed a couple of hundred titles, and both were exit surveys – so readers had to generalize on the basis of titles returned on the same day. It would be useful to have further research, based on a large sample of specific titles as they are *returned* to the library.

The hunt for new authors is a persistent, and often frustrating, activity for fiction readers in public libraries. 'I liked the author's other books' is constantly cited as a motive for choice. Authors' names are also important for the sizeable numbers of people – between 14% and 29% of all fiction borrowers in four different surveys – who select from libraries on behalf of others. It seems that many users are hard pressed to identify new authors. Some have a small list of favourites – often names discovered years earlier – and are at a loss if they cannot find books by any of these on the shelves. Spiller's report[6] of a man of 30 who knew only two authors – Edgar Wallace and G K Chesterton – both recommended by his mother, poignantly symbolizes a fairly common sense of helplessness.

In terms of 'availability on the shelf', three surveys summarized by Goodall reported 43%, 52% and 54% of users searching unsuccessfully for fiction authors. The failure rate is high (given the choice of titles for each author), but in surveys failure can often be disguised by the high rate of substitutability which is possible between fiction authors. Oddly, in view of these figures, few fiction readers use the reservation service.

The problem readers have in finding new authors is clear, but the library solution to it is not. Several of the surveys found that only a small proportion of readers made use of library booklists, though this was partly because the books in 'new additions' lists were rarely on the shelves when new. Spiller found that 20% and 13% respectively of those surveyed were influenced by books recommended or serialized on TV or radio, which suggests that librarians need to keep in touch with the media's treatment of fiction. A great many library users said that they followed up recommendations from friends. Roy and Jeanne Huse's *Who else writes like* (Huse and Huse, 1999) incorporates recommendations from a number of librarians by listing 1200 fiction authors and, under each one, suggesting several other authors who 'write like' them. The book is widely purchased by public libraries, and usually located near fiction sections; it is also available for electronic manipulation on Whitaker bibliographical products.

These measures aside, libraries can perhaps best serve their fiction readers by taking practical measures to help them to browse more efficiently. For instance, by far the largest factor in browsing is the blurb on the jacket of the book, with up to 80% of users in surveys rating it as important. Most librarians see blurbs as dubious instruments for choosing novels – but it looks as if they should be retained, at least on library fiction.

A factor affecting many users (29% in one survey) is the height of the library shelves – both high and low shelves being ruled out by a gamut of medical conditions. This problem can be softened if libraries avoid extremes of shelving for certain types of stock – ie stock for which browsing is a major feature in user selection.

The age of fiction is also a factor. As might be expected, users make heavier use of recent novels. Sumsion[9] found that, in 20 libraries, 55% of loans derived from books published in the previous five years (34% of total stock); 26% of loans from the 24% of stock which was 6–10 years old; and 11% of loans from the 18% of stock that was 11–15 years old. The figures suggest a need for a continuous supply of new titles. But older material of quality is not neglected. Smith[3] cited Public Lending Right figures for 1995–96, which estimated that Jane Austen and Thomas Hardy each generated between 200,000 and 600,000 loans a year in public libraries. He also checked on the shelf availability in his authority's libraries of titles by 25 20th-century 'literary' authors – Kafka, Hesse, Virginia Woolf and so on. Of 1125 copies of these authors' works in stock, 31% were on loan, indicating that demand for them was much the same as for fiction as a whole.

Surprisingly, Spiller[6] found that only one person in three referred to the text when browsing, which seems to suggest that for most readers literary style is not a preoccupation. It is hard to know what use to make of this (rather dispiriting) information in practical selection terms.

The subject of fiction display was thoroughly explored by Sear and Jennings, who took the admirable and unusual step of investigating a problem in one piece of research,[5] and a solution in a second[10] which described the setting up of public library browsing areas in which stock was arranged under a number of themes. The exercise made heavy use of staff time, but the results were largely positive. Some 40% of people interviewed said they had found the area easier to use than the A–Z sequence, and the satisfaction with books chosen was higher than the authors had found in the first survey (though, on the debit side, 30% of those interviewed said they had not noticed the area).

There is much discussion in professional literature about whether to *categorize* fiction – ie arrange together all books of the same genre (romance, mystery etc). Goodall[4] summarized some of the contributions. In short, categorization appears to be better for those who read only one genre, whereas the A–Z sequence is better for those who normally seek particular authors. A majority of readers seem to prefer categorization, but there are some who definitely do not. It is possible to combine the two methods by some system of colour coding genres within the A–Z sequence.

Finally, the surveys indicated that very few readers asked library staff for help in finding fiction: 16% in the Sear and Jennings survey, and 4% in Spiller's survey. This was partly because of the personal nature of fiction selection, but there also appeared to be low expectations of success. Given the importance of fiction provision amongst public library services, there is a strong case for readers advisors who *can* give users meaningful advice on selecting novels – but in most authorities this would need a big change of approach.

Fiction provision in libraries

Though it is helpful for librarians to examine surveys of fiction reading, they still face several intractable problems when the actual process of selection begins. Evaluating fiction is a highly subjective process – more so than for most other types of book – so that comparisons between authors or titles are especially difficult. Fiction in libraries is often shelved in a single A–Z sequence, so cannot easily be broken down, as non-fiction can, into manageable subgroups. And with fiction, establishing a balance between user demand and a representative variety of stock (a problem discussed in Chapter 5) is an acute problem: librarians face, on the one hand, intense demand for recreational reading from a relatively small group of users; and on the other, pressure to stock and sustain the full gamut of 'literary' fiction.

Given these real difficulties, it is hard enough for librarians – let alone the general public – meaningfully to measure the success (or failure) of their fiction provision. But as already observed, fiction use in libraries is plummeting, and we have to consider whether this is a function of inadequate provision and/or part of an overall fashion in the use of leisure time. Some possible changes of direction towards a different kind of provision are summarized below.

Arriving at a sensible policy for recreational reading (or 'light fiction') within the overall fiction stock is a necessary starting point. Of course, 'light' fiction melts, at some point, seamlessly into 'literary' fiction; but most examples of light and literary fiction are easily distinguishable. The case for providing good light fiction in libraries is a powerful one. Demand for it is heavy, and most library users – whatever their regular reading tastes – want recreational reading at one time or another. At one level, light fiction contributes to sustaining literacy (although a majority of romance and mystery readers come from the literate middle classes).

The question is not whether libraries should provide light fiction, but how much funding should be allocated to it, in proportion to 'literary' fiction. A judgement has to be made, backed up by a policy statement, and preferably by allocation guidelines. Some librarians (including the writer) favour a heavy weighting for 'literary' novels. This is partly because genre fiction offers readers a much higher level of acceptable substitutability between authors than 'literary' fiction, with its attempt – however flawed – at originality. More than that, much light fiction is readily available in bookshops and other retail outlets, whilst all but the best known literary fiction is not. And making a wide variety of authors and titles available in libraries is more important than maximizing issues with multiple copies of light reading titles. Library performance measures for 'the number of fiction titles' in stock (and/or added during one year) would reinforce this approach.

Another possible measure involves taking lists of literary authors recommended by experts, and measuring stock holdings and use (*and* shelf representation) against titles on the list. The lists can cover – in addition to front-rank literary authors – some of the less-trumpeted names, such as up-and-coming literary authors, first novelists, prize-winners, novelists in translation, short story writers and so on. A rare example of this approach was Sumsion's paper at the 1992 'Reading the future' seminar.[11] He took 1985 Public Lending Right (PLR) data for novel titles from four groups – literary authors (split male/female), 'less well known' literary authors, and American literary authors – and measured their representation in the stock of nine libraries, and average annual issues per volume. The average issues – between six and twelve issues per copy for nearly all the titles – demonstrated the relatively high use that such apparently 'non-popular' material can achieve. This is so even though the top hundred PLR authors rarely if ever include a 'literary' novelist.

Current library policies of buying large numbers of paperback editions – see Reuben and Spiller's study[12] – probably affect adversely the variety of stock on the shelf. Though most fiction still appears in the traditional sequence – hardback first, followed by paperback – a number of titles appear *only* in hardback (and a number *only* in paperback). Heavy paperback buying can depress purchases of novels which only appear in hardback. A Heinemann fiction editor, (Fraser, 1992) lamented the meagre purchasing by public libraries of new novelists in hardback. (On average, some 200 copies were sold to libraries of a 750-copy imprint – a pathetic number, given the 4700 public library service points in the UK.)

One other approach to sustaining variety in the fiction stock is to have a good system for retaining last copies of titles in the authority. This is important, given the restrictions on borrowing fiction through interlending systems. (The British Library Document Supply Centre does not lend fiction, and the percentage of failed fiction requests from all sources tried is high, at 15%.[13] Moreover, some libraries do not accept reservations for fiction at all.

We have stressed that there are choices to be made between different types of fiction, and further choices between different authors within types. Another sort of choice – between different titles by the same author – is often neglected. Many library authorities place pre-publication orders for titles by established authors, leaving no room to distinguish between the first-rate and the pot-boiler. Few authorities have systematic procedures for taking reviews into account, even though most new literary fiction *is* reviewed soon after publication[7, 14] (Spiller, 1979). The upshot can be that important authors are represented on the shelves only by minor or discredited works.

Over the years there have been occasional articles in the professional literature arguing for a more systematic approach to fiction provision.[11, 15, 16] But declining issue figures nationally, not to mention the condition of the fiction shelves in many public libraries, still suggest that this service is seldom taken seriously. There is an urgent requirement for some quantitative research on a national scale. We also need local initiatives on performance measurement which (as in the PLR exercise above) delve beyond the summary figures and lead on to providing a greater variety of stock – in the catalogue and on the shelf – as well as more measures for promoting quality writers who are not in the best-seller lists.

Non-fiction and reading for pleasure

In the same way that some users visit a public library to borrow 'a novel' to read for pleasure, others borrow types of non-fiction for the same reason. Prominent amongst these types is 'biography', and to some extent 'travel literature' – though the latter is hard to distinguish, in the classification schedules, from the more practically oriented travel guides to tourist destinations.

Luckham's celebrated 1971 survey of library use (see Appendix) found that 10% of users were borrowing biographies, 10% geography and travel, and 5% history (compared to 72% borrowing fiction). In the 1988 Euromonitor study (Euromonitor Publications, 1989), 8% of respondents, asked what they were reading at the time, replied 'biography'. From a different angle, a study of non-fiction lending, Timperley[17] found that 14% of 400 titles analysed were borrowed primarily 'for pleasure', of which by far the greater proportion – 56% – were biographies. (Of course, user motivations for borrowing are often mixed – so that, for instance, biographies are borrowed for personal learning purposes as well as for pleasure.)

A recent survey of library acquisitions over time[18] found that biography acquisitions in public libraries had more than trebled in 14 years, from 3% of all acquisitions in 1984 to 10% in 1998. This in itself was a reflection of an extraordinary increase in the publication of biographies – 45% during the period 1991–98. But the splurge in biography acquisition (often fuelled by reservations pressure via broadsheet reviews) may not be justified when related to long-term library use. Smith's study of non-fiction management information in one authority[19] found 'biography' to have the fourth-largest subject stock in the authority (after literature, travel and history), but to be 27th in terms of popularity – with 24% of stock on loan, compared to (for instance) 80% of computer stock, 49% of 'the paranormal' and 34% of travel. See Chapter 5 for further comment on over- and underprovision in non-fiction categories.

Little has been written on the use of biography in libraries. Spiller[14] suggested features for identifying biographies of lasting quality – amongst them, the objectivity of the biographer (or 'honesty', in the case of an autobiography), the occupation and celebrity of the subject, originality of treatment, and the extent to which biography successfully amalgamates the private and public lives of the biographee.

As with fiction provision, there is a strong argument for cutting down on trivial material, and including a large proportion of classic or long-lasting biography (or travel literature, etc). Richard Hoggart[20] has written widely on this theme, and Lord Quinton, in a stirring speech – later an article[21] – referred to 'the best that has been thought and said'. He went on:

> The most serious threat to culture at the present moment is the assault against the idea that there is any canon at all, any objectively definable elite of books which should be addressed in preference to others . . .

13
Materials for children

Library materials for children are provided through both the children's and adult sections of public libraries, and through the libraries of primary and secondary schools of all types. Much of the commentary on public libraries elsewhere in this book is relevant to provision for children, so in this chapter we concentrate on provision in schools – although coordination between materials in school and public libraries is important (see below).

One service straddling both these sectors is the Schools Library Service (SLS), which provides long-loan batches of stock to primary and secondary schools in many areas of the UK. Creaser's annual survey (Creaser, 1999) found a high take-up of SLS in 1997–98: by 90% of primary LEA schools in areas where SLS was available, and 83% of secondaries – plus some independents. In total, SLS held 27 million stock items in that year, of which 96% were books; 62% of these were on loan. This stock represented 3.3 items per pupil served, compared to 2.2 items per resident child in the public library service. Evaluation of the impact of SLS is perhaps overdue, but there is some evidence[1] to suggest that a school's access to SLS does lead to pupils being more satisfied with their library's stock.

Impact of materials provision

There has been much recent discussion of the long-term impact of providing materials for children. Two good summaries of the background issues are in the Department of National Heritage's (DNH) 1995 report *Investing in children,*[2] and Kinnell's *Managing library resources in schools.*[3] The DNH report highlighted the importance of supporting literacy programmes, observing that a third of 14-year-olds had a reading age of 11, and that 40% of 16–19-year-olds lacked basic literacy and numeracy skills.

There is an important role in school libraries for print and electronic materials to be used for recreational purposes, but it seems clear that the main function should be, and is, in support of curriculum studies. The National Curriculum was introduced in England and Wales following the 1988 Education Reform Act, and marked a move away from the former priority of content towards the process of learning. A 1994 survey by Heeks and Kinnell[4] found that 87% of teachers in 12 state schools perceived the National Curriculum as generating an increased need for information skills in pupils; these included computer literacy, as well as obtaining information from printed materials.

Spreadbury in her 1998 survey of secondary school library users[1] interviewed 400 pupils across four schools (two state, two independent). She found that 51% of all pupils interviewed were using the library for schoolwork, 18% for 'pleasure', and 31% for both. The percentage for schoolwork increased with the age of pupils. In the Heeks and Kinnell survey the curriculum function also predominated, with 82% of pupils saying they used the library for schoolwork, 46% for leisure reading and 30% for private study.

Given the predominance of curriculum-related library use, the key contacts for librarians in schools are with teachers and members of curriculum forums; and the crucial forms of promotion for the library are teachers urging their pupils to use it. Price made the point in her article 'The role of the library in the effective primary school' (Price, 1999). In practice, teacher/library contacts are not always as close as they should be. Spreadbury[1] enquired of pupils whether teachers asked them to use the library to help with schoolwork: 25% did so 'always or most of the time', and 43% 'sometimes'; but 32% did so 'not very often or never'. She found a close correlation between the subject areas where teachers were library-oriented and actual use by subject. Heeks and Kinnell[4] put similar questions to the teachers. Some 6% of teachers said they 'rarely' directed pupils to library resources, whilst 39% said 'sometimes' and 55% 'often'.

Shakeshaft's *Survey of independent school libraries*[5] found that only 10% of the 177 librarian respondents attended curriculum or senior management meetings. The situation is slightly better in state school libraries: The Library Association's wide-ranging *Survey of secondary school libraries in the UK*[6] found that 20% of all the librarians (ie in state and independent schools) attended curriculum development meetings 'most of the time', but 52% 'not at all'. A comment from one of the librarians in the Shakeshaft survey – 'I have repeatedly asked to become a member of the Curriculum Committee, but without success; frankly, there is very little interest from colleagues' – seemed fairly characteristic, and underlined a problem which just has to be overcome if library materials are to reflect what teachers and pupils really need.

Despite the difficulties described in the surveys, pupils' views on the availability of curricular information were reasonably encouraging. In the Spreadbury report,[1] 18% of pupils said they could 'always' find something, 56%

said 'most of the time', 21% said 'sometimes' and 4% 'not very often'. To a more general question in the Heeks and Kinnell survey[4] – 'How often do you find what you want?' – only 8% replied 'rarely', 47% 'sometimes', and 45% 'often'.

If children's requirements in school libraries are naturally dominated by curricular materials, the main preoccupation in public libraries is 'reading for pleasure'. (A 1996 survey in all of Birmingham's public libraries[7] found that only 28% of children took books 'to help with homework', whereas 60% took fiction to read for pleasure, and 37% information books for the same reason.) Cooperative acquisition arrangements in any context are generally fraught with difficulties, but in the case of provision for children they must be worth considering – given such a clear division of needs and use. The DNH report[2] recommended that local authorities should develop integrated strategies for young people. Few observers would suggest an either/or strategy for providing schoolwork/recreational materials; but local cooperation could define the emphasis given to the two strands of provision, in ways that would be cost-effective for both public and school libraries in an area.

User surveys

In the context described above, knowing about children's use of different libraries in an area is important. Spreadbury[1] asked whether pupils used a public library in addition to their school library: 56% said 'yes', 15% 'sometimes' and 29% 'no' – with much higher proportions of pupils saying 'no' in the two independent schools. In two of the schools (one state, and one independent), pupils were asked where they got most of the books they read – and 'home' was added to the list of prompted answers. Most of the pupils plumped for just one location: 34% cited the school library, 29% home and 21% the public library; 9% said school and home, and 7% school and the public library. Use of books from the home was predictably much higher amongst independent school pupils.

If the findings of Shakeshaft's independent schools survey[5] were typical, most school libraries keep only rudimentary performance data. She found that issue statistics were often the only measure used – and even they were not kept in 20% of the schools surveyed. Subanalysis of issues by features such as pupil age-group or the subject of books was rare (made by 10% and 9% respectively). This is a missed opportunity in a sector where stock records are highly automated, but the stock itself receives relatively low use – suggesting that management information could be the most profitable application for the automation systems. Shakeshaft also found that only 5% of the independent schools measured use of the electronic resources; and there was no mention at all of in-house use scrutiny, although this must be an important feature in school libraries, with their captive readership.

The *Investing in children* report[2] emphasized the need for the measurement of performance and for the development of performance indicators. At least two UK public library authorities have developed – through their schools library services – benchmarking systems for schools in their areas, comparing local performance with national benchmarks taken from the Library Association survey.[6] The results are highly informative, and this is an initiative worth pursuing on a broad scale.

Given the lack of information, Spreadbury's survey findings on the types of material used[1] made interesting reading: on the day she interviewed them, 39% of the children were borrowing books, 14% were making use of materials in-house, 12% using the computers, and 11% the magazines. There were no takers at all for the videos or cassettes. In the Heeks and Kinnell survey,[4] pupils were asked which of the services they used regularly: 87% borrowed books, 39% used the computers, 22% consulted magazines, and 3% used cassettes. The very low use of cassettes in both surveys suggests that collection development in this area – or having a collection at all – is an issue that needs rethinking.

Asked which improvements they would like to see in their libraries, 52% of pupils in Spreadbury's survey[1] said 'more books' and 39% 'more computers'. To a similar question in the Heeks and Kinnell survey,[4] 16% said 'more recent books', 12% 'more books of a specific type', 10% 'a larger library', and 7% 'more computers'. Responses of teachers to the same question were 22% 'more recently published books', 20% 'a larger library', 17% 'more stock in specific categories', and 7% 'more computers'.

Information about user preferences and satisfaction with stock can only be obtained through surveys of the Spreadbury and Heeks type, and there can be few school libraries which would not benefit from conducting similar surveys which address local concerns about provision. Findings are much more informative if they can be compared with findings in similar schools – ideally, through cooperative surveys conducted in schools of the same type or in the same geographical area. In public libraries the CIPFA PLUS survey was extended to children in 1999,[8] and the first findings are now becoming available, permitting local results to be compared with national averages.

Reading for pleasure

Several surveys over the past 30 years have looked into children's reading habits: how often they read, what they choose and how they choose. Heather's *Young people's reading*,[9] based on interviews with 60 children, was published in 1981 by the University of Sheffield. Carter[10] summarized the findings of several surveys. The Roehampton Institute's *Contemporary juvenile reading habits*,[11] published in

1994, interviewed 321 pupils across 12 schools. Spreadbury[1] also investigated leisure reading.

The Roehampton survey asked children 'Do you ever borrow books?' Amongst the boys, the percentage answering 'often' declined from 28% for the 4-7 age range to 21% for those aged 11-16. With girls, the percentage who often borrowed was higher and more constant (40–43% for the three age ranges studied). These responses accord with other findings that boys read less than girls, and that their reading falls away with age. That said, the percentages who 'never' borrowed were relatively small for both sexes: between 9% and 22% for boys (rising with age across three age ranges), and between 6% and 7% for girls. However, Spreadbury found that amongst pupils in years 10–13 a third or more 'never' read for pleasure – largely because of pressures of the curriculum.

The question of *how* children choose books to read is of keen interest to librarians selecting and displaying stock. Carter observed that young children were heavily influenced by the format and appearance of books, together with their length and the number of illustrations. Prior familiarity with an author was a factor for all ages. Heather's respondents rated the influences, in order of importance, as: familiarity with the author; books recommended; titles identified through the mass media; books of a particular type; and scanning information on the cover. The Roehampton survey investigated these influences by age range. For the 4–7 and the 7–11 age ranges, amongst both boys and girls, the main influences mentioned were the books' illustrations and titles. The title was also the main influence for boys aged 11–16, followed by 'recommendations'; for girls in this age bracket, recommendations were most important, followed by the blurbs on the covers of books.

The same report also looked at *who* made the reading recommendations. For the 4–7 age group, parents naturally predominated. For the 7–11 group, parents were still influential, but friends and teachers also had a big say in choice. By the time children had reached the 11–16 group, parents took a back seat to friends. It is perhaps of some concern that school librarians and staff in public libraries played only a small part in recommending books – being mentioned by no more than 16% of children in any group.

Finding new books to read is a perennial problem – for adults as well as children (see Chapter 12). A 1999 guide titled *Who next?* (Irvin and Cooper, 1999) deserves prominent display in libraries for children; it lists children's authors by age range, and under each name suggests other authors who write in a similar way.

Spreadbury's analysis[1] of recreational reading by 'fiction' and 'non-fiction' categories confirmed the commonly held view that boys read more non-fiction than girls. Amongst girls, 67% read 'mostly fiction', only 2% 'mostly non-fiction' and 31% a mixture; amongst boys, only 18% read 'mostly fiction', 17% 'mostly non-fiction' and 64% a mixture. The Heather, Roehampton, and Spreadbury surveys all carried out further analysis of fiction reading. The findings were fairly consistent over the years, with both sexes reading adventure books, thrillers and mysteries, boys favouring science fiction and humour, and girls preferring 'family/friendship' books, animal stories and romances (amongst older girls). The main change over the years has been the recent fashion for 'horror' books, currently read by both sexes with a morbid enthusiasm which has projected R L Stine into the top ten authors listed by the Public Lending Right scheme.

Spreadbury's further analysis of children's non-fiction preferences produced fairly predictable findings, with boys favouring sport, computers, cars and factual books, and girls 'real life stories'. Both sexes wanted comedy and humour books. In the Roehampton survey, boys of all ages gave 'hobbies' as their first preference; younger girls favoured 'animals/plants', whilst older girls mentioned 'other parts of the world', and famous people.

A very substantial survey – now little referred to – was carried out in 1973 on the instigation of the then Department of Education and Science (DES, 1973). The responses to questions to users aged 14 or under gave a different perspective: 62% of them regularly sought 'any novel of interest' and 37% 'any non-fiction of interest; 26% regularly sought specific information, 14% books by a specific author and 12% a specific book.

Serials have an important role in libraries for children, and are generally stocked in respectable numbers. Carter[10] observed that young people of both sexes spent a lot of time reading comics and magazines. Heather's survey[9] found that 78% of pupils read magazines. The Library Association survey[6] noted that over half of all secondary schools stocked between 10 and 50 magazines and newspapers; in independent secondary schools, Shakeshaft[5] found that 55% stocked 16 or more magazines, and that 41% had five or more newspapers.

Selection mechanics

Published information about the process of selecting material for children is relatively limited. Chambers and Stoll[12] gave some feel of what happens in selection meetings. Their report commented that children's librarians 'tend to have a much more judgemental approach to book selection than adult librarians', and 'a much stronger educational as well as moral sense to their aims'. The report also commented on a unique feature of children's book selection – the local 'reviewing' by librarians of new books. A number of librarians handling adult materials were reported to be sceptical about this approach, but children's librarians were on the whole left to handle an area which was felt to be too specialized for 'adult' librarians to grasp (or want to grasp) fully.

To this author, there seem to be both advantages and disadvantages to the different approach of children's librarians. They are willing to take responsibility for their special group of users, who certainly need – up to a point – more spoon-feeding than an adult clientele; and their close interest in the books themselves is heartening in an era when materials often seem to be the last thing on librarians' minds. On the debit side, children's librarians who are too bossy in their selection can exclude a lot of material which users want to read, but which is considered 'not to be good for them'; and the prospect of hundreds of individual children's librarians all over the UK 'reviewing' books – presumably with varying degrees of success – must prompt serious questions about cost-effectiveness.

There have been recent developments on the 'reviewing' front. The Place for Children project (Library and Information Statistics Unit, 1998) asked public library authorities to give an 'importance rating' to a number of different selection sources. The overall ratings, in descending order of importance, were: approvals from library suppliers 4.9, internal reviews 4.4, selective bibliographies 4.1, journals 4.0, CD-ROMs from library suppliers 3.9, library supplier lists 3.7, publisher lists 3.6, trade bibliographies 3.4, national bibliographies 2.7.

It is encouraging to note the high ratings for evaluative sources such as journals and selective bibliographies; but we also note with mixed feelings the relatively high use of services from library suppliers. Doubts about these services centre on two features: the quality of information provided (see below) and their comprehensiveness. Concern about the latter is enhanced by the low priority given to national and trade bibliographies, and the steadily increasing numbers of children's titles published – 8400 in 1998 (Library and Information Statistics Unit, 1999b, 198).

The quality of information provided by library suppliers has recently improved in at least one case: the *Children's ROMREAD* CD-ROM provided on a fortnightly basis by Peters Library Services. This tool is seen by Peters as an alternative to a hard-copy approvals service and includes – probably for the first time in a supplier service – a one-sentence *evaluation* of each title, provided by qualified librarians on Peters' staff. Factors taken into consideration include: for fiction, plot, characterization, illustrations, 'appeal', production and literary style; and for non-fiction, currency, the quality and relevance of illustrations, the text, layout and production.

Catherine Blanshard's[13] 1997 article described why her English county had switched from local reviewing to using the Peters CD-ROM. Prominent amongst the reasons were the high cost (in terms of staff time) of local reviewing, including the reviewing of many titles which were not subsequently put into stock, and delays in the local reviewing process, which resulted in out-of-print reports for short print-run titles. Blanshard estimated that about £15,000 a year would be saved by using the CD-ROM, probably rising to £25,000 when an interface with the library's computer system had been sorted out.

This may be the direction in which children's selectors move. If so, both the comprehensiveness of the CD-ROM database and the quality of the evaluations need to be kept under very close review.

Electronic materials

School libraries already have a reasonable representation of electronic materials – which started with CD-ROMs and is increasingly extending to the Internet. The Library Association's 1997 survey[6] found that 88% of secondary schools provided access to at least one CD-ROM player, and 30% had access to the Internet. The numbers of workstations available in the schools at that time ranged between 0 and 19; a quarter of schools had 5–9 workstations, and only 9% had none. But we know very little about how the electronic sources are used. Shakeshaft,[5] for instance, found that only 5% of independent secondary schools in her 1998 survey monitored CD-ROM use.

Spreadbury[1] studied quite closely the use of CD-ROMs in the two state and two independent secondary schools in her survey. Asked whether they used the CD-ROMs in the library, 31% of pupils said 'yes' and 32% 'sometimes; 37% did not make use of them, but two-thirds of these said they used CD-ROMs elsewhere. The unexpected finding was the extent to which CD-ROM use declined with age: almost half of year-7 pupils used the service, compared to about one-fifth of years 10–13. It became clear that the CD-ROMs stocked were not detailed or sophisticated enough for many of the older pupils' curriculum-related needs – and also that many of the younger pupils used the medium for game-playing. Spreadbury also had some useful information about the *way* that CD-ROMs were used: there was a good deal of printing out of material without proper, prior scanning, and the most appropriate use of the medium was found in the one school which had carried out proper training sessions on using CD-ROMs.

Herring's recent book[14] contains a good summary of the role to date of CD-ROMs in schools. Amongst the first suitable materials to appear in this format were encyclopaedias, which provided sophisticated searching procedures to content, and a combination of text, graphics, photographs and video clips which were attractive to school audiences. Newspapers on CD-ROM are also widely available in schools, providing important support for curricular subjects needing up-to-date information. And there is a wide variety of subject-based CD-ROMs which library staff need to acquire in close cooperation with teaching staff.

Writing in 1999, Herring observed that CD-ROM was still the key electronic resource in most school libraries, and was likely to remain in use for some years – although Internet resources could be expected gradually to move centre-stage. He identified the key qualities for selection of CD-ROMs in schools as being: relevant to curriculum studies; appropriate in terms of level; user-friendly; of high quality; and suitable for the UK culture (ie largely avoiding products for the American market).

Information technology is already a pervasive feature of teaching and learning in schools: a subject on the curriculum, a tool which provides teachers with a variety of options, and a one-to-one child–computer personal learning tool which offers some advantages over the one-to-30 child–teacher relationship. The way forward for school libraries is to have the library computers connected to school-wide networks, and it is important that library staff should be participants in school-wide ICT planning. The 1997 Library Association survey[6] found that 39% of library computers were connected to networks, but that 57% were run as autonomous library management systems. The dangers of being sidelined are all too evident. An important independent report to the Government in 1997[15] made no mention of school libraries, and included no librarians amongst the 100 people contacted in drawing up the report.

In the immediate future a good deal of the speculation about electronic materials will be concentrated on the immense potential of the Internet for teaching and learning purposes. Informative recent sources are Herring,[14] Small[16] and Jervis and Stegg's 1997 survey of Internet provision.[17]

Jervis and Stegg found that 83% of the 116 schools surveyed had some kind of Internet connection, while only 3% had no plans to connect. The majority of schools had connections for only one or two standalone computers. Of those with connections, 71% provided supervised pupil access, and only 6% allowed unsupervised access. Unsuitable access was restricted by the Internet service provider (in 44% of cases) and by filtering software (in 18%). As many as 80% of pupils used the Internet facilities for individual research, 46% for directed class research, 41% for class e-mail projects, and 35% for undirected class research. Little serious curriculum work was being done at that time. Computers with Internet connections were located in three main places: computer rooms (in 59% of schools), libraries and resource centres (34%), and staff areas (34%). The report commented that information about the Internet in schools was often based upon a few well-funded, well-publicized projects – a feature which intimidated many other, less-advanced schools.

The main problem about selecting material from the Internet – and this affects all users, whether in libraries or not – is the enormous amount of information, of widely varying quality (see Chapter 4). In school libraries, where pupils need to be protected – to an extent – from inaccurate or misleading (not to mention offensive) information, the problem is particularly acute. Small[16] identified three possible solutions: supervising access at all times (which is usually impractical), teaching pupils how to use the Internet intelligently, or creating an intranet.

Intranets are already used in a number of schools – 23% of those in the Jervis and Stegg survey.[17] Websites thought suitable for local use are downloaded onto a closed local or wide-area network. Herring[14] recommended that teachers and librarians should work together in creating intranets, which he felt were bound to develop in many – but probably not all – schools. Selected websites should be downloaded on the basis of a number of criteria: accuracy, authority, objectivity, currency, coverage, level, and ease of use. It would also be helpful if the sites were an advertising-free zone. The difficulties involved in creating school intranets should not be underestimated: they are time-consuming to create and to maintain; they also sacrifice the Internet's main advantages of size and variety, and preclude pupils from learning how to use a key information tool of the 21st century.

Web information on school intranets is likely to be combined with various other types of information: networked CD-ROMs, the library OPAC, administrative and curriculum information, and news releases. The Jervis and Stegg survey found that 81% of the existing school intranets stored downloaded web pages, 57% were used as internal school noticeboards, and 33% displayed examples of pupils' work.

One Internet initiative which is expected to impact heavily upon schools, and upon school libraries, is the UK government's National Grid for Learning project. The 1997 consultation paper[18] described the grid as 'a way of finding and using online learning materials', and 'a mosaic of interconnecting networks and educational services, based on the Internet, which will support teaching, learning, training and administration in schools, colleges, universities, libraries, the workplace and the home'. Examples given of pupil-related activities were children doing history or geography homework with access to world-wide resources, and children participating remotely in science experiments. But despite the all-embracing description, the early thrust of the project appears to be on teacher-training and school administration. The project model was launched in 1998, and the schedule anticipates that all schools will be connected by the year 2002.

14
Foreign language materials

Special problems connected with the provision of foreign language materials can be split into two main categories: provision for research, and provision for immigrant communities.

Provision for research

Surveys in the 1970s[1,2] attempted to quantify the amount of foreign language material relevant to research needs. At that time anything between 20% and 70% (depending upon the subject field) of references in abstracting services were to articles published in languages other than English. The most significant, after English, were French, German, Russian and Japanese, though big variations were apparent for specific subject areas.

The surveys also showed clearly that language barrier problems prevented many researchers from consulting relevant literature. (Only with French did British researchers appear to have attained a reasonable command of another language.) A number of solutions to the problem were put forward – improvement of language qualifications amongst research workers, more cover-to-cover translations of journals, better and more widely publicized translation agencies, fuller English language abstracts of foreign language articles – some of them pursued, though without real success.

In the circumstances, individual academic and workplace libraries tend to minimize holdings of foreign language materials, and lean heavily on national interlending systems. Most journals and conference proceedings published outside the UK are readily available, since the British Library Document Supply Centre collects these formats irrespective of language – though it is not possible for them to follow this policy for monographs.

Nevertheless, the demand is relatively small. A 1981 survey of interloans at the University of Dundee by Roberts and Cameron[3] was one of the few surveys to analyse material by language. Of 2300 interloans analysed, only 9% of all serial requests were in a foreign language, and 5% of monograph requests. Most of the serials requests were for German material (7% of the 9% in all languages), with 1% for French articles. Of monograph requests, 1.9% were for German language material, and 1.8% for French. The figures were somewhat distorted by an unusually large demand from the foreign languages department, which accounted for one-third of all French and German requests. The arts and social science departments absorbed most of the remainder. Science-based faculties were barely represented.

Despite the likelihood of limited use, some libraries do need to acquire some foreign materials for their own stock. A useful working tool by Bloomfield[4] outlined the problems of acquisition for particular regions of the world, and suggested some solutions to these. Several writers referred to the problems caused by delays in the appearance of national bibliographies and the inadequacies of their coverage. (These features tend to be particularly acute in developing countries.) The most common alternative to selection from lists and bibliographies is the commissioning of an agent in the country concerned to make a selection of material on behalf of the purchasing library – an arrangement which requires a good deal of confidence in the agent. Dilution of the agent's responsibility can be managed by requesting from agents lists of publications from which the library makes a choice.

Provision for immigrant communities

Some British public library authorities receive quite heavy demand for foreign language materials from immigrant communities. The first serious investigation into immigrant reading requirements in the UK was by Clough and Quarmby in 1978.[5] Two studies by Elliott in the 1980s[6,7] indicated some of the problems. Cooke[8] provides a more recent survey of the UK situation.

The demand for immigrant-language provision affects a surprisingly large number of languages, including a contingent from the Indian subcontinent. Cooke received 83 responses from a questionnaire to 110 public library authorities in England, Wales and Scotland. In all, 27 languages were reported, of which the most commonly mentioned (together with the numbers of authorities which specified them) were: Urdu 47, Bengali 42, Punjabi 40, Gujarati 39, Chinese 36, Hindi 38, German 25, French 25, Spanish 24, Vietnamese 19. A total of 27 languages were mentioned altogether.

Cooke found that the average annual expenditure (in 1993) on purchase of materials in these languages exceeded £5,000 in only 13 authorities – and four of these were predominantly books in Welsh. The survey's conclusions were that provision was 'fragmentary and under-resourced', and almost entirely confined to public libraries, and that there was a need for a national vision on an infrastructure for provision to ethnic minorities.

A small survey of 28 authorities in 1996 (Spiller and Creaser, 1999) found that only six of them could provide stock and issues information for minority languages material for the year 1995–96. The annual turnover of this stock (ie the average number of issues per book per year) was quite low: 2 and 1.8 issues a year in two London boroughs; 0.8 in a metropolitan district; and 1.5 in an English county. (The turnover of Welsh-language stock in two Welsh authorities was even lower – 0.5 and 0.4.) Low use would be expected – relative to English-language stock – because of the relatively small numbers of users in any one authority. Even so, the figures suggest that some further investigation is necessary, to ensure that stock goes beyond a political gesture to provide the right types of material in the right languages – with the size of stock in any one language matched to the amount of use.

Barron's 1996 survey of user surveys (see Appendix), which received responses from 74% of UK public library authorities at that time, found that only three reported having carried out a survey of ethnic minority users. One of these – High's 1995 survey of 450 Asian-origin users at Hounslow[9] – provided much useful information. She found that 59% of those interviewed used the Asian-language collections, but 41% did not – and most of the latter were not interested in doing so. Of those who used the Asian-language services, about half were satisfied with the range of books, but a third were dissatisfied (a high proportion in a satisfaction survey). Asked how the collections could be improved, nearly half the respondents asked for 'more books', and 38% for a broader range of authors. By far the most popular subjects requested were religion and the philosophy of religion (by nearly 60% of those using the books), followed by history.

Of the respondents, 56% said that they also read the Asian magazines and newspapers – a very high proportion compared to public library users whose first language is English. Almost half of the respondents used them on a weekly basis. The main improvements requested were a greater variety of titles, and more copies of the main titles already stocked.

The report commented that there was a clear library culture for older male users: spending time in the library reading newspapers to keep up-to-date about their country of origin, and using books for historical and religious analysis.

Use of the libraries by children of Asian origin was even more clearly defined. There were 129 parents or carers answering questions on behalf of children under 14. Of these, 83% said the children borrowed books in English, and only 14% borrowed books in the language of their country of origin; 61% of the children could only read English.

We cannot know how typical these responses were for the UK's Asian and other immigrant communities in general, but the Hounslow survey certainly provided food for thought. Authorities providing services to immigrant communities may be advised to carry out a detailed survey of user needs, enquiring (as Hounslow did) about English-language as well as first-language needs, and paying particular attention to children's requirements – which will dictate future service provision. If Hounslow is typical, the need for foreign-language material may – at least for some cultures – fade entirely after a few decades.

Meanwhile, some attention needs to be given to stock for existing adult users. As with all areas of minority provision, maintaining freshness of stock is a problem, and stock exchanges between service points are common (see Chapter 5). For some languages it is possible to borrow loan collections periodically from an outside cooperative scheme – notably the Library of Asian Languages at Birmingham Public Library, and the Polish Central Circulating Library in London.

Bibliographical information for other-language publications is a problem, and many libraries lean heavily on selection by UK-based specialist booksellers, whose numbers have increased in the past couple of decades. Elliott[6] in 1984 listed 40 specialist bookshops. He also reported an increase in UK indigenous publishing for ethnic minority groups, identifying 105 publishers, in a large number of different languages, and guessing that at least 200 more were in existence. But their output was small: Elliott recorded 27 publishers producing a total of 354 book titles in the course of five years. He estimated that perhaps 50% of the UK-published immigrant language books at that time appeared in the national bibliography.

The users of common European languages such as French, German and Spanish include British nationals who are studying a language or who have in the past achieved fluency in a language and still enjoy reading in it. Most UK public libraries provide small collections in these languages at their larger libraries, as do university departments of modern languages. Marcan (1986) provided some useful practical information on building up collections of this kind. Libraries need to hold the basic bibliographies for the languages in question, together with surveys of their respective literatures. There are several reputable UK booksellers dealing in European languages who are willing to offer advice. Stock usually includes prize-winning books. Stock mobility is again essential within the library system.

15
Out-of-print materials

Ranganathan (1966) decreed that in a 'service' library there was no place for books selected for their 'oldness of physique'. If this is accepted, then the private collector's interest in acquiring books according to their rarity, reputation, physical condition, provenance (previous whereabouts) or the fluctuations of fashion has no direct part to play in selection for 'service' libraries. Books are acquired so that users may consult them for their content.

Rarity is a relative concept. Any out-of-print book is rare in that it is more difficult to obtain than a work which is in print, and (usually) more expensive. The condition of 'rarity' as defined by an antiquarian bookseller depends primarily upon the size of the book's original edition, the subsequent fluctuations in the work's reputation, the number of surviving copies, and demand. A work may be difficult to find, but if it is not sought after it cannot be described as 'rare'. A great many works are out of print, but if there are still large numbers of copies in circulation they would merely be described as 'out-of-print' or 'second-hand'. Some of the books sought by librarians fall into this category.

Most types of 'service' library have occasion, at one time or another, to search for out-of-print books to add to their stock. For some – for instance, university or learned society libraries – the acquisition of out-of-print material forms an important and recurrent feature of their work. Some public libraries – notably those in the large cities – also have outstanding collections of rare books; these are the exception rather than the rule, though every public library authority periodically needs to acquire out-of-print books for local history collections, or to make good omissions which have become apparent in the stock. Cave's *Rare book librarianship*[1] is a good introduction to the subject. Cox's article on rare books and special collections[2] gives a valuable account of how this aspect of work is managed in a university library.

Out-of-print books are purchased by libraries in one of three main ways: by visiting second-hand bookshops; by marking up dealers' catalogues; or by preparing desiderata lists (lists of wanted titles) to submit to dealers.

Dealers can broadly be classified into the rare book specialists and those who deal with the whole gamut of second-hand books – whatever their price or vintage. Where time permits, visits to both categories of dealer often prove worthwhile; they give an opportunity to examine stock on the bookseller's shelves, and they also strengthen the library's hand in bidding for stock for which other customers are also in the market. To capitalize on visits of this kind, librarians need an excellent knowledge of their own stock.

Booksellers' catalogues list materials which have come into their possession recently (sometimes in the form of a large special collection), and which are being offered for sale. The catalogue quotes the bibliographical details of each book, the price, and – in the case of rare books – gives an indication of physical condition.

The crucial requirement for checking dealers' catalogues is speed. They have to be read through on receipt and checked against the library's desiderata file. Orders should be conveyed immediately to the dealer; delay invariably means that some of the works listed will be taken by other customers.

A desiderata file is the library's lists of wants: titles previously sought for one reason or another – perhaps because of readers' requests which could only be satisfied through the interlending system – and found to be out of print. The list should note the bibliographical details of each book, when it went out of print, the reason it was required and its importance to the library, and any action taken so far.

As well as checking desiderata lists against dealers' catalogues, libraries may periodically send them to one or more dealers, with instructions to search for titles on behalf of the library. After checking their own holdings, dealers then advertise for the wanted titles – in the UK this is usually done through the weekly journal called *The Clique* – and refer back with details of the price and condition quoted. (Alternatively, libraries may suggest automatic purchase below a given price.) While not obliged to purchase works identified by dealers in this way, most librarians would regard themselves as morally bound to do so, as long as the price and condition of the works are reasonable. The use of a single dealer (rather than several) is usually preferred, to avoid multiple advertising for the same titles.

The desiderata file of a British university might typically run to some 2000 items. Files are periodically revised, in association with academic staff, to see whether listed items are still wanted (or have already been added to stock). An article by Cameron and Roberts[3] described this process at Dundee University.

Ground rules for putting a price on an out-of-print book cannot be definitively stated. A useful guideline can be taken from reference books which record the actual prices registered in recent sales (*Book Auction Records*, annual). But judgement of 'a fair price' depends upon a number of factors in addition to rarity, and the records of other sales – if used without considering other background details – can be misleading. Fashions in book buying come and go. The condition of a book, and its provenance, can both have a big influence upon price. Buyers are advised to enter each transaction with a good knowledge of both dealer and book, to avoid paying a badly inflated price for an inferior product.

The condition of a rare or second-hand book is less important to librarians than to private collectors. Cave[1] defines 'good condition' in a book as 'complete and undisturbed in its original binding . . . and clean and sound throughout'. In view of the fact that the condition of a library copy will – if it is used at all – soon decline, purchase of slightly inferior copies is justified, and may achieve a substantial overall saving on expenditure.

Lists of the very large number of dealers, together with their specializations, are widely available. In addition to the general dealers in rare and second-hand books, there are specialists for most subject areas. Experience over time shows which dealers offer an efficient service, and if more than one dealer is used, libraries should keep a record which enables them to compare the proportion of titles supplied from wants lists, the average delay in supply, and other details.

Donations

All types of library are liable to receive unsolicited donations of material from time to time, varying in size from a handful of books to large and important special collections (the latter often forming a notable part of university and research library collections).

An offer of a large special collection raises major policy issues in the 'receiving' institution. But to some extent, the issues involved differ only in scale from those raised by any proposed donation. Is the donation suitable for the library? Can the material be properly housed and indexed? Are there any special limitations attached to the gift, and if so is the library prepared and able to meet them? Can the library afford the high cost of maintaining special collections, especially if they require extra security, air conditioning, and separate reading rooms and exhibition areas? And perhaps most important, will the donated material be used? A survey by Diodata and Diodata (1983) in a medium-sized academic library found that purchased books circulated four times more often than donations. Arfield's stock analysis at the University of Reading[4] found that much of the unborrowed stock turned out to have been donated.

If these questions cannot be resolved satisfactorily, the library should be prepared to redirect potential donors to other locations.

16
Paperbacks

Publishing of paperbacks

Paperbacks are big business in the UK book trade, comprising (in 1998) 61% of all titles published – 67% of fiction, 56% of academic and professional books, 65% of other non-fiction, and 55% of children's books (Library and Information Statistics Unit, 1999b, 198–9).

In recent years, the 'traditional' pattern of publishing – where a hardback edition was published first, and sometimes followed by a paperback – has diversified considerably. Reuben and Spiller[1] investigated this feature through four small samples of books published in 1995 (fiction, genre fiction, biographies and medical texts). They found that the 'hardback then paperback' sequence was still common (in 60% of general fiction, 42% of genre fiction and 35% of biographies), but that a lot of titles only appeared in paperback (28% of general fiction 27% of genre fiction and 19% of biographies). It was rare for hard and paperback editions of titles to appear simultaneously (occurring in only 8% of cases in all three of these categories), and relatively rare for hardbacks not to be followed by a paperback (occurring in 4% of general fiction, 15% of genre fiction and 38% of biographies). Many of the paperback versions of hardbacks appeared within 18 months of the original, and most appeared within three years.

Overall, 96% of fiction, 85% of genre fiction and 62% of biographies appeared at some point in paperback, whilst 72% of general fiction, 73% of genre fiction and 81% of biographies appeared at some point in hardback.

The format situation was much clearer for the sample of medical textbooks: essentially, titles were published either in hardback (in 54% of cases) or paperback (38%) – rarely in both.

Library practice in purchasing paperbacks

At one time it was the norm for public libraries to buy the hardback edition of a title, where one existed – and the paperback only where it did not. Surveys in the 1980s by Capital Planning Information[2] and Hart[3] revealed changes in this practice, with some public librarians still sticking to the traditional approach, but with others buying up to 20–30% of all acquisitions in paperback – many of these intended for recreational reading and purchased in bulk.

In the 1990s, the pendulum swung further towards paperback provision. Matthews (1994) reported that in 1992–93, Essex acquired about 70% of all adult fiction and 60% of non-fiction in paperback. Reuben and Spiller[1] found that on average 46% of books purchased by public libraries were paperbacks, though there was considerable variation amongst authorities. Asked about their preferred formats for purchasing different book categories, a majority of authorities said they had no preferences – except in the case of 'light fiction', where 49% favoured paperbacks, against 41% expressing no preference. The only category where a preference for hardbacks substantially outweighed paperbacks was reference material.

A survey of public and academic library acquisitions during the period 1984–98[4] found that, since 1991, more than half of public library acquisitions had been paperbacks (56% in 1998). Surprisingly, throughout the period 1984–98, there were more acquisitions in paperback for non-fiction than for fiction. The situation was different in academic libraries, where more than half of all acquisitions for the same period were in hardback (for all but one year). The 1998 proportions were 56% in hardback and 43% in paperback.

In Reuben and Spiller's survey, 97% of authorities said they opted for a paperback edition when there was 'a large price difference', and it is clear that one of the main reasons for libraries ordering paperback editions (where the option exists) is that it is often more economical to do so. Several surveys by practitioners have tried to compare the cost-effectiveness of hardbacks and paperbacks, among them work by Head (1996), Matthews (1994) and Eaton (1983). This kind of investigation often gets drawn into costings for the different reinforcement methods used for paperbacks.

Reuben and Spiller[1] took this approach a step further, by giving a 'condition' grading to library shelf stock in four different groups (hardbacks, and paperbacks in three different kinds of covering), then combining this information with cost data to measure cost-effectiveness. They concluded that the paperback edition is usually more cost-effective than the hardback, but that 'where the hardback is less than about 1.6 times the cost of the paperback, the hardback is more cost-effective'.

Reuben and Spiller reported several other circumstances which prompted paperback purchase in public libraries – all directly or indirectly associated with cost-effectiveness: for disposing of waiting lists (by 83% of authorities); where there is a limited readership (by 90%); and for works which date quickly (by 9%).

Library users and paperbacks

What are the views of library users on these matters? Surveys carried out in the 1980s[5, 6, 7] all found a majority of respondents with a preference for hard over paperback – although invariably, greater proportions of the young library users preferred paper. Those younger users from the 1980s appear to be carrying their preferences through into middle age because, in the user survey conducted by Reuben and Spiller,[1] 47% of respondents preferred the paperback format for fiction, whilst only 35% preferred the hardback and 19% had no preference. The comparable preferences for non-fiction were hardback 40%, paperback 33% and no preference 28%. The single reason most often given for preferring paperbacks was that they were 'easier to read in bed'; whilst for hardbacks comments on 'larger print size' and 'it looks like a proper book' (and similar observations) were most often reported.

Conclusions

Research into cost-effectiveness and user preferences is certainly helpful; but in practice, format provision is bedevilled by uncertainty about the order in which formats will be published. Where a title appears in paperback and hardback simultaneously, decisions on format are easily taken. But where a title appears first in hardback, purchasers cannot be sure that a paperback version will follow. If they think it will, they can make a modest initial investment in the hardback, and a greater investment subsequently in the paperback. If there is to be no subsequent paperback, they must try to anticipate this and invest in the hardback immediately. Sometimes the guesses will be wrong.

In summary, there is clearly a good case for investing in paperbacks – because a lot of users like them, and because they are more often than not cost-effective. Where there is a big price difference between hard and paper editions, paper should usually be the choice – though there are exceptions to this (for instance, when illustrations are important to the book). But when there is no likelihood of a paperback follow-up to an initial hardback, libraries must invest in the hard-cover edition.

Reuben and Spiller[1] also looked at the effectiveness of different methods of reinforcing paperbacks. Plastic sleeves appeared to be highly efficient, but they recommended that libraries should carry out their own studies of the different methods. It seems that most paperbacks now purchased for libraries *are* reinforced in one way or another. Publishers do not like the practice, and few paperbacks appear without a printed warning on the reverse of the title page forbidding such reinforcement – a warning so far widely ignored without penalty.

17
Videos and recorded sound

Videos

The relatively low price of video brings it within the purchasing range of most kinds of library. Two surveys in the 1980s showed that academic libraries had moderate collections of videos, many of these deriving from the production departments of their own or other academic institutions: Heery's 1983 survey[1] covered polytechnics and colleges; and Thompson's 1988 survey (Thompson, 1988) of audiovisual provision in the higher education sector reported that 22 institutions (nearly all universities) held mostly print collections, whilst 52 (comprising polytechnics, colleges of higher education, and universities) were multimedia. Since the 1980s, interest in audiovisual materials in the academic sector appears to have been overtaken by the digital revolution, and little has been written or researched on the way that videos and recorded sound materials are being used.

By contrast, videos in public libraries have flourished. Pinion's survey (Pinion, 1983) found that in 1983 only 25 out of the 160 public library authorities surveyed offered video lending services, mostly of feature films. Just 17 years later, videos are an important service for most authorities, and use of these collections has been on an upward trend for the past decade. In the period 1988–98, video additions to public libraries increased by 1,150%; over the 5-year period leading up to 1998, video issues increased by 138% (Library and Information Statistics Unit, 1999b, 55–70). One feature driving this development is that video services can be charged for, and so have become a major source of income – much of which is presumably ploughed back into the video service itself (though there are no transparent data on this). A 1995–96 survey found that a range of 6–50% of total revenue income in 21 authorities derived from video fees, with a mean of 22% (Spiller and Creaser, 1999).

All the same, video remains a minority service in public libraries. The CIPFA

PLUS archive for 1997[2] found that 5.3% of users visited their libraries to borrow or return videos – compared to 78% borrowing or returning books. Video issues per head of population in 1997–98 were 0.19, compared to 8.1 for books – a ratio of 1:42. This compares oddly with expenditure per capita on audiovisual materials as a whole: £0.24 compared to £1.53 for books – a ratio of 1:6.

Though a number of authorities have carried out user surveys on audiovisual materials – Barron (see Appendix) found that more had surveyed this aspect of service than any other – little of this research has found its way into print, and we remain largely unsighted about the detail of video and recorded sound services. Fortunately Smith[3] conducted an analysis of audiovisual service management information in a London borough. He noted that the authority's video stock of 12,000 items comprised 3–4% of all lending stock, but accounted for 9% of all issues; the high rate of use was confirmed by the 'average annual issues per item' figure of 18 – much higher than the rate for any category of books.

The circulation of videos was dominated by feature films, which took 71% of all issues despite comprising only 61% of all video stock – even though feature films were charged and non-features were loaned free. Children's videos took 15% of issues, and non-feature videos took 14%. Of the feature film issues, two-thirds were of 15 and 18 certificate ratings. Of the non-feature film issues, the 'body and mind' category made up 18% of the total (mostly on health and fitness subjects), whilst 'travel' and 'nature' made up 10% each. Borrowing took place mainly at weekends, irrespective of prices charged, and films were most popular when new.

Smith mentioned four factors which influenced the use of the video service: the library's performance compared to the local commercial market; charging policies and loan periods; the quality of stock; and the presentation and quality of access to stock.

Some further research into video services in public libraries is perhaps long overdue. A number of questions need to be addressed:

1 What is the make-up of existing collections in terms of feature and non-feature videos, and further subdivisions of those categories – for instance, how do feature films break down between 'popular' and 'classic'?
2 How does the content of videos stocked support the overall aims of the authority, and relate to other stock formats held?
3 What proportion of existing users are interested in the video service, or might be interested if content were adapted/expanded?
4 What proportion of library non-users would be interested in videos, and how many of them are aware of the service? Howkins (1999) found that only a

third of non-users of Leicester's libraries were aware of the feature films service, although 43% of them said they were 'likely to use' it.

5 What proportion of video revenue is ploughed back into the video service itself? Is the service genuinely self-financing (in terms of staff costs and overheads, as well as materials)?

More information on these points could fuel a proper discussion of key issues. For instance, one can argue very strongly that video services should be central to an authority's overall objectives, and not an add-on designed merely to generate revenue. Libraries are not funded to compete (and on advantageous terms) with commercial suppliers to provide popular material, especially if those services interest only a small minority of their customers. On the other hand, if video services are completely self-financing and all revenue is ploughed back into videos, then there is no argument for using videos as a revenue source for more 'mainstream' library services.

Recorded sound

Sound recordings have been a component of public library services for several decades, so recent developments have been less dramatic than those in video services. The total 'audio' stock of UK public libraries in 1998 – 5.9 million items – is an increase of 16% on stock a decade earlier, but stock has fallen slightly over the past five years (Library and Information Statistics Unit, 1999b, 56). Issues of audio materials over the five years up to 1997–98 increased by 3.4%, but fell by the same percentage in the last year of the period (Library and Information Statistics Unit, 1999b, 70). According to data which are only available for the last three years, music recording issues are falling, but this is counterbalanced by an increase in the issues of talking books. If we look at 'annual issues per head of population', both music and talking book recordings are used at about the same rate as videos (between 0.19 to 0.23 issues). But the numbers are small compared to 'issues per head' for books (at 8.1); the CIPFA PLUS archive for 1997[2] found that 6.6% of library users were visiting public libraries to borrow or return cassettes (compact discs were not mentioned), compared to 77.6% borrowing or returning books.

We know relatively little about the content of these public library collections of recordings. The last published survey by Saddington and Cooper (1984) predated the compact disc, which reveals its antiquity. But Smith's 1997 analysis[3] of management information on music recordings in a London borough was very informative. He noted that the authority had 27,000 music recordings in stock, which comprised 8% of all materials and accounted for 7% of total issues. Music issues had been in decline since 1991–92. Table 17.1 gives his analysis of percentages of stock and issues by type:

Table 17.1 *Percentage of music stock and issues analysed by type*

	stock	issues 1996–97	percentage of category on loan 1996
classical	39%	28%	29%
pop	43%	48%	46%
easy listening	4%	6%	35%
jazz	8%	8%	36%
other	6%	10%	38%

It is clear from Table 17.1 that classical recordings issued less frequently than any of the popular music categories – a feature which one would expect to be replicated in other authorities.

Although the authority found that 40% of their customers borrowed music recordings at one time or another, an analysis on one particular day showed that only one in 20 customers had a music item on loan.

As with video, recorded sound lending is usually a charged service (charged for the loan of each item). But Smith noted that revenue from the service was easily absorbed by the staff costs of running it – unlike video services, where revenue outweighed service costs.

A couple of background points should be made about selecting sound recordings. Because of the existence of the *Gramophone* and other good reviewing journals, review coverage of music – particularly the classical repertoire – is almost comprehensive for British recordings. Reviews cover both performance and technical features, and are published soon enough for selection to be based upon their appearance. For popular music and jazz, these sources are supplemented by specialized journals such as *Melody Maker*. Selection of recordings is also greatly helped by the regular appearance of excellent selective guides to classical music and jazz, which compare different recordings and recommend 'the best'.

Selection of classical music is characterized by one unusual feature: the *content* of collections is fairly stable, comprising the well-known classical repertoire, augmented periodically by new music or revivals of lesser-known pieces. The evaluation process therefore concentrates mainly upon the *performance* of pieces rather than on musical content. To an extent this means that provision is about achieving a balance within the traditional repertoire, as earlier additions to stock wear out and new performances replace them.

There are several policy considerations peculiar to this area, which need to be resolved by a combination of asking users and making value judgements:

Format

Gramophone records are no longer used for library lending, but both compact discs and cassettes are. At the point where technologies change, decisions sometimes need to be made between two or more formats, but in the year 2000 there is a fairly distinct division between spoken-word material (which usually appears only on cassette) and music (which is generally only on compact disc). Though compact disc is more expensive than its precursor formats, it is also more cost-effective because of better sound quality and greater longevity.

Content

Perhaps the most intractable consideration concerns the relative priority to be given to different categories of recordings – particularly classical music vis-à-vis different types of popular music. User preferences (as determined through management information and surveys) play a part in this, but most library authorities are also likely to make a value judgement about the importance of different types of content. There is no intrinsic reason why classical music should be considered more significant than popular music – though that judgement may nevertheless often be made. The rapid commercial development of talking-book recordings is an additional complicating factor; the extent to which this service is used by partially sighted library users (or potential users) is perhaps the most important factor in fixing the size of talking book collections.

Bargain versus expensive labels

In the classical music area in particular, there are large numbers of bargain items. Performances on these are rarely 'the best' available (in the view of the critics), but bargain items are usually a more cost-effective buy than the latest (expensive) recordings. Given a shortage of library funding, establishing the repertoire in libraries seems more important than having in stock relatively minor differences in interpretation.

Old versus new

As noted above, selecting classical recordings is often a matter of choosing between new versions of an 'old' repertoire. This is not the case with pop/rock albums where the 'new' is invariably what is in most demand. Very new albums cannot – by law – be purchased by libraries; but in any case there is a strong case for libraries to concentrate on the older 'repertoire' of pop/rock music, given the ubiquitous availability of new albums, and the rapid fall-off of interest in most of them during the first few months after they are issued.

Appendix

Surveys of users

Aslib (1995) *Review of the public library service in England and Wales: final report*, Aslib.

Bohme, S and Spiller, D (1999) *Perspectives of public library use 2: a compendium of survey information*, Library and Information Statistics Unit.

Book Marketing Ltd (1998) *Household library use survey 1998*, Book Marketing Ltd.

Craghill, D (1988) *Public library user studies: what we have learned and where do we go from here?*, Dept of Information Studies, University of Sheffield.

England, L and Sumsion, J (1995) *Perspectives of public library use: a compendium of survey information*, Library and Information Statistics Unit.

Erens, B (1996) How recent developments in university libraries affect research, *Library management,* **17** (8), 5–16.

Luckham, B (1971) *The library in society: a study of the public library in an urban setting*, The Library Association.

Surveys of libraries

Barron, E (1999) User consultation. In Bohme, S and Spiller, D *Perspectives of public library use 2: a compendium of survey information*, Library and Information Statistics Unit, 30–32.

Council of Academic and Professional Publishers (1995) *Survey of acquisitions in special libraries*, CAPP/Publishers Association.

Creaser, C and Spiller, D (1997) *TFPL survey of UK special library statistics*, Library and Information Statistics Unit.

Spiller, D et al (1998) *Libraries in the workplace*, Library and Information Statistics Unit.

Spiller, D and Creaser, C (1999) Pilot of proposed new measures for CIPFA public library statistics. In Bohme, S and Spiller, D *Perspectives of public library use 2: a compendium of survey information*, Library and Information Statistics Unit, 60–68.

Sumsion, J (1994) *Survey of resources and uses in higher education libraries in UK*, Library and Information Statistics Unit.

Wallace, W and Marden, D (1999) *Library and learning resources in further education: the report of the 1996–97 survey*, The Library Association, available at:

http://www.la-hq.org.uk/directory/prof_issues/linfe.html

Further reading

Chapter 1
Library policy and provision

1 National Committee of Inquiry into Higher Education, *Higher education in the learning society (Dearing report): summary report,* HMSO, 1997.

2 National Committee of Inquiry into Higher Education, *Higher education in the learning society (Dearing report). Report 2: Full and part-time students in higher education: their experiences and expectations* (Claire Callender, Policy Studies Institute), HMSO, 1997.

3 Pickering, H et al, *The stake-holder approach to the construction of performance measures*, Caledonian University, 1996.

4 Joint Funding Council's Library Review Group, *Report (Follett Report)*, HEFCE, 1993.

5 Alston, S and Nicholson, H, Gauging the value of research periodicals, *SCONUL Newsletter*, **16** (Spring), 1998, 5–8.

6 Department of National Heritage, *Guidance for local authorities*, HMSO, 1995.

7 Department of Culture, Media and Sport, *Comprehensive spending review*, HMSO, 1998.

8 Timperley, P and Spiller, D, *The impact of non-fiction lending from public libraries*, Library and Information Statistics Unit, 1999.

9 Totterdell, B and Bird, J, *The effective library: report of the Hillingdon project on public library effectiveness*, The Library Association, 1976.

10 Department of National Heritage, *Investing in children: the future of library services for children and young people*, HMSO, 1995.

11 Spreadbury, H and Spiller, D, *Survey of secondary school library users*, LISU, 1999.

12 Shakeshaft, G, *Survey of independent school libraries*, MA dissertation, LISU, 1997. Summarized in Spiller, D and Shakeshaft, G, Libraries in UK independent schools, *New Review of Children's Literature and Librarianship*, **3**, 1997, 75–92.

13 Spiller, D J, Libraries for all?, *Library Association Record*, **90** (4), 1998, 217–8 (plus correspondence on censorship in subsequent issues).
14 Capital Planning Information Ltd, *Information used in public library book selection*, CPI, 1998.
15 National Acquisitons Group, *Public library stock management*, BNB Research Fund report 90, National Acquisitions Group, 1998.
16 Futas, E (ed), *Collection development policies and procedures*, 3rd edn, Oryx Press, 1995.
17 Wood, R and Hoffman, F, *Library collection development policies: a reference and writers' handbook*, Scarecrow Press, 1996.
18 Cole, N and Usherwood, B, Library stock management: policies, statements and philosophies, *Public Library Journal*, **11** (5), 1996, 121–5.
19 Capital Planning Information Ltd, *Trends in public library selection policies*, BNB Research Fund, 1987.
20 Snow, R, Wasted words? The written collection development policy and the academic library, *Journal of Academic Librarianship*, **22** (3), 1996, 191–4.

Chapter 2
Budgeting

1 Baker, D, *Resource management in academic libraries*, Library Association Publishing, 1997.
2 Ford, G, Finance and budgeting. In Jenkins, C and Morley, M, *Collection management in academic libraries*, Gower, 1999, 36–69.
3 Breaks, M, Management of electronic information. In Jenkins, C and Morley, M, *Collection management in academic libraries*, Gower, 1999, 107–34.
4 Graham, T W, University library finance in the 1980s. In Dyson, B, *The modern academic library*, Library Association Publishing, 1989, 32–56.
5 Fletcher, J, Financial management systems. In Line, M B, *Academic library management*, Library Association Publishing, 1990, 215–22.
6 Hutchins, J, Allocating funds for purchasing resources. In Baker, D, *Resource management in academic libraries*, Library Association Publishing, 1997, 111–18.
7 Budd, J M, Allocation formulas in practice, *Library Acquisitions*, **13** (4), 1989, 381–90.
8 Yeadon, J and Cooper, R, Book selection and bookfund management at Imperial College libraries, *New Review of Academic Librarianship*, **1**, 1995, 33–40.
9 McClellan, A W, Systematic stock control in public libraries. In McClellan, J W, *The reader, the library and the book*, Bingley, 1973, 83–105.

10 Houghton, T, *Bookstock management in public libraries*, Bingley, 1985.
11 Capital Planning Information Ltd, *Trends in public library selection policies*, BNB Research Fund, 1987.
12 Department of National Heritage, *Investing in children: the future of library services for children and young people*, HMSO, 1995.
13 Valentine, S, Total collection management: the Hertfordshire approach. In Barton, D, *Stock management in libraries: a holistic approach*, Capital Planning Information Ltd, 1997.

Chapter 3
Evaluating print materials

1 Capital Planning Information Ltd, *Information used in public library book selection*, CPI, 1998.
2 Council of Academic and Professional Publishers, *Survey of acquisitions in special libraries*, CAPP/Publishers Association, 1995.
3 Chambers and Stoll, *Book selection in public libraries*, British Library Research and Development Department, 1996.
4 Chapman, A and Spiller, D, *Trend analysis of monograph acquisitions in public and university libraries in the UK*, Library and Information Statistics Unit, 2000.
5 Peasgood, A N, Towards demand-led book acquisitions?: experiences in the University of Sussex library, *Journal of Librarianship*, **18** (4), 1986, 242–56.
6 Smith, I, Adult non-fiction and the public library. In Bohme, S and Spiller, D, *Perspectives of public library use 2: a compendium of survey information*, Library and Information Statistics Unit, 1999, 161–6.
7 Spiller, D, The provision of fiction for public libraries, *Journal of Librarianship*, **12** (4), 1980, 238–66.
8 Roberts, D H E, An analysis of the request and reservation service of Nottinghamshire County Library, *Journal of Librarianship*, **5** (1), 1973.
9 Smith, I, *Customer requests in Westminster libraries*, unpublished, 1999.
10 Institute of Public Finance, CIPFA PLUS archive for 1997. In Bohme, S and Spiller, D, *Perspectives of public library use 2: a compendium of survey information*, Library and Information Statistics Unit, 1999, 52–9.
11 Sear, L and Jennings, B, *How readers select fiction*, Kent County Council, 1986.
12 Smith, I, Adult fiction and the public library. In Bohme, S and Spiller, D, *Perspectives of public library use 2: a compendium of survey information*, Library and Information Statistics Unit, 1999, 167–72.
13 Chapman, A, *Bibliographic record provision in the UK: measuring availabil-*

ity against demand, UK Office for Library and Information Networking, University of Bath, 1998.

14 Arthur, M, Supplier selection, *Taking Stock*, 8 (2), 1999, 7–11.

Chapter 4
Evaluating electronic materials

1 Ajibade, B and East, H, Characteristics of BIDS-ISI users: 'real-time' surveys of networked on-line use. In East, H et al, *Developments of database access in universities: studies in use, expenditure, pricing and benefits*, BLRIC report 140, British Library Research and Innovation Centre, 1998.

2 Ajibade, B and East, H, Pricing JISC database services. In East, H et al, *Developments of database access in universities: studies in use, expenditure, pricing and benefits*, BLRIC report 140, British Library Research and Innovation Centre, 1998.

3 Ajibade, B and East, H, Research assessment exercise and usage of BIDS-ISI. In East, H et al, *Developments of database access in universities: studies in use, expenditure, pricing and benefits*, BLRIC report 140, British Library Research and Innovation Centre, 1998.

4 Batt, C, *Information technology in public libraries*, 6th edn, Library Association Publishing, 1998.

5 Leach, K, A constant demand for new services: a survey of CD-ROM acquisitions in UK academic institutions, 1996. In East, H et al, *Developments of database access in universities: studies in use, expenditure, pricing and benefits*, BLRIC report 140, British Library Research and Innovation Centre, 1998.

6 Library Association, *Survey of secondary schools in the UK*, The Library Association, 1997, available at:
http://www.la-hq.org.uk/
Executive summary available from The Library Association.

7 Spreadbury, H and Spiller, D, *Survey of secondary school library users*, LISU, 1999.

8 *Connecting the learning society: National Grid for Learning,* the Government's consultation paper, DfEE, 1997.

9 Library and Information Commission, *New library: the people's network*, Library and Information Commission, 1997.

10 Capital Planning Information Ltd, Exit survey, 1997. In Bohme, S and Spiller, D, *Perspectives of public library use 2*, Library and Information Statistics Unit, 1999, 141–6.

11 Cooke, A, *A guide to finding quality information on the Internet: selection and*

evaluation strategies, Library Association Publishing, 1999.

12 Nisonger, T E, The Internet and collection management in academic libraries. In Gorman, G E and Miller, R H, *Collection management for the twenty-first century: a handbook for librarians*, Greenwood Press, 1997, 29–57.

13 Bertha, E, Comparison of pricing structures of information on various electronic media, *Aslib Proceedings*, **50** (2), 1998.

14 Craig, G M, Information available on UK agricultural Web sites, *Aslib Proceedings*, **51** (5), 1999, 155–66.

15 Breaks, M, Management of electronic information. In Jenkins, C and Morley, M, *Collection management in academic libraries*, Gower, 1999, 107–34.

16 Nicholas, D, Developing a testing method to determine the use of Web sites: case study newspapers, *Aslib Proceedings*, **51** (5), 1999, 144–54.

17 Lancaster, F W, Evaluating the digital collection. In *Proceedings of 2nd Northumbria International Conference on Performance Management*, Dept of Information and Library Management, University of Northumbria at Newcastle, 1998, 47–57.

Chapter 5
Stock logistics and stock revision

1 McClellan, A W, *The logistics of a public library bookstock*, Association of Assistant Librarians, 1978.

2 McClellan, A W, *The reader, the library and the book*, Bingley, 1973, 83–105.

3 Chapman, A and Spiller, D, *Trend analysis of monograph acquisitions in public and university libraries in the UK*, Library and Information Statistics Unit, 2000.

4 Timperley, P and Spiller, D, *The impact of non-fiction lending from public libraries*, LISU, 1999.

5 Smith, I, Adult non-fiction and the public library. In Bohme, S and Spiller, D, *Perspectives of public library use 2: a compendium of survey information*, Library and Information Statistics Unit, 1999, 161–6.

6 Houghton, T, *Bookstock management in public libraries*, Bingley, 1985.

7 Moore, N, Systematic bookstock management in public libraries, *Journal of Librarianship*, **15** (4), 1983, 262–76.

8 Betts, D and Hargrave, R, *How many books?*, MCB Publications, 1983.

9 Kerr, G, Get to know your stock, *Library Association Record*, **100** (2), 1998, 78–81.

10 Smith, I, Library use – frequency of borrowing. In Bohme, S and Spiller, D, *Perspectives of public library use 2: a compendium of survey information*,

Library and Information Statistics Unit, 1999, 173–5.

11 Valentine, S, Total collection management: the Hertfordshire approach. In Barton, D, *Stock management in libraries: a holistic approach*, Capital Planning Information Ltd, 1997.

12 Audit Commission, *Due for renewal: a report on the library service*, Audit Commission, 1997.

13 Lumb, C I, *Practical stock management and stock rotation on mobile libraries*, MA dissertation, Department of Information Science, Loughborough University, 1998. Summarized in Bohme, S and Spiller, D, *Perspectives of public library use 2: a compendium of survey information*, Library and Information Statistics Unit, 1999, 182–7.

14 Fussler, H H and Simon, J L, *Patterns in the use of books in large research libraries*, University of Chicago Press, 1969.

15 Kent, A L, *Use of library materials: the University of Pittsburgh study*, Dekker, 1979.

16 Arfield, J, Pruning, weeding and grafting: strategies for the effective management of stock, *Library management*, **14** (3), 1993, 9–15.

17 Peasgood, A N, Towards demand-led book acquisitions?: experiences in the University of Sussex library, *Journal of Librarianship*, **18** (4), 1986, 242–56.

18 Day, M and Revill, D, Towards the active collection: the use of circulation analyses in collection evaluation, *Journal of Librarianship and Information Science*, **27** (3), 1995, 149–57.

19 Jacobs, N A, Students' perceptions of the library service at the University of Sussex: practical quantitative and qualitative research in an academic library, *Journal of Documentation*, **52** (2), 1996, 139–62.

20 Wall, T, A comparative approach to assessing the performance of a short-loan collection, *Journal of Librarianship and Information Science*, **26** (4), 1994, 193–200.

21 Yeadon, J and Cooper, R, Book selection and bookfund management at Imperial College libraries, *New Review of Academic Librarianship*, **1**, 1995, 33–40.

22 JISC, *The impact of on-demand publishing and electronic reserve on students, teaching and libraries in higher education in the UK*, JISC, 1997.

23 Kingston, P, Short loan collections. In Spiller, D, *Academic library surveys and statistics in practice*, Library and Information Statistics Unit, 1998, 51–66.

24 Buckland, M, An operational research study of a variable loan and duplication policy at the University of Lancaster, *Library Quarterly*, **42**, 1972, 97–106.

25 Buckland, M, *Book availability and the library users*, Pergamon, 1975.

26 Wall, T, Availability, accessibility and demand for recommended books in academic libraries, *Journal of Librarianship and Information Science*, **31** (3), 1999, 145–51.

27 Jacobs, N A, Book availability surveys. In Spiller, D, *Academic library surveys and statistics in practice*, Library and Information Statistics Unit, 1998, 43–6.

28 Book Industry Communication, *Availability and value of library management information: a feasibility study*, Book Industry Communication, 1992.

Chapter 6
Stock evaluation and performance measures

1 Batt, C, *Information technology in public libraries*, 6th edn, Library Association Publishing, 1998.

2 Joint Funding Council's Library Review Group, *Report (Follett Report)*, HEFCE, 1993.

3 Joint Funding Council, *The effective academic library: a framework for evaluating the performance of UK academic libraries*, HEFCE Publications, 1995.

4 Barton, J and Blagden, J, *Academic library effectiveness: a comparative approach*, British Library Research and Innovation Centre, 1996.

5 Department of National Heritage, *Reading the future*, DNH, 1997.

6 Library Association, *Survey of secondary schools in the UK*, The Library Association, available at:
http://www.la-hq.org.uk/
executive summary available from The Library Association, 1997.

7 Wallace, W and Marden, D, *Library and learning resources in further education: the report of the 1996–97 survey*, The Library Association, 1999.

8 Ward, S, *Library performance measures and library management tools*, European Commission, 1995.

9 Harnesk, J, The ISO standard on library performance indicators (ISO 11620). In *Proceedings of 2nd Northumbria International Conference on Performance Measurement*, Dept of Information and Library Management, University of Northumbria at Newcastle, 1998.

10 Book Industry Communication, *Availability and value of library management information: a feasibility study*, Book Industry Communication, 1992.

11 Smith, I, Adult non-fiction and the public library. In Bohme, S and Spiller, D, *Perspectives of public library use 2: a compendium of survey information*, Library and Information Statistics Unit, 1999, 161–6.

12 Smith, I, Adult fiction and the public library. In Bohme, S and Spiller, D,

Perspectives of public library use 2: a compendium of survey information, Library and Information Statistics Unit, 1999, 167–72.

13 Smith, I, Library use – frequency of borrowing. In Bohme, S and Spiller, D, *Perspectives of public library use 2: a compendium of survey information*, Library and Information Statistics Unit, 1999, 173–5.

14 Audit Commission, *Due for renewal: a report on the library service*, Audit Commission, 1997.

15 Peasgood, A N, Towards demand-led book acquisitions?: experiences in the University of Sussex library, *Journal of Librarianship*, **18** (4), 1986, 242–56.

16 Day, M and Revill, D, Towards the active collection: the use of circulation analyses in collection evaluation, *Journal of Librarianship and Information Science*, **27** (3), 1995, 149–57.

17 Shakeshaft, G, *Survey of independent school libraries*, MA dissertation, LISU, 1997. Summarized in Spiller, D and Shakeshaft, G, Libraries in UK independent schools, *New Review of Children's Literature and Librarianship*, **3**, 1997, 75–92.

18 Goodall, D, *Browsing in public libraries*, Library and Information Statistics Unit, 1989.

19 Timperley, P and Spiller, D, *The impact of non-fiction lending from public libraries*, LISU, 1999.

20 Baker, S L and Lancaster, F W, *The measurement and evaluation of library services*, 2nd edn, Information Resources Press, 1991.

21 Ford, G, *Review of methods employed in determining the use of library stock*, BNB Research Fund. 1990.

22 Lancaster, F W, *If you want to evaluate your library . . .*, 2nd edn, Library Association Publishing, 1993.

23 Kent, A L, *Use of library materials: the University of Pittsburgh study*, Dekker, 1979.

24 Rubin, R, *In-house use of materials in public libraries*, University of Illinois, Graduate School of Librarianship and Information Science, 1986.

25 Harris, C, *The subject intensity of library use: some aspects of polytechnic library use*, Newcastle-upon-Tyne Polytechnic Library, 1975.

26 Selth, J, The use of books within the library, *College and Research Libraries*, **53**, 1992.

27 Schofield, J L, Evaluation of an academic library's stock effectiveness, *Journal of Librarianship*, **7**, 1975, 207–27.

28 Van House, N A, *Measuring academic library performance: a practical approach*, American Library Association, 1990.

29 Kantor, P B, *Objective performance measurement for academic and research libraries*, Association of Research Libraries, 1984.

30 Mansbridge, J, Availability studies in libraries, *Library and Information Science Research*, **8** (4), 1986, 299–314.

31 Line, M B, The ability of a university library to provide books wanted by researchers, *Journal of Librarianship*, **5**, 1973, 37–41.

32 Revill, D, Availability as a performance measure, *Journal of Librarianship*, **19** (1), 1987, 16–30.

33 Revill, D, An availability study in co-operation with a school of librarianship and information studies, *Library Review*, **37** (1), 1988, 17–34.

34 Jacobs, N A, Book availability surveys. In Spiller, D, *Academic library surveys and statistics in practice*, Library and Information Statistics Unit, 1998, 43–6.

35 Institute of Public Finance *CIPFA public library user survey*. General information from the Institute of Public Finance, 7th floor, NLA Tower, 12–16 Addiscombe Road, Croydon, CRO OXT.

36 Institute of Public Finance CIPFA PLUS archive for 1997. In Bohme, S and Spiller, D, *Perspectives of public library use 2: a compendium of survey information*, Library and Information Statistics Unit, 1999, 52–9.

37 Spreadbury, H and Spiller, D, *Survey of secondary school library users*, LISU, 1999.

38 Pickering, H et al, *The stake-holder approach to the construction of performance measures,* Glasgow Caledonian University, 1996.

39 Wressell, P (ed), *Proceedings of 1st Northumbria International Conference on Performance Management*, Department of Information and Library Management, University of Northumbria at Newcastle, 1995.

40 *Proceedings of 2nd Northumbria International Conference on Performance Management*, Dept of Information and Library Management, University of Northumbria at Newcastle, 1998.

41 Capital Planning Information Ltd, Exit survey, 1997. In Bohme, S and Spiller, D, *Perspectives of public library use 2*, Library and Information Statistics Unit, 1999, 141–6.

42 Orr, R H, Measuring the goodness of library services: a general framework for considering qualitative measures, *Journal of Documentation*, **29** (3), 1973, 315–32.

43 Johnson, H, User satisfaction surveys over five years: a college of higher education experience. In Spiller, D, *Academic library surveys and statistics in practice*, 1998, 23–31.

44 Line, M B, *Library surveys: an introduction to their use, planning, procedure and presentation*, 2nd edn, Bingley, 1982.

45 Hayden, M, Satisfaction surveys using Libra software and focus groups. In Spiller, D, *Academic library surveys and statistics in practice*, 1998, 33–42.

46 Lancaster, F W, Evaluating the digital collection. In *Proceedings of 2nd Northumbria International Conference on Performance Management*, Dept of Information and Library Management, University of Northumbria at Newcastle, 1998, 47–57.

47 Brophy, P and Wynne, P, *Management information systems and performance measurement for the electronic library*, Centre for Research in Library and Information Management, Manchester Metropolitan University, 1997.

48 Nicholas, D, Developing a testing method to determine the use of Web sites: case study newspapers, *Aslib Proceedings*, **51** (5), 1999, 144–54.

49 Spiller, D, Benchmarking in practice. In *Proceedings of 2nd Northumbria International Conference on Performance Management*, Dept of Information and Library Management, University of Northumbria at Newcastle, 1998, 431–9.

Chapter 7
Managing the provision of materials

1 Chambers and Stoll, *Book selection in public libraries*, British Library Research and Development Department, 1996.

2 Capital Planning Information Ltd, *Information used in public library book selection*, CPI, 1998.

3 Valentine, S, Total collection management: the Hertfordshire approach. In Barton, D, *Stock management in libraries: a holistic approach*, Capital Planning Information Ltd, 1997.

4 McClellan, A W, The organisation of a library for subject specialisation. In McClellan, A W, *The reader, the library and the book*, Bingley, 1973.

5 Hindle, A, *Developing an acquisitions system for a university library*, British Library, 1977.

6 Higham, N, *The library and the university: observations on a service*, Deutsch, 1980.

7 Martin, J V, Subject specialisation in British university libraries: a second survey, *Journal of Librarianship and Information Science*, **28** (3), 1996, 159–69.

Chapter 8
Weeding

1 Slote, S J, *Weeding library collections: library weeding methods*, 4th edn, Libraries Unlimited, 1997.

2   Williams, S, Stock revision, retention and relegation in United States aca-
    demic libraries. In Jenkins, C and Morley, M, *Collection management in
    academic libraries*, Gower, 1999, 205–24.

3   Buckland, M, An operational research study of a variable loan and duplica-
    tion policy at the University of Lancaster, *Library Quarterly*, **42**, 1972,
    97–106.

4   Heaney, H, Acquisition and retention policies. In LINC, *Library service
    provision for researchers: proceedings of the Anderson Report seminar,* LINC,
    1997, 15–20.

5   Arfield, J, Pruning, weeding and grafting: strategies for the effective man-
    agement of stock, *Library management*, **14** (3), 1993, 9–15.

6   Taylor, C and Urquhart, N C, *Management and assessment of stock control in
    academic libraries: a report on a research project*, British Library, 1976.

7   Capital Planning Information Ltd, *Disposal of printed material from
    libraries*, BNB Research Fund, 1995.

8   Chapman, A and Spiller, D, *Trend analysis of monograph acquisitions in pub-
    lic and university libraries in the UK*, Library and Information Statistics
    Unit, 2000.

9   Smith, I, Library use – frequency of borrowing. In Bohme, S and Spiller,
    D, *Perspectives of public library use 2: a compendium of survey information*,
    Library and Information Statistics Unit, 1999, 173–5.

10 University Grants Committee, *Capital provision for university libraries:
    report of a working party*, the Atkinson Report, HMSO, 1976.

11 Steele, C, *Steady state, zero growth and the academic library*, Bingley, 1978.

12 Douglas, I, Effects of a relegation programme on borrowing of books, *Jour-
    nal of Documentation*, **42** (4), 1986, 252–71.

13 Fussler, H H and Simon, J L, *Patterns in the use of books in large research
    libraries*, University of Chicago Press, 1969.

14 Trueswell, R W, Determining the optimal number of volumes for a library's
    core collection, *Libri*, **16**, 1966, 49–50.

15 Line, M B and Sandison, A, Obsolescence and changes in the use of litera-
    ture with time, *Journal of Documentation*, **30** (3), 1974, 283–350.

16 Reuben, J and Spiller, D, *Paperbacks in public libraries*, Library and Infor-
    mation Statistics Unit, 1999.

17 Duckett, B, Beyond the stacks, *Library Association Record*, **92** (6), 1990,
    433–5.

18 Burrows, J and Cooper, D, *Theft and loss from UK libraries: a national sur-
    vey,* Police Research Group, Home Office Police Department, 1992.

Chapter 9
Holdings versus access

1 Parry, D, *Why requests fail: inter-library lending and document supply request failures in the United Kingdom and Ireland*, Information North for CONARLS, 1997.

2 Sykes, J, Document delivery strategies. In Jenkins, C and Morley, M, *Collection management in academic libraries*, Gower, 1999, 183–203.

3 Rowley, J, *The electronic library*, Library Association Publishing, 1998, 365–90.

4 Finnie, E, *Document delivery*, Aslib, 1998.

5 Morris, A and Blagg, E, Current document delivery practices in UK academic libraries, *Library Management*, **19** (4), 1998, 271–80.

6 Line, M B, Access v ownership, *IFLA Journal*, **22** (1), 1996, 35–41.

7 Roberts, M and Cameron, K J, A barometer of 'unmet demand': inter-library loans analysis and monograph acquisitions, *Library Acquisitions*, **8** (3), 1984, 31–42.

8 McClellan, A W, *The reader, the library and the book*, Bingley, 1973, 72–82.

9 Bevan, S J, BIODOC: the transition from research project to fully-fledged services, *Serials*, **11** (2), 1998, 152–62.

10 Brown, A J, Some library costs and options, *Journal of Librarianship*, **12** (4), 1980, 211–16.

11 Line, M B, Co-operation: the triumph of hope over experience?, *Interlending and Document Supply*, **25** (2), 1997, 64–74.

Chapter 10
Serials

1 Horwill, C, Periodicals reviewing by voting. In Corrall, S, *Collection development; options for effective management*, Taylor Graham, 1988, 102–10.

2 Kent, A L, *Use of library materials: the University of Pittsburgh study*, Dekker, 1979.

3 Harris, C, *The subject intensity of library use: some aspects of polytechnic library use*, Newcastle-upon-Tyne Polytechnic Library, 1975.

4 What is quality in an established academic journal?, *Library Review*, **43** (7), 1994, 12–45.

5 Lancaster, F W, *If you want to evaluate your library . . .*, 2nd edn, Library Association Publishing, 1993, 87–108.

6 Scales, P A, Citation analyses as indicators of the use of serials: a comparison of ranked title lists by citation counting and from use data, *Journal of*

Documentation, **32** (1), 1976, 17–25.

7 Clarke, A, The use of serials at the British Library Lending Division, *Interlending Review*, **9** (4), 1981, 111–17.

8 Kefford, B and Line, M B, Core collections of journals for national interlending purposes, *Interlending Review*, **10** (2), 1982, 35–43.

9 Line M B, Changes in rank lists of serials over time: interlending vs citation data, *Interlending and Document Supply*, **12** (4), 1984, 145–7.

10 Kushkowski, J D, A method for building core journal lists in interdisciplinary subject areas, *Journal of Documentation*, **54** (4), 1998, 477–88.

11 Line, M B, Rank lists based on citations and library users as indicators of journal usage in individual libraries, *College Management*, **2**, 1978, 313–6.

12 Alston, S and Nicholson, H, Gauging the value of research periodicals, *SCONUL Newsletter*, **16** (Spring), 1998, 5–8.

13 Fishwick, F, *Scholarly electronic journals: economic implications*, Joint Information Systems Committee (TBC Distribution), 1998.

14 Graham, G, *As I was saying*, 1994, 235–9.

15 Buckland, M, An operational research study of a variable loan and duplication policy at the University of Lancaster, *Library Quarterly*, **42**, 1972, 97–106.

16 Fussler, H H and Simon, J L, *Patterns in the use of books in large research libraries*, University of Chicago Press, 1969.

17 Taylor, C and Urquhart, N C, *Management and assessment of stock control in academic libraries: a report on a research project*, British Library, 1976.

18 Line, M B and Sandison, A, Obsolescence and changes in the use of literature with time, *Journal of Documentation*, **30** (3), 1974, 283–350.

19 Breaks, M, Management of electronic information. In Jenkins, C and Morley, M, *Collection management in academic libraries*, Gower, 1999, 107–34.

20 JISC, *Impact of electronic and multi-media journals on scholarly communications*, Joint Information Systems Committee, 1997.

21 Johnston, C, Electronic technology and its impact on libraries, *Journal of Librarianship and Information Science*, **30** (1), 1998, 7–24.

22 McKnight, C, User studies of commercial and free electronic journals. In Spiller, D, *Academic library surveys and statistics in practice*, Library and Information Statistics Unit, 1998, 71–6.

23 Institute of Public Finance, CIPFA PLUS archive for 1997. In Bohme, S and Spiller, D, *Perspectives of public library use 2: a compendium of survey information*, Library and Information Statistics Unit, 1999, 52–9.

24 Oldman, C M and Davinson, D, *The usage of periodicals in public libraries: an investigation carried out in 1972–3*, Leeds Polytechnic Department of Librarianship, 1975.

25 Users' needs for newspapers and magazines: sampling error. In England, L and Sumsion, J, *Perspectives of public library use: a compendium of survey information*, Library and Information Statistics Unit, 1995.

26 Matchett, S, A study of the provision and usage of periodicals in public libraries, using six libraries in the Midlands as case studies. In Bohme, S and Spiller, D, *Perspectives of public library use 2: a compendium of survey information*, Library and Information Statistics Unit, 1999, 188–91.

27 Brunskill, K, *Electronic serials in public libraries*, British Library Research and Innovation Centre, 1998.

Chapter 11
Reference and research materials

1 Smith, I, Adult non-fiction and the public library. In Bohme, S and Spiller, D, *Perspectives of public library use 2: a compendium of survey information*, Library and Information Statistics Unit, 1999, 161–6.

2 Nolan, C W, The lean reference collection: improving functionality through selection and weeding, *College and Research Libraries*, **52** (1), 1991, 80–92.

3 Stacey, M, Assessing our sources: the information professional's search for authenticity, *Refer*, **16** (1), 2000, 1–9.

4 Chapman, A and Spiller, D, *Trend analysis of monograph acquisitions in public and university libraries in the UK*, Library and Information Statistics Unit, 2000.

5 Marcella, R and Baxter, G, Citizenship information: a national survey of the citizenship information needs of the general public. In Bohme, S and Spiller, D, *Perspectives of public library use 2: a compendium of survey information*, Library and Information Statistics Unit, 1999, 231–6.

6 Meadows, A J *Communicating research*, Academic Press, 1998.

7 LINC, *Library service provision for researchers: proceedings of the Anderson Report seminar*, LINC, 1997.

8 Anderson, M, The Anderson Report: an overview. In LINC, *Library service provision for researchers: proceedings of the Anderson Report seminar*, LINC, 1997.

9 Joint Funding Council's Library Review Group, *Report (Follett Report)*, HEFCE, 1993.

10 Love, C and Feather, J Special collections on the World Wide Web: a survey and evaluation, *Journal of Librarianship and Information Science*, **30** (4), 1998, 215–22.

11 Feeny, M *Digital culture: maximising the nation's investment – a synthesis of*

JISC/NPO studies on the preservation of electronic materials, National Preservation Office, 1999.

12 Parry, D Virtually new: creating the digital collection, 1998, available at: **http://www.ukoln.ac.uk/services/lic/digitisation** Summary in Bohme, S and Spiller, D *Perspectives of public library use 2: a compendium of survey information*, Library and Information Statistics Unit, 1999, 129–34.

Chapter 12
Reading for pleasure

1 Dixon, J, *Fiction in libraries*, Library Association Publishing, 1986.

2 Kinnell, M, *Managing fiction in libraries*, Library Association Publishing, 1991.

3 Smith, I, Adult fiction and the public library. In Bohme, S and Spiller, D, *Perspectives of public library use 2: a compendium of survey information*, Library and Information Statistics Unit, 1999, 167–72.

4 Goodall, D, *Browsing in public libraries*, Library and Information Statistics Unit, 1989.

5 Sear, L and Jennings, B, *How readers select fiction*, Kent County Council, 1986.

6 Spiller, D, The provision of fiction for public libraries, *Journal of Librarianship*, **12** (4), 1980, 238–66.

7 Turner, S E, *A survey of borrowers' reaction to literary fiction in Beeston Library, Nottinghamshire*, MA dissertation, Department of Library and Information Studies, Loughborough University, 1987.

8 Spenceley, N, *The readership of literary fiction: a survey of library users in the Sheffield area*, MA dissertation, Postgraduate School of Librarianship, Sheffield University, 1980.

9 Sumsion, J, *Public Lending Right in practice: a report to the Advisory Committee*, 2nd edn, Public Lending Right, 1991.

10 Sear, L and Jennings, B, *Novels ideas: a browsing area for fiction*, Kent County Council, 1989.

11 Sumsion, J, Who reads what in libraries? In Van Riel, R, *Reading the future: a place for literature in public libraries*, 1992, 47–57.

12 Reuben, J and Spiller, D, *Paperbacks in public libraries*, Library and Information Statistics Unit, 1999.

13 Parry, D, *Why requests fail: inter-library lending and document supply request failures in the United Kingdom and Ireland*, Information North for CONARLS, 1997.

14 Spiller, D, A strategy for biography provision in public libraries, *Library Review*, **37** (1), 1988, 40–4.

15 McClellan, A W, The reading dimension in effectiveness and service, *Library Review*, **30** (Summer), 1981, 77–86.

16 Olle, J G, Fiction – the missing service, *New Library World*, **82** (972), 1981, 101–4.

17 Timperley, P and Spiller, D, *The impact of non-fiction lending from public libraries*, LISU, 1999.

18 Chapman, A and Spiller, D, *Trend analysis of monograph acquisitions in public and university libraries in the UK*, Library and Information Statistics Unit, 2000.

19 Smith, I, Adult non-fiction and the public library. In Bohme, S and Spiller, D, *Perspectives of public library use 2: a compendium of survey information*, Library and Information Statistics Unit, 1999, 161–6.

20 Hoggart, R, *A local habitation*, Oxford University Press, 1989, 183–5.

21 Quinton, Lord, The cultural value of books, *Library Association Record*, **91** (11), 1989, 645–51.

Chapter 13
Materials for children

1 Spreadbury, H and Spiller, D, *Survey of secondary school library users*, LISU, 1999.

2 Department of National Heritage, *Investing in children: the future of library services for children and young people*, HMSO, 1995.

3 Kinnell, M, *Managing library resources in schools*, Library Association Publishing, 1994.

4 Heeks, P and Kinnell, M, *School libraries at work*, British Library, 1994.

5 Shakeshaft, G, *Survey of independent school libraries*, MA dissertation, LISU, 1997. Summarized In Spiller, D and Shakeshaft, G, Libraries in UK independent schools, *New Review of Children's Literature and Librarianship*, **3**, 1997, 75–92.

6 Library Association, *Survey of secondary schools in the UK*, The Library Association, 1997, available at:
http://www.la-hq.org.uk/
executive summary available from The Library Association.

7 Birmingham City Council Report of a survey of children using the library. In Bohme, S and Spiller, D, *Perspectives of public library use 2: a compendium of survey information*, Library and Information Statistics Unit, 1999, 77–80.

8   Institute of Public Finance, *CIPFA public library user surveys*. General information from the Institute of Public Finance, 7th floor, NLA Tower, 12–16 Addiscombe Road, Croydon, CRO OXT.

9   Heather, P, *Young people's reading: a study of the leisure reading of 13–15 year olds*, Centre for Research on User Studies, University of Sheffield, 1981.

10 Carter, C J, Young people and books: a review of the research into young people's reading habits, *Journal of Librarianship*, **18** (1), 1986, 1–22.

11 Roehampton Institute, *Contemporary juvenile reading habits: a study of young people's reading at the end of the century*, Children's Literature Research Centre, Roehampton Institute, 1994.

12 Chambers and Stoll, *Book selection in public libraries*, British Library Research and Development Department, 1996.

13 Blanshard, C, The electronic approval system, *Library Association Record*, **99** (1), 1997, 36–7.

14 Herring, J E, *Exploiting the Internet as an information resource in schools*, Library Association Publishing, 1999.

15 *Information and communications technology in schools: an independent inquiry*, The Independent ICT in Schools Commission, 1997.

16 Small, G, The Internet and the school library, *School Librarian*, **47** (2), 1999, 62–3, 65–6.

17 Jervis, A and Stegg, T, *The Internet in secondary schools*, University of Manchester, 1998.

18 *Connecting the learning society: National Grid for Learning,* the Government's consultation paper, DfEE, 1997.

Chapter 14
Foreign language materials

1   Ellen, S R, Survey of foreign language problems facing the research worker, *Interlending Review*, **7** (2), 1979.

2   Hutchins, W J, *The language barrier: a study in depth of foreign language methods in the research activity of an academic community*, Postgraduate School of Librarianship and Information Science, University of Sheffield, 1971.

3   Roberts, M and Cameron, K J, A barometer of 'unmet demand': inter-library loans analysis and monograph acquisitions, *Library Acquisitions*, **8** (3), 1984, 31–42.

4   Bloomfield, B C, *Acquisition and provision of foreign books by national and university libraries in the UK*, Mansell, 1972.

5   Clough, E and Quarmby, J, *A public library service for ethnic minorities in*

Great Britain, Library Association, 1978.

6 Elliott, P, *Public libraries and self-help ethnic minority organisations*, School of Librarianship, Polytechnic of North London, 1984.

7 Elliott, P, *Access to ethnic minority materials*, School of Librarianship, Polytechnic of North London, 1986.

8 Cooke, M, The management of stock in minority languages, *Journal of Librarianship and Information science*, **25** (2), 1993, 79–84.

9 High, E, Different language, different needs?: a survey of Asian library users, 1995. In Bohme, S and Spiller, D *Perspectives of public library use 2: a compendium of survey information*, Library and Information Statistics Unit, 1999, 84–93.

Chapter 15
Out-of-print materials

1 Cave, R, *Rare book librarianship*, 2nd edn, Bingley, 1982.

2 Cox, D, Rare books and special collections. In Stirling, J F, *University librarianship*, Library Association Publishing, 1981.

3 Cameron, K J and Roberts, M, *Desiderata file maintenance: purging and its policies*, *Journal of Librarianship*, **14** (2), 1982.

4 Arfield, J, Pruning, weeding and grafting: strategies for the effective management of stock, *Library management*, **14** (3), 1993, 9–15.

Chapter 16
Paperbacks

1 Reuben, J and Spiller, D, *Paperbacks in public libraries*, Library and Information Statistics Unit, 1999.

2 Capital Planning Information Ltd, *Trends in public library selection policies*, BNB Research Fund, 1987.

3 Hart, M, *The use of paperbacks in public libraries in the UK: a review of research*, Centre for Library and Information Management, University of Loughborough, 1983.

4 Chapman, A and Spiller, D, *Trend analysis of monograph acquisitions in public and university libraries in the UK*, Library and Information Statistics Unit, 2000.

5 Spiller, D, The provision of fiction for public libraries, *Journal of Librarianship*, **12** (4), 1980, 238–66.

6 Harrison, K M, *Paperback books in public libraries*, Masters dissertation,

Department of Information and Library Studies, Loughborough University, 1984.

7 Goodall, D, *Browsing in public libraries*, Library and Information Statistics Unit, 1989.

Chapter 17
Videos and recorded sound

1 Heery, M J, Audiovisual materials in academic libraries: preliminary report of a survey conducted on behalf of the Library Association Audiovisual Group, *Audiovisual Librarian*, **9** (4), 1983, 183–92.

2 Institute of Public Finance, CIPFA PLUS archive for 1997. In Bohme, S and Spiller, D, *Perspectives of public library use 2: a compendium of survey information*, Library and Information Statistics Unit, 1999, 52–9.

3 Smith, I, Audio-visual materials. In Bohme, S and Spiller, D, *Perspectives of public library use 2: a compendium of survey information*, Library and Information Statistics Unit, 1999, 152–60.

References

Acorn project at Loughborough University, available at:
http://acorn.lboro.ac.uk

Aslib (1995) *Review of the public library service in England and Wales: final report*, Aslib, 37.

Atton, C (1994) Beyond the mainstream: examining alternative sources for stock selection, *Library Review*, **43** (4), 57–64.

Benge, R C (1963a) *Bibliography and the provision of books*, Association of Assistant Librarians, 153–203.

Benge, R C (1963b) *Libraries and cultural change*, Bingley.

Blake, M and Meadows, A J (1984) Journals at risk, *Journal of Librarianship*, **16** (2), 118–28.

Blond, A (1971) *The publishing game*, Cape.

Bohme, S and Spiller, D (1999) *Perspectives of public library use 2: a compendium of survey information*, Library and Information Statistics Unit.

Book Auction Records (annual), Stevens and Stiles.

Book Industry Communications, tel 020 7607 0021.

Bookseller (weekly). Average book price information is published biannually.

Brophy, P (1985) *The effectiveness of library expenditure: investigations into the selection of books and their subequent use*, Bristol Polytechnic Library.

Bryant, P (1983) The use of cataloguing-in-publication in United Kingdom libraries, *Journal of Librarianship*, **15** (1), 1–18.

Butcher, J E (1988) British Library bibliographic services. In Greenwood, D, *Bibliographic records in the book world: needs and capabilities*, BNB Research Fund, 104–8.

Chambers, J (1999) End-user document supply or who needs an inter-library loans service?, *Interlending and Document Supply*, **27** (2), 71–9.

Chartered Institute of Public Finance and Accountancy (annual) *Public library statistics: actuals, and estimates*, CIPFA.

Clinton, P (1999) Charging users for inter-library loans in United Kingdom university libraries: a survey, *Interlending and Document Supply*, **27** (1), 17–29.

Creaser, C (1999) *Survey of public library services to schools and children in the UK 1997–98*, Library and Information Statistics Unit.

Cronin, B (1988)   The uncontested orthodoxy, *British Journal of Academic Librarianship*, **3** (1), 1–8.

Crump, M L and Freund, L (1995) Serials cancellations and inter-library loan, *Serials Review*, **21** (2), 29–36.

Department of Education and Science (1973)   *Public libraries and their use*, HMSO, 23.

Department of Education and Science (1962) *Standards of public library service in England and Wales* (the Bourdillon Report), HMSO.

Diodata, L W and Diodata, V P (1983) The use of gifts in a medium-sized university library, *Collection Management*, **5** (1/2), 53–71.

Distributed National Electronic Resource: http://www.jisc.ac.uk/index.html

Eaton, R (1983)   Paperback format research project. In Hart, M, *The use of paperbacks in public libraries in the UK: a review of research*, Centre for Library and Information Management, Loughborough University, 50–59.

England, L and Sumsion, J (1995) *Perspectives of public library use: a compendium of survey information*, Library and Information Statistics Unit.

Euromonitor Publications (1989) *The book report 1989*, Euromonitor.

Evans, G E (1970)   Book selection and book collection usage in academic libraries, *Library Quarterly*, **40** (3), 297–308.

Everest, K (1999)   Devolved budgeting workshop, *SCONUL Newsletter*, **16** (Spring), 40–41.

Ford, G (1988) A review of relegation practice. In Corrall, S, *Collection development*, Taylor-Graham, 71–87.

Ford, G (1980) Stock relegation in some British university libraries, *Journal of Librarianship*, **12** (1), 42–55.

Foster, C (1996) Determining losses in academic libraries and the benefit of theft detection systems, *Journal of Librarianship and Information Science*, **28** (2), 93–104.

Francis, J P E (1996) The complete library, *Public Library Journal*, **11** (4), 111–15.

Fraser, H (1992) In Van Riel, R, *Reading the future: a place for literature in public libraries*, 81.

Gilder, L (1980) *The relegation and storage of material in academic libraries: a literature review*, Centre for Library and Information Management, University of Loughborough.

Goodall, D (1989) *Browsing in public libraries*, Library and Information Statistics Unit, 92–3.

Gore, D (1976) *Farewell to Alexandria: solutions to space, growth and performance problems of libraries*, Greenwood Press, 164–80.

Gossen, E A and Irving, S (1995) *Library resources and technical services*, **39** (1), 45–52.

Harris, C (1977) A comparison of issues and in-library use of books, *Aslib Proceedings*, **29** (3), 118–26.

Hart, M (1986) *Book selection and use in academic libraries*, Centre for Library and Information Management.

Head, M P (1996) Stock protection put to the test, *Library Association Record*, **98** (7), 364–5.

Heaney, H (1987) The university research library. In Corrall, S, *Collection development: options for effective management*, Taylor-Graham.

Hertfordshire Library Service (1984) *Statistical approaches to stock management: measures of current performance in Hertfordshire*, Hertfordshire Library Service.

Higginbottom, J (1987) The subject librarian. In Revill, D H, *Personnel management in polytechnic libraries*, Gower.

Higher Education Funding Council Colleges Learning Resources Group (annual) *Statistics*, available from Angela Conyers, Head of Learning Resources, Canterbury Christ Church College, North Holmes Road, Canterbury, CT1 1QU.

Hoggart, R (1993) *An imagined life*, Oxford University Press, 70.

Horrocks, A (1998) What do students want? Using priority search surveys to determine user satisfaction with library services, *SCONUL Newsletter,* **15** (Winter), 21–4.

Houghton, B and Prosser, C (1974) Survey of the opinions of BLLD users in special libraries and the effects of non-immediate access to journals, *Aslib Proceedings*, **26** (9).

Houghton, T (1985) *Bookstock management in public libraries*, Bingley, 71.

Howkins, H (1999) *A survey of non-users of Leicester's public libraries*, MA dissertation, Dept of Information Science, Loughborough University, 59.

Huse, R and Huse, J (1999) *Who else writes like?: a reader's guide to fiction authors*, Library and Information Statistics Unit.

Institute of Public Finance Ltd (1999) CIPFA PLUS archive for 1997. In Bohme, S and Spiller, D, *Perspectives of public library use 2: a compendium of survey information*, Library and Information Statistics Unit, 52–9.

Irvin, N and Cooper, L (1999) *Who next?: a guide to children's authors*, Library and Information Statistics Unit.

Jones, A and Pratt, G (1974) The categorisation of adult non-fiction, *Journal of Librarianship*, **6** (2), 91–8.

Kibby, P and White, M (1999) *TFPL/Blackwell's guide to electronic journals management*, TFPL.

King, D W and Griffiths, J M (1995) Economic issues concerning electronic publishing and distribution of scholarly articles, *Library trends*, **43** (4), 713–40.

Kingma, B (1997) Inter-library loan and resource sharing, *Library Trends*, **45** (3), 518–30.

KnowUK, available at:
http://www.knowuk.co.uk

Kohl, D (1997) Resource sharing in a changing Ohio environment, *Library Trends*, **45** (3), 435–47.

Kohut, J (1974) Allocating the book budget: a model, *College and Research Libraries*, **35** (May), 192–9.

Library and Information Statistics Unit (twice yearly) *Average prices of British academic books*, LISU.

Library and Information Statistics Unit (1998) *Place for Children Project* Unpublished work by the Library and Information Statistics Unit, Loughborough University.

Library and Information Statistics Unit (1999a) *Library and Information Statistics Tables* (brochure), LISU.

Library and Information Statistics Unit (1999b) *LISU annual library statistics 1999*, LISU.

Library and Information Statistics Unit (annual) *Public library materials fund and budget* survey, LISU.

LINC (1997) *Library service provision for researchers: Proceedings of the Anderson Report seminar*, LINC, 18.

Line, M B (1983) Access to collections, including inter-library loans. In Parker, J S, *Aspects of library development planning*, Mansell.

Loughborough University (1998) Unpublished undergraduate project at Huntingdon Public Library.

McClellan, A W (1973) The reader, the library and the book, Bingley, 45.

McGrath, W (1975) A pragmatic book allocation formula for academic and public libraries, with a test for library effectiveness, *Library Resources and Technical Services*, **19** (4), 357–67.

Marcan, P (1986) In Dixon, J, *Fiction in libraries*, Library Association Publishing, 93–103.

Matthews, I (1994) The issue life of bookstock, *Public Library Journal*, **9** (5), 123–5.

Neilson, K and Willett, P (1999) UK regional newspapers on the World Wide Web, *Aslib Proceedings*, **51** (3).

Nicholas, D and Boydell, L (1996) BLAISE-LINE: enigma, anomaly or anachronism?, *Aslib Proceedings*, **48** (3), 55–9.

Noll, R and Steinmueller, W E (1992) An economic analysis of scientific journal prices, *Serials review*, **18** (1, 2), 32–7.

Payne, G and Willers, J (1989) Using management information in a polytechnic library, *Journal of Librarianship*, **21** (2), 19–35.

Peasgood, A N (1988) Acquisition/selection librarians: academic libraries. In Greenwood, D, *Bibliographic records in the book world: needs and capabilities*, BNB Research Fund, 38–44.

Pinion, C F (1983) Video home lending services in public libraries, *Audiovisual Librarian*, **9** (1), 18–23.

Price, G (1999) The role of the library in the effective primary school, *School Librarian*, **47** (3), (Autumn), 119–20.

Prowse, S W (1999) A review of interlending in the UK in 1998, *Interlending and Document Supply*, **27** (2), 80–88.

Public Libraries and Museums Act (1964), HMSO.

Public libraries in Australia: report of a committee of inquiry into public libraries (1976), Government Printer of Australia.

Raffell, J A and Shishko, R (1969) *Systematic analysis of university libraries*, MIT Press.

Ranganathan, S R (1966) *Library book selection*, 2nd edn, Asia Publishing House.

Rowley, J (1998) *The electronic library*, Library Association Publishing.

Russell, J (1999) Collection profiling, *SCONUL Newsletter*, **16** (Spring), 26–30.

Saddington, G H and Cooper, E (1984) *Audio cassettes as library materials: an introduction*, 2nd edn, *Audiovisual Librarian*.

SCONUL (annual) *Annual statistics*, SCONUL, 102 Euston Street, London, NW1 2HA.

Smith, M (1979) Book selection sources, *Library Association Record*, **81** (3), 31.

Spiller, D (1979) The provision of fiction for public libraries, MLS dissertation, Loughborough University of Technology.

Spiller, D (1980) The provision of fiction for public libraries, *Journal of Librarianship*, **12** (4) 238–66.

Spiller, D and Creaser, C (1999) Pilot of proposed new measures for CIPFA public library statistics. In Bohme, S and Spiller, D, *Perspectives of public library use 2: a compendium of survey information*, Library and Information Statistics Unit, 60–68.

Steptowe, C G (1987) *A case study of fiction provision in a public library*, MA dissertation, Dept of Library and Information Studies, Loughborough University.

Stock relegation in practice in major academic libraries in N E England (1982), The Library Association, Universities Section.

Sumsion, J (1996) *LISU review of CIPFA public library statistics*, Library and Information Statistics Unit.

Sweeney, R (1977) *International target audience code (ITAC): a proposal and report on its development and testing*, IFLA International Office for UBC.

Thompson, A H (1988) Relationships between academic libraries and audio-visual production services: the facts, Part 1, *Audiovisual Librarian*, **14** (3), 136–41.

UK Office for Library and Information Networking (UKOLN): information provided, January 2000.

Urquhart, J A and Schofield, J L (1972) Overlap of acquisitions in the University of London libraries, *Journal of Librarianship*, **4** (1), 32–47.

Usherwood, B (1989) *The public library as public knowledge*, The Library Association.

Wenger, C B and Childress, J (1977) Journal evaluation in a large research library, *Journal of the American Society for Information Science*, **28** (5), 293–9.

Whitaker, D E (1988) The Whitaker approach to bibliographical content. In Greenwood, D, *Bibliographical records in the book world*, BNB Research Fund.

White, B (1986) *Interlending in the UK*, British Library.

Williams, S R (1986) Weeding an academic library using the Slote method, *British Journal of Academic Librarianship*, **1** (2), 147–59.

Wilson, T D and Masterston, W A J (1974) *Local library co-operation*, University of Sheffield Postgraduate School of Library and Information Science.

Wood, R J (1996) The Conspectus: a collection analysis and development success, *Library Acquisitions*, **20** (4), 429–53.

Woodhead, P A and Martin, J V (1982) Subject specialisation in British university libraries, *Journal of Librarianship*, **14** (2).

Woodward, A M (1978) *Factors affecting the renewal of periodical subscriptions: a study of decision making in libraries with special reference to economics and inter-lending,* Aslib, 1978.

Index

International Yearbook of Library and Information Management 2000: Collection Management

GENERAL EDITOR: DR G E GORMAN FLA, FRSA

About the series: *The International Yearbook* is essential reading for anyone who wants to keep up-to-date with recent developments in library science and information management on a global basis. Each thematic volume will include papers covering current issues, emergent debates, models of best practice and likely future developments, contributed by an internationally respected panel of researchers, practitioners and academics.

The first volume of this authoritative annual publication provides a timely and forward-looking focus on the theme of collection management. This broad subject area will be examined from a variety of perspectives including a narrative bibliography on the topic supported by a range of historical, analytical, evaluative and provocative essays that tell us where we have been, where we are and where we seem to be going. Individual contributions will cover:

- the access-ownership debate • acquisitions and access • censorship • collection assessment
- collection development programmes in Africa and Asia • collection management in school libraries
- the impact of digital information on the roles of collection managers • cooperative collection development • economics of collection development • electronic publications • managing government documents collections • policy issues in collection management • preservation management • selection in an electronic environment • serials management • storage facilities and services • the role of archives in the information age and their influence on collection management • weeding.

These substantive chapters will comprise a mix of research-based, practice-based or reflective scholarly studies and they will report on developments internationally.

The series editor: **Dr G E Gorman BA MDiv STB GradDipLib MA ThD FLA FRSA** is senior lecturer in library and information science at Victoria University of Wellington in New Zealand. He has published extensively in the field of library and information work and he is a regular contributor to scholarly and professional journals. The Editorial Board of the International Yearbook series includes members from Australia, New Zealand, China, Vietnam, India, Pakistan, Singapore, UK and USA.

October 2000; c352pp; hardback; 1-85604-366-5; c£60.00

The Public Librarian's Guide to the Internet

SALLY CRIDDLE, ALISON MCNAB, SARAH ORMES AND IAN WINSHIP

Society is moving rapidly towards the networked delivery of information, educational and entertainment services, and public libraries are beginning to meet this challenge by developing and delivering an essential range of networked information services on the web.

This introductory guide aims to get public librarians familiar with using the Internet, in order to help in their everyday information work, both directly through their own expertise, and indirectly by passing on their searching skills to the user.

While it cannot cover all the Internet user will ever need to know, it does demonstrate the main procedures and sources that will help in learning to explore the Internet. An invaluable resource guide points to key sources unlikely to be covered in other guides, including the most important collections of subject information. The public librarian will find help with:

- what the Internet is and how it can assist you
- understanding and using Internet addresses
- public access issues
- essential communication skills on the Internet
- net techniques explained
- tips on browsing for (subject) information
- tips on searching for information
- developing public library web services
- professional use
- creating a public library web site
- design and web management issues.

This deskbook is an essential companion for all public librarians with little or no experience of the Internet. It covers all the issues affecting public library use as well as identifying key resources in: reference (sport, travel, history, etc), literature, children's work including homework, family history, community information, business information, and lifelong learning. The text will prove invaluable to all public librarians facing the challenge of ICT training guidance.

Sally Criddle MSc is Resource Co-ordinator, UK Office for Library and Information Networking (UKOLN). **Alison McNab MA MSc MIInfSc ALA** is Academic Services Manager, Pilkington Library, Loughborough University. **Sarah Ormes MA** is Public Library Networking Focus Officer, UKOLN. **Ian Winship BA MA ALA** is Electronic Services Manager, Learning Resources Department, University of Northumbria at Newcastle.

June 2000; 264pp; paperback; 1-85604-328-2; £19.95 Published in association with UKOLN

The Serials Management Handbook
A practical guide to print and electronic serials management

EDITED BY TONY KIDD AND LYNDSAY REES-JONES

Serials information management has changed beyond recognition in recent years, and is playing a major part in revolutionizing the nature of scholarly communication. Journals and other serials now encompass a wide range of forms: print, electronic, microform, CD-ROM and web-based formats; and they are distributed variously through local holdings, inter-library loan and electronic document delivery.

This timely publication, compiled in association with the UK Serials Group, provides a much needed overview of best practice in the many different aspects of serials management. Contributed by experienced professional and strategic players from a range of academic and commercial backgrounds, it takes a problem and solution approach, rather than a step-by-step, 'how to' one, to the processes and materials available.

While there is substantial emphasis on electronic developments throughout, this is not at the expense of print journals, which still contain the highest percentage of serials information delivered in most libraries. The book is written with an awareness of the paramount importance of user requirements, remembering that processes are not ends in themselves, but means to deliver information to end-users. The chapters cover:

- why do we need serials?
- how serials are produced
- serial information delivery options
- budgeting, ordering and payment
- acquisition methods

- processing
- stock management
- exploitation and usage analysis
- signposts to the future.

Whilst it primarily highlights practice in the UK, the material is, by its nature, of wide multinational interest. Addressing the strategic as well as the practical issues, this book is required reading for serials managers and information professionals across all library sectors. It is also of major interest to serials providers, publishers and subscription agents, systems developers and all players in the serials information industry.

Tony Kidd MA ALA is Head of Serials at Glasgow University Library and is also a UKSG Committee Member. **Lyndsay Rees-Jones** BA ALA FRSA is Professional Adviser, Special Libraries and Information Services at The Library Association and a UKSG Committee Member

2000; 176pp; hardback; ISBN 1-85604-355-X; £39.95   Published in association with The UK Serials Group